The Treaty of Frankfort

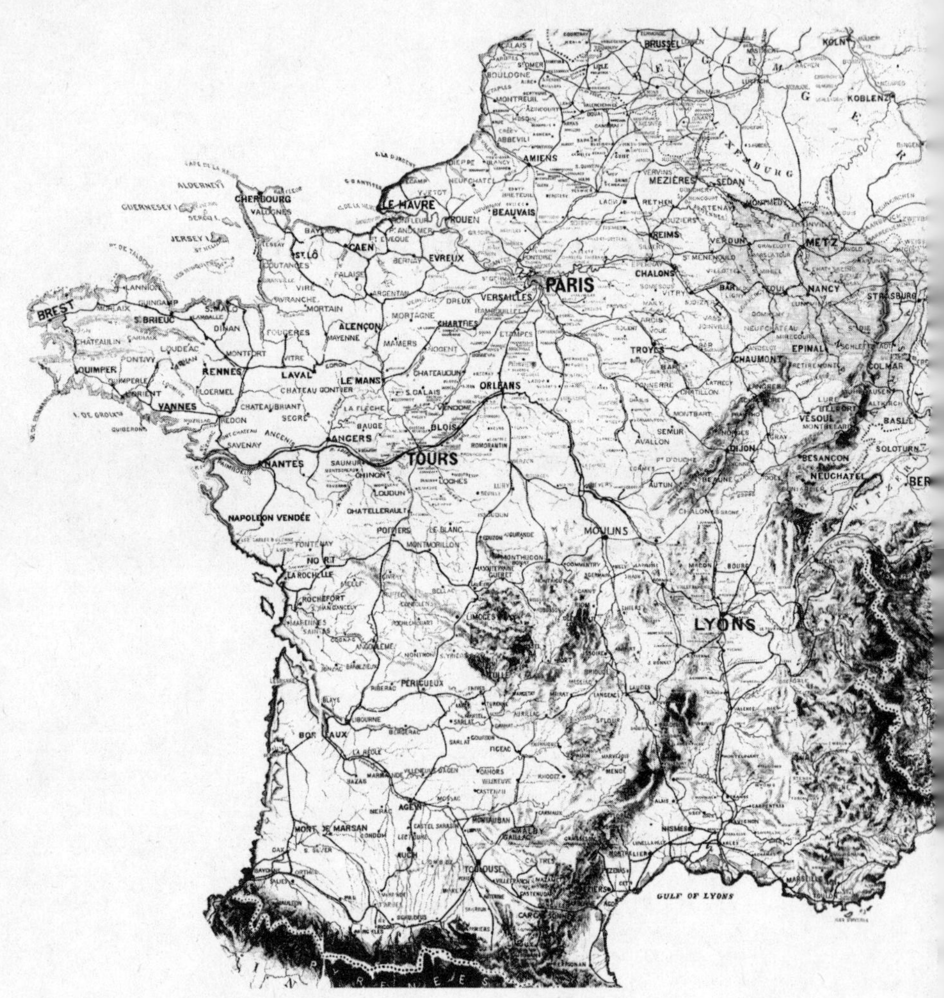

War map of France. (Map Collection, New York Public Library)

The Treaty of Frankfort

A Study in Diplomatic History
September 1870—September 1873

By

Robert I. Giesberg

Philadelphia

University of Pennsylvania Press

Published in Great Britain, India, and Pakistan by the
Oxford University Press London, Bombay, and Karachi

Library of Congress Catalogue Card Number: 64–21088

7454
Printed in the United States of America

To My Father
and the Memory of My Mother

Acknowledgments

MUCH OF THE RESEARCH for this volume was made possible through the grant of a Penfield Fellowship by the University of Pennsylvania. The award made possible a year's study in Europe during which I was able to consult the diplomatic archives of France, Germany, and England.

It would not have been possible to write this book without the assistance of the staffs of various archives and libraries: the Bibliothèque Nationale, the Bibliothèque Thiers, the Archives Nationales, the Archives du Ministère des Affaires Etrangères in Paris; the Public Record Office and the British Museum in London; the Library of the University of Texas; and the M.D. Anderson Memorial Library of the University of Houston. The University of Houston generously extended me a leave of absence to pursue my doctoral work, of which this book is the product. I must also extend my thanks to Mrs. Joanna Armstrong of Houston without whose assistance the mysteries of German hand-script would be mysteries still.

The help, advice, and encouragement of so many people go into the writing of a book that one runs the risk of seeming to be ungrateful when one singles out certain individuals for special mention. Nevertheless, I must express my special thanks to Dr. Floyd S. Lear, of Rice University, a great historian and a great teacher who had faith in me and to Dr. Lynn M. Case of the University of Pennsylvania who gave unstintingly of his time and advice in the direction of the dissertation which was the genesis of this book. My greatest debt of gratitude is to my wife for reasons which I could never effectively put into words.

Robert I. Giesberg

Fordham University
New York, 1963

Contents

List of Illustrations

This war represents the German Revolution, a greater political event than the French Revolution of last century. There is not a diplomatic tradition which has not been swept away. You have a new world, new influences at work, new and unknown objects and dangers with which to cope, at present involved in that obscurity incident to novelty in such affairs. . . . But what has really come to pass? The balance of power has been entirely destroyed.

Benjamin Disraeli
February 9, 1871

The Treaty of Frankfort

I

Sedan to Ferrières

The Government of National Defense, which assumed power in Paris on September 4, 1870, was, said a contemporary, "better suited to adorn the French Academy than to fill . . . the breach."[1]

The new government was faced with a situation which bordered on chaos. Everywhere in northern France the German armies held the initiative while France's finest armies were either in retreat or penned uselessly inside their fortresses. It was a situation which would have tested the abilities of men long familiar with the problems of war and diplomacy. This government, upon which power had devolved so suddenly, was composed largely of men who, whatever their patriotism, had little or no practical experience in governing.

France's new minister of foreign affairs was Jules Favre,[2] whose only qualification for this difficult office seems to have been that he was briefly an under-secretary of foreign affairs in the government of the Second Republic.[3] A German who came to know Favre well said that he was "the typical French avocat" who "because he was able to hold forth on everything . . . imagined he could really understand everything." He felt that Favre was "on the whole . . . an honourable man, actuated by good motives but quite unpractical in the ordinary affairs of life, and too easily the victim of tearful moods."[4] Lord Lyons, the British ambassador to France, conceded that Favre was an "excellent man" but had serious faults as a diplomat since he "was too much led away by his feelings to be a man of business."[5]

Favre said that when he assumed office he was willing to do anything to gain an honorable peace.[6] The Austrian ambassador, Prince Richard Metternich, put it more bluntly when he said that "Jules is dying to make peace."[7] His efforts to this end were sincere but they led him, at the very outset of his diplomatic career, to take an ill-advised step which was to earn for him considerable abuse.

At the morning session of the government on September 6, Favre read to his colleagues a circular which he proposed to send to French representatives abroad. In it Favre stated that France was willing to negotiate [*traiter*] with Prussia for terms of peace, but only on the basis of the territorial integrity of France. In spite of some objections from the minister of finance, Ernest Picard, who felt the language somewhat too intransigent, the proposed circular met with "a lively approval."[8] That very day Favre issued the circular, proclaiming in resounding terms that France would "cede neither an inch of our territory nor a stone of our fortresses."[9]

Favre later said that he had intended the circular to show that France was fighting to protect her soil and that, since he had assurances that the governments of Europe would never tolerate a peace which mutilated France, he was speaking the sentiments of France and of all Europe.[10] While he was certainly not speaking for all of Europe, what Gladstone called the "Pouce and Pierre" doctrine[11] was enormously popular in France. One observer said that "no diplomatic document ever enjoyed more favor in France. . . . Paris received it with a

Jules Favre (Picture Collection, New York Public Library)

kind of frantic exaltation."[12] Indeed, so strong was public feeling that Favre considered his use of the word *traiter* to be "rather a bold step towards accustoming the people of Paris to the idea of treating while the Prussians are still on French soil."[13]

In any event, the circular had been issued. Whatever its merits or failings, it returned to haunt him. When the day finally came to sign a peace treaty ceding territory to Germany, a leader of the legitimist faction in the assembly said that "it seemed just that the treaty which was going to despoil us be signed by the author of the imprudent and resounding formula: 'Not an inch of our territory, not a stone of our fortresses'."[14]

That the German authorities were already thinking in terms of war aims and that territorial annexations played a large part in them is well established, although the scope of territorial gains was less clear. For years there had been scattered demands for the "return" of Alsace and Lorraine to Germany,[15] and plans for their acquisition were openly discussed in some Berlin circles,[16] but no vast popular movement seems to have been created. Bismarck was not a supporter of annexation for its own sake, nor did he break easily under pressure when matters of policy were concerned, as his behavior in 1866 amply demonstrated. After the crushing defeat of Austria at Königgrätz, demands for great territorial annexations flooded into Prussian headquarters.[17] Among the military there had been considerable demand for south German and Bohemian annexations,[18] but Bismarck was not to be goaded into demands which he considered excessive. Prussia would one day need Austria, he argued,[19] and he complained of his "thankless task" of convincing others that "we don't live alone in Europe, but with three other Powers who hate and envy us."[20] The King of Prussia also wanted more annexations than, in fact,

Prussia got, feeling that the army would feel cheated after its great victory, but Bismarck finally won him over to accepting smaller but still substantial areas.[21] Bismarck came in for some further criticism at the time of the Luxembourg Crisis of 1867 on the grounds that he had surrendered German territory out of weakness.[22]

During the diplomatic crisis which preceded the outbreak of the Franco-German war there was no general outcry for the annexation of Alsace and Lorraine.[23] In the first two weeks after the war began, two weeks when south Germany lay open to French invasion, Sir Robert Morier, British minister to Stuttgart, reported a growing demand for Alsace and Lorraine, not by newspapers, "but by earnest men well versed in military questions."[24] By the beginning of August the cry had been taken up by the popular press.[25]

By late August and early September the sentiment for harsh peace terms, including extensive annexations, was growing daily more voluble throughout Germany.[26] Meetings of influential Prussians were held to urge the king to obtain from France guarantees for her future conduct.[27] Although there were those who were concerned about possible pro-French views of Alsatians and Lorrainers, German writers tended to consider as "German" lands, those areas which had been German-speaking at the time of their absorption by France during the seventeenth and eighteenth centuries.[28] Historians such as Sybel and Treitschke pointed out that Alsace and Lorraine had been parts of the Holy Roman Empire[29] and refused to accept the principle of self-determination, arguing instead that "this territory is ours by the right of the sword, and annexation follows from the right of the German nation to prevent the loss of any of its sons."[30] Amid such clamor, the voices of those who protested were scarcely heard.[31] Bismarck was scornful of such arguments, which he called "Professors' Ideas,"[32] but the

Bismarck in 1877 (Picture Collection, New York Public Library)

Napoleon III and Bismarck conferring near Sedan, 1870. (Picture Collection, New York Public Library)

Crown Princess of Prussia may well have been correct when she wrote that she did not see "how the Government are to resist the resolute determination of the German nation to wrest them [Alsace and Lorraine] back at all hazards!"[33]

There is no evidence that the Prussian government had any intention of resisting the demand even though Bismarck did not base his claims on anything so ephemeral as national sentiment. At least as early as August 7 Bismarck told a confidant that he proposed to secure Alsace as well as Metz.[34] On August 14 a statement from German headquarters declared that "Alsace and, so far as it is German, Lorraine also must be taken."[35] Two military governments were established for the provinces of Alsace and Lorraine.[36] The next week, following a council of war at Pont-à-Mousson, at which it was decided that Alsace and Metz would definitely be retained,[37] a new decree was issued detaching five *arrondissements* from the government of Lorraine and attaching them to that of Alsace, thus placing under one government the area which Germany proposed to annex.[38] In the weeks that followed, Bismarck directed his propagandists to stress the German determination to have the fortresses of Strasbourg and Metz, and he so far forgot his contempt for "Professors' Ideas" as to tell them to recall that the region had once been German and was still German in language. Subsequently he de-emphasized this idea to stress that the winning of Metz was "indispensable" to the generals.[39]

The inclusion of Metz in Bismarck's demands is interesting since even some of the most ardent nationalists were willing to concede that it was well beyond the linguistic border between France and Germany,[40] and the propriety of including it in the annexation plans stirred up considerable debate in the German press.[41] The question of defending Germany from future French invasion was an important consideration in Bismarck's thinking,[42] and the question of Metz was to become of major importance in the final peace negotiations. On September 2 the government of Baden submitted to King William a memorandum concerning the moving westward of the borders of Germany[43] and on that same day, at Sedan, Bismarck declared that to assure German security "we must have between France and ourselves a barrier: we need a territory, some fortresses and frontiers which serve us forever as a refuge from all attack on her part."[44] He is said to have remarked that Prussia would demand Strasbourg, Metz, Alsace, Lorraine, and four billion francs.[45] On the very day that Favre issued his circular, Bismarck told a friend that the powers must soon be prepared for the idea that peace could not be made without Strasbourg and Metz, "not to bring Alsace and Lorraine to Germany again, but only to guard against a new French offensive war must we possess the two fortresses."[46]

Thus, at the very moment that Prussian policy-makers were discussing territorial changes in public and in private, the hasty and ill-timed circular of September 6 stopped discussion on a point which would obviously be considered in peace negotiations. The circular committed the Government of National Defense to a policy totally unsupported by the fortunes of war and it was never able to avoid completely the effects of its own early intransigence.

Having issued the circular, Favre proceeded to take more practical steps to try to end hostilities. His plan, if such a word can be used for actions which seem too often motivated entirely by impulse, had two objectives: to enlist the aid of the neutral powers on behalf of France, while at the same time, trying to establish direct communications with Prussian headquarters in an attempt to reach an armistice agreement. Occasionally the two aims overlapped and became confused with each other.

He first turned to the neutrals in an attempt to secure their good offices on behalf of an armistice. Italy, Spain, and Turkey were willing enough to take some form of diplomatic action, but they pointed out that nothing could be hoped for unless Russia and England joined such a move.[47]

Favre told Lyons that France "would certainly agree to an armistice if proposed by a neutral," and said that mediation on the basis of the territorial integrity of France should be offered,[48] a step which would virtually commit the neutral powers to support the French claims. The three great neutral powers refused so to commit themselves. The British government indicated that it was prepared to do no more than to receive propositions from *both* sides so as to work toward an exchange of ideas.[49] Russia gave little more encouragement. Prince Gorchakov assured Gabriac, first secretary of the embassy at St. Petersburg, that the Czar was not prepared to take up arms to support French territorial integrity.[50] From Austria, Favre was able to obtain no more than Count Beust's offer to relay to Berlin any communication which he might choose to send.[51]

On September 8 Metternich told Favre that Beust was of the opinion that Favre should approach Prussia directly to find out her terms of peace.[52] At a meeting of the government that same night Favre reviewed the diplomatic situation. There followed an exchange of views of the bases upon which France might deal with Prussia, including an inconclusive discussion of the possibility of surrendering the French fleet. The notes of this meeting give no indication that Favre told his colleagues of Beust's suggestion of direct negotiations,[53] but the fact was that Favre had decided to seek a personal meeting with Bismarck. Whether the idea first came to him as a result of Beust's suggestion we do not know but, having determined upon a course of action, Favre was prepared to follow it up immediately.

On September 9 Favre asked Lyons to forward a note to Lord Granville, British foreign secretary, for Bismarck at Prussian headquarters. The note asked of Bismarck if and with whom he was prepared to enter into discussions concerning an armistice and conditions of peace.[54] That same evening, in the course of his report to the government on the diplomatic situation, Favre asked if, in the event the King of Prussia should refuse to receive a foreign diplomat speaking on behalf of France, it would not be better if he were to go personally to Prussian headquarters. The proposal was rejected on the grounds that it would be useless and would compromise France's future position. Again, the notes give no hint that Favre mentioned his action of that day in initiating a personal meeting with Bismarck,[55] but the fact that he raised the question at all seems to indicate that he was sounding his colleagues for their reaction.

While Favre waited for a reply to his note he played yet another card in his game of trying to get the aid of the neutrals. He proposed to send to London some influential Frenchman who might be able to influence the future action of the British government. The council refused to approve Michel Chevalier, Favre's first choice, but did approve the nomination of Louis Adolphe Thiers.[56] On the evening of September 11 it was announced that Thiers's mission would include visits to St. Petersburg and Vienna as well as London.[57]

That same day, in a communiqué issued from Prussian headquarters, Bismarck at last broke his silence. He denied that any mediation had been undertaken by foreign powers and said that any such attempt would fail unless "the bases of an arrangement" were discussed with Germany. In German eyes, he said, the French imperial government was "the only one . . . which is authorised to enter into negotiations of an international character." "By what right," he asked, could the German governments "negotiate with a power which . . . represents only a part of the left of the former legislative body at Paris."[58] Favre was in a dilemma. Bismarck had rebuffed the claims of the Government of National Defense to be the legally constituted authority in France, but he had not given a specific answer to Favre's note.

Favre had not long to wait, however, for something more specific upon which to act. The day after he had issued the communiqué, Bismarck wired Bernstorff, Prussian minister in London, warning him not to give the overtures of the provisional government the importance "which an overture made by the French government would have." The emperor was, he said, the only repository of sovereignty from the point of view of foreign powers. At the same time he instructed Bernstorff to ask what guarantees the Paris Government could give that a convention negotiated by it would be respected throughout France.[59]

Granville relayed this message to Lord Lyons for delivery to Favre and, in an attempt to facilitate a meeting between Favre and Bismarck, he authorized Lyons to send someone to Bismarck to inquire if Favre would be received at Prussian headquarters.[60] Favre was, of course, already determined to get in touch with Bismarck directly,[61] and he seized the opportunity presented by Granville's offer. He said that he was anxious to learn from Bismarck his conditions for an armistice and, if possible, for a peace treaty.[62] He also sent via London his answer to Bismarck's guarantees demand:

> The guarantees justly claimed by Count Bismarck can be furnished from a double point of view, political and military. From the political point of view, the Government of National Defense will sign an armistice and afterward will call an assembly which

will ratify the treaty which will be agreed to between the Prussian and French governments. From the military point of view, the Government of Defense offers the same security as a regular government since the minister of war is obeyed in all orders which he gives. Everything which would be regulated in this regard by an armistice would thus be punctually executed without any delay.[63]

When the council met that night at 9.50 Favre reported that Lyons had received permission to send an agent to Prussian headquarters, but he apparently did not tell his colleagues that the purpose of the agent was to determine if Bismarck would receive an emissary of the Paris government nor of his own determination to seek a personal interview.[64] His reticence may well have been due to the cold reception given to such a plan a few nights before by his colleagues.

Lyons' emissary left Paris that very evening. He was Edward Malet, a second secretary of the British embassy, chosen because of his knowledge of German and a prior acquaintance with Bismarck.[65] Prussian headquarters was then located at Meaux and there, on September 15, Malet had a long interview with Bismarck, who had already received Favre's reply to his guarantees demand.[66] The chancellor told Malet that, while a representative of the Paris government would be properly received, he would not consider granting an armistice since it could only work to the advantage of France. He rejected the French argument that the French people should be exonerated from guilt for the war and he said that the Government of National Defense was "speaking most deceitfully" in encouraging the French people to hope for the mediation of the neutrals. He had, he said, no intention of dictating France's future choice of government: the fact that in those provinces under German control the emperor was still recognized as sovereign was an "act of courtesy and not intended to indicate a policy."

Bismarck spoke with passion about his war aims. This was the "twenty-seventh war" in two centuries waged by France against Germany, "and a peace concluded now, leaving France in its former territorial conditions, would simply be an armistice lasting till they had recruited their forces and obtained allies." Germany, he said, must protect herself against future French attack:

> We do not ask for Alsace or Lorraine; France may keep them under conditions which would render them useless as a lever in making war against us, but we must insist on Strassburg and Metz. . . .
>
> Would they have hesitated for a moment to exact the complete disintegration of Germany? And they ask us to accept money, of which we are not in want, and to leave France just as it was when the war began.
>
> I pray of you to say, when you go back, that we are neither children nor fools.[67]

Malet then left for Paris, arriving late in the afternoon of September 16. That night, at the British Embassy, he told Favre what Bismarck had said. However, he deliberately omitted any reference to Bismarck's peace terms, for he and Lord Lyons agreed that foreknowledge of such terms would unnecessarily prejudice the slight chance of peace and might even result in Favre being forbidden to go to Prussian headquarters.[68]

Although Bismarck was said to be "by no means ill-disposed" to receiving Favre and had advised King William to receive him,[69] there was certainly reason for Lyons's pessimism regarding any favorable outcome to a meeting between Favre and Bismarck. Not only were the two men poles apart on the issue of territorial cessions, there was also no meeting of minds as to the object of any negotiation. Favre was thinking in terms of an armistice in "general terms" to permit the neutrals to be consulted about peace terms[70] and to allow the election of an assembly to determine the issue of war or peace. Bismarck, on the other hand, had spoken to Malet entirely in terms of a discussion of peace terms, and he was irritated by the action of the Paris government in rejecting out of hand the bases for a peace acceptable to Germany and in agitating for neutral intervention.

Although Favre very much wanted to see Bismarck, he yet felt himself to be in an anomalous position. He had received no reply to his "guarantees" message of September 14, and he had only an oblique invitation from Bismarck through Malet. Twice on September 17 he was with Lyons, nervously questioning Malet about his interview with Bismarck and, as though seeking reassurance, stating that if an answer from Prussian headquarters were delayed too long he would go without waiting for one. Lyons encouraged him in this determination and assured him that he need feel no embarrassment in seeking out Bismarck without a formal invitation.[71] At last he made up his mind to go. He drew up a note for the *Journal officiel* of the following day. In it, as a means of preparing the French for the idea of paying a war indemnity, he threw the entire responsibility for the war on the government of Napoleon III.[72] He also directed Count Chaudordy, his "chef de cabinet," to go to Tours to represent the foreign office with the governmental delegation which had been established in that city.[73] That night he attended a meeting of the government but apparently he said nothing of his plans to seek out Bismarck.[74]

Shortly before seven o'clock on the morning of September 18, unsure of the exact location of Prussian headquarters,

Favre left Paris. He traveled in strict secrecy[75] and his suite consisted of his deputy chief clerk Baron de Ring, his secretary, M. Hendlé, a captain from the general staff, and a M. Lutz from the foreign ministry.[76]

At Villeneuve-Saint George, Favre learned that headquarters were still located at Meaux. A note forwarded to Bismarck elicited a courteous reply asking Favre to call on him the next day at Meaux.[77] At nine o'clock in the morning of September 19 Favre, together with his companions and their escort, left by carriage, arriving at Meaux in mid-afternoon. Favre found waiting for him a note asking him to proceed to the Rothschild chateau of Ferrières, where Bismarck proposed to spend the night.[78] Favre caught up with Bismarck's party near the village of Montry. He and Bismarck immediately adjourned to the nearby chateau of Haute-Maison, where they held their first conversation in a debris-littered salon.[79]

Favre began by speaking of France's desire for peace. Bismarck replied that he would be glad to sign a peace treaty if a lasting one could be obtained. He questioned, however, the stability of the Paris government and said that, since Favre represented only an "imperceptible minority," Prussia must have adequate guarantees.[80]

Favre offered Bismarck a monetary idemnity but said that he could go no farther.[81] Several times Bismarck said that France must surrender Strasbourg but he refused to be more specific than that. Upon being pressed, Bismarck said, according to Favre's account, that "the two departments of the Bas- and Haut-Rhin, a part of that of the Moselle with Metz, Château-Salins and Soissons" were "indispensable" to him.[82] (Bismarck denied that he had asked for Soissons and said that instead he had discussed Saaregemünd.[83]) Favre said: "Then it is Alsace and Lorraine." Bismarck answered that he had not mentioned Lorraine, but "as to Alsace I am determined" for it was "[is] absolutely indispensable to our defense."[84] When Favre expressed doubt that the people of the region would give their assent to any such transfer of sovereignty, Bismarck replied that he was under no illusions as to the Germans being wanted by the people of those provinces but that it was an unavoidable, dirty job which had to be done, since "I am sure that very soon we will have a new war with you and we want to do so with all the advantages."[85] Favre called on morality and European public opinion to support his contention that a cession of territory should be approved by the whole nation, and he pleaded for Bismarck to "let us call an assembly, we will turn our powers over to it, it will name a definitive government which will judge your conditions." Bismarck cut off this line of argument with the curt remark that such a plan presupposed an armistice "and I don't want that at any price."[86]

Although this first discussion had generated some heat, it had been conducted courteously. As evening came on, Favre asked for a second interview, and the two men parted. They met again at 9.30 the same evening, this time at the lavish chateau of Ferrières, where Bismarck was staying, and the interview lasted until nearly midnight.

Favre immediately restated the case for granting an armistice and, unlike the earlier interview, met with no objections. Bismarck appeared to have become convinced of the need for convoking an assembly, and he willingly discussed questions attendant upon an armistice for the purpose of electing an assembly. He had certain conditions which he set forth: the right to occupy the fortresses of the Vosges and of Strasbourg, leaving Metz in a state of siege and without permitting it to be reprovisioned. Both sides, he insisted, must have a free hand where Metz was concerned. Favre then set out his terms for an armistice: Paris to be neutralized and revictualled; safe conducts to be allowed candidates going to the departments and members coming back from Paris; the armistice to last two weeks.[87] Bismarck refused to commit himself until he had consulted the king about the guarantees to be asked in return for granting an armistice.[88] The two men broke up their meeting agreeing to see each other at eleven o'clock the next morning.

The following day, Bismarck conferred with the king, Roon, and Moltke, and arrived at his meeting with Favre about forty-five minutes late. He brought with him a text written in German from which he proceeded to read the terms for an armistice. According to Favre, he demanded the occupation of Strasbourg, Toul, and Phalsbourg.[89] (Bismarck later said that he had demanded Strasbourg, Toul, and Verdun or Bitsche instead of Phalsbourg.[90]) Moreover, should the new assembly meet at Paris, he demanded as security a fort dominating that city, and he mentioned Mont Valerien. This last demand brought from Favre an anguished protest that no French assembly could meet under German guns, and the observation that he could not bring himself to repeat to his colleagues Bismarck's demand. Favre then mentioned the possibility of convening the assembly at Tours and, in that event, of exacting no security. Bismarck agreed to speak to the king about this. He returned to the question of Strasbourg, saying that it must be occupied and its garrison be made prisoners of war since, he said, it must fall to the German armies eventually. At this, Favre rose and announced that it would be an act of cowardice to surrender so heroic a garrison. Bismarck agreed only to speak to the king about this demand. He left the room, returning a quarter of an hour later to announce that the king had agreed to the proposal concerning Tours (by which, apparently, no security would be exacted for Paris), but that he insisted on the imprisonment of the Strasbourg garrison.[91]

Favre was noted for his public demonstrations of tears, and this announcement provoked another one. Since he absolutely refused to concede the surrender of Strasbourg, an impasse had been reached, and discussions were broken off. Favre left immediately for Paris, arriving there the same day.

The governmental council met late in the evening of September 20 to hear the story of his trip. Favre told them that he had not revealed his intentions because he wanted to assume responsibility for making a "supreme effort" to achieve an honorable peace or at least an armistice.[92] The council refused to meet Bismarck's demands and communicated their decision to the chancellor by letter on September 21.[93] On the same day, a note was published in the *Journal officiel* stating in rather extreme terms Bismarck's demands, including retention of both Alsace and Lorraine by right of conquest, and at the same time restating the determination to make no territorial cessions whatsoever.[94] Favre's account of the Ferrières interview was published, and copies of it were sent out of Paris by balloon.[95] In Tours, Gambetta ordered all departmental prefects to publish the account in every commune of France in order to stimulate patriotic ardor.[96]

Favre's account of the interview reached Prussian headquarters on September 23, and it was received with what seemed a mixture of disappointment and relief. The crown prince said that although there had not been hopes that Prussia's conditions would be accepted immediately, "Favre's moderation had led to hopes for further negotiations."[97] Bismarck had been under enormous strain during the negotiations and had been "out of sorts physically and mentally," but he became "more benign and cheerful" after they were broken off.[98] Busch noted that Favre's letter was to be given to the press along with hints that Napoleon III was not, after all, too bad, and he might still be of use to Prussia.[99]

The first phase of negotiations looking toward an armistice and eventual peace had ended in failure. Favre had entered office proclaiming his desire for peace and there is no reason to doubt his sincerity. Nor had his efforts to that end been completely useless. He had not got the intervention of the neutrals that he had hoped for. He had, however, received England's assistance in putting him into direct relations with Bismarck. Bismarck himself had come around to the point of conceding an armistice rather than the final peace that he had originally demanded. There is then reason to think that the war might have ended in September 1870 had not Favre been committed to his unfortunate formula refusing absolutely to concede any French territory to the Germans. Just as that condition precluded any final peace, Favre's refusal to surrender the garrison of Strasbourg prevented an armistice which could have permitted the elections which Favre himself desired. In short, Bismarck had made more concessions than had Favre. It was a missed opportunity.

The question arises whether the fear of revolution in Paris justified Favre's stubborn stand. There is no question that this was a matter constantly in the minds of the Government of National Defense. The notes of its meetings are full of references to concern over Parisian reaction to governmental decisions. In the light of the events of the Commune one wonders if France would have been worse off if surrender had come in September 1870 rather than in January 1871. The question is raised, of course, with the advantages of hindsight. Too many intangibles are involved and the question can never be answered conclusively.

The first phase was over. The second was about to begin.

NOTES TO CHAPTER I

1. Ernest Alfred Vizetelly ["*Le petit homme rouge*"], *Republican France, 1870–1912* (London: 1912), p. 9.

2. The members of this government were General Trochu (president), Favre, Arago, Crémieux, Ferry, Gambetta, Garnier-Pagès, Glais-Bizoin, Pelletan, Picard, Rochefort, and Simon. In addition to Favre and Trochu, the council of ministers consisted of Crémieux (justice), General Le Flô (war), Admiral Fourichon (navy and colonies), Gambetta (interior), Picard (finance), Dorian (public works), Magnin (agriculture and commerce), Simon (public instruction and cults),. (France. *Almanach National. Annuaire officiel de la République française* [Paris: 1872 ff.], 1871–1872, pp. xvii–xviii).

3. Vizetelly, p. 9.

4. Alfred Waldersee, *A Field-Marshal's Memoirs* (London: 1924), p. 108. This work is an abridgment of *Denkwurdigkeiten des General-Feldmarschalls Alfred Grafen von Waldersee* (Stuttgart and Berlin: 1923–1925). Where I have used the German original I have indicated that fact as follows: Waldersee (Germ.).

5. Lyons to Granville, Paris, Sept. (N.D.), 1870, and Sept. 12, 1870, Lord Edmond Fitzmaurice, *The Life of Granville* (3d. ed.; London: 1905), II, 55.

6. Jules Favre, *Le gouvernement de la défense nationale* (Paris: 1871–1875), I, 125.

7. Metternich to Beust, Paris, Sept. 8, 1870, J. P. T. Bury, *Gambetta and the National Defence* (New York and London: 1936), p. 78.

8. A. Dréo, *Gouvernement de la défense nationale. Procès-verbeaux des séances du conseil d'après les manuscrits origineaux de M. A. Dréo*, ed. Henri des Houx (Paris: 1905), pp. 78–80. Dréo said that his notes of these meetings were "completely personal," had no official character, and were never read in council or to any member of the government (France, Assemblée Nationale, *Enquête parlementaire sur les actes du govérnement de la défense nationale* [Paris: 1872–1875], Dépositions, II, 58–62, hereafter cited as *Enq. parl.*). Favre apparently drew up the circular on his own initiative (Jules Valfrey, *Histoire de la diplomatie du Gouvernement de la défense nationale* [Paris: 1871–1872], I, 10–11.

9. *Archives diplomatiques* (Paris: 1861–1914), 1871–1872, II, 511–513, no. 415, hereafter cited as *AD*.

10. Favre, I, 121–122.

11. Gladstone to Granville, Hawarden Castle, Oct. 7, 1870, Agatha Ramm (ed.), *The Political Correspondence of Mr. Gladstone and Lord Granville* ("Camden Third Series," LXXXI–LXXXII) (London: 1952), I, 138.

12. Valfrey, *Gouvernement*, I, 10–11.

13. Lyons to Granville, Paris, Sept. 6, 1870, Thomas Wodehouse Legh,

2d Baron Newton, *Lord Lyons* (London: 1913), I, 312–313. The American minister to France stated bluntly that "the Prussians demanded territory, and no government could yield to such a demand and live a day in France" (Elihu B. Washburne, *Recollections of a Minister to France, 1869–1877* [New York: 1887], I, 144).

14. Vicomte de Meaux, *Souvenirs politiques, 1871–1877* (Paris: 1905), p. 36.

15. In August 1866 the *Fränkische Zeitung* said that Prussia should demand Alsace and Lorraine in answer to Napoleon III's demands for compensations following the Prussian victory at Königgrätz (E. Malcolm Carroll, *Germany and the Great Powers,* 1866–1914 [New York: 1938], p. 31). In April 1867 the *Korrespondent von und für Deutschland* of Nuremberg spoke of "the possession of Metz and Strassburg" as the "rewards of a challenge to France" (*ibid.,* p. 37). As early as 1840 Prince William of Prussia—later Emperor William I—wrote a poem part of which was as follows:

> Peuple des Vosges et des Ardennes!
> Nous voulons te délivrer du joug de l'étranger.
> Ecoute donc l'appel des Allemands unis!
> Aie honte de l'esclavage dont les Francs t'oppriment;
> Mais si tu ne nous écoutes pas, si tu n'as pas honte d'être esclave,
> Nous saurons te contraindre à remplir ton devoir de fils de la patrie
> Afin qu'un jour tes enfants soient Allemands
> Et remercient les conquérants de leurs pères.

This poem and some other items concerning German demands for Alsace and Lorraine are contained in Paul Pilant, "Genèse des projets d'annexion de l'Alsace et de la Lorraine en 1870-1871," *Revolution de 1848,* 1934, vol. 31, pp. 155–169.

16. Wemyss, Rosslyn, *Memoirs and Letters of the Right Hon. Sir Robert Morier, G.C.B. from 1826 to 1876* (London: 1911), II, 179.

17. Carroll, *Germany,* pp. 26–27.

18. Gordon A. Craig, *The Politics of the Prussian Army, 1640–1945* (Oxford: 1955), p. 199.

19. Frederic B. M. Hollyday, *Bismarck's Rival: a Political Biography of General and Admiral Albrecht von Stosch* (Durham: 1960), p. 39.

20. Bismarck to his wife, July 9, 1866, Craig, p. 200.

21. *Ibid.,* p. 203. Concerning the pressures to which Bismarck was subjected see also Bismarck, Otto, *Bismarck, the Man and the Statesman* (New York and London: 1899), II, 43–53; Moritz Busch, *Our Chancellor* (New York: 1884), I, 387–389; Anneliese Klein-Wuttig, *Politik und Kriegführung in den deutschen Einigungskriegen 1864, 1866 und 1870/71* (Berlin: 1934), pp. 47–51.

22. Carroll, *Germany,* p. 41.

23. *Ibid.,* p. 75.

24. Morier memorandum, Wemyss, II, 171.

25. Carroll, *Germany,* p. 75.

26. Weymss, II, 172; Carroll, *Germany,* p. 73.

27. Dora N. Raymond, *British Policy and Opinion During the Franco-Prussian War* (New York: 1921), p. 160.

28. Richard Hartshorne, "The Franco-German Boundary of 1871," *World Politics,* II (January, 1950), p. 216.

29. Erich Eyck, *Bismarck* (Zurich: 1943), II, 508.

30. Carroll, *Germany,* p. 77.

31. Professor Hermann Baumgarten of Karlsruhe doubted the advisibility of a policy of annexation (Eyck, II, 508). The Central Committee of the Socialist Party issued a manifesto protesting the annexation of Alsace and Lorraine. The signers of the manifesto were arrested (*ibid.*, 511; Raymond, pp. 160–161) as was the Radical Dr. Johann Jacoby, who spoke out against Prussian territorial annexations (Raymond, p. 162).

32. Eyck, II, 508.

33. Crown Princess of Prussia to Queen Victoria, Homburg, Sept. 6, 1870, *Letters of Queen Victoria,* second series, 1862–1885, ed. George Earle Buckle (London: 1926–1928), II, 58–61, hereafter cited as *LQV.*

34. Hartshorne, *Loc. cit.,* p. 229.

35. *Ibid.,* p. 215.

36. *Ibid.,* p. 211, fn. 4.

37. *Ibid.,* p. 229.

38. *Ibid.,* p. 211.

39. *Ibid.,* p. 229.

40. Charles Downer Hazen, *Alsace-Lorraine Under German Rule* (New York: 1917), pp. 93–94.

41. Hartshorne, *loc. cit.,* p. 217; Carroll, *Germany,* p. 79.

42. Bismarck emphasized to Russia that Prussia would not make a final peace without acquiring territory to protect South Germany (W. E. Mosse, *The European Powers and the German Question, 1848–1871* [Cambridge, England: 1958], p. 334), and he instructed the North German envoy to Munich to give assurances that he fully intended to regulate the border in the interest of South German security (Eyck II, 508).

43. Moritz Busch, *Bismarck in the Franco-German War, 1870–1871* (New York: N.D.), II, 166–167.

44. General A. A. Ducrot, *La journée de Sedan* (Paris: 1871), p. 59.

45. Ducrot, p. 62; General E. F. de Wimpffen, *Sedan* (Paris: 1871), p. 242, quoted in Paul Deschanel, *Gambetta* (New York: 1920), p. 129.

46. F. M. L. Robert von Keudell, *Fürst und Fürstin Bismarck* (Berlin and Stuttgart: 1901), quoted in Otto von Bismarck, *Die gesammelten Werke,* ed. H. von Petersdorf, F. Thimme, and others (Berlin: 1924–1935), VII, 338–339, no. 256, hereafter cited as *GW.*

47. Favre, I, 126.

48. Lyons to Granville, Paris, Sept. 6, 1870, Public Record office, London, MSS, Foreign Office 27/1814, hereafter cited as PRO, FO.

49. Tissot to Favre, Sept. 9, 1870, Archives du ministère des affaires étrangères, Paris, MSS, Correspondance politique (Angleterre), Vol. 753, fols. 238–240. These materials were examined at the French foreign ministry archives, Paris. The pertinent archival materials are divided

into "Correspondance politique" and "Mémoires et documents." These documents will be cited as MAE, CP or MAE, MD, followed by the appropriate national section, volume and folio number.

50. Gabriac to Favre, St. Petersburg, Sept. 10, 1870, MAE, CP (Russie), 244: 270–273.

51. Dréo, p. 85.

52. Lyons to Granville, Paris, Sept 8, 1870, PRO, FO 27/1814.

53. Dréo, pp. 87–91.

54. Lyons to Granville, Paris, Sept. 9, 1870, PRO, FO 27/1815.

55. Dréo, pp. 94–96.

56. *Ibid.*, pp. 99–102.

57. *Ibid.*, pp. 105–109.

58. Communiqué from German General Headquarters, Rheims, Sept. 11, 1870, *AD*, 1871–1872, II 543–544, no. 458; Albert Sorel, *Histoire diplomatique de la guerre Franco–Allemande* (Paris: 1875), I, 331 and 340.

59. Bismarck to Bernstorff, Sept. 12, 1870, *AD*, 1871–1872, II, 547, no. 465.

60. Sorel, I, 311.

61. Favre to Gabriac, Paris, Sept. 13, 1870, MAE, CP (Russie), 244; 284–285. Thiers had encouraged Favre in his scheme (Favre, I, 130), and it was Thiers's revelation of the plan which prompted Granville's offer (Granville to Lyons, London, Sept. 13, 1870, *AD*, 1871–1872, II, 563–564, no. 477).

62. Lyons to Granville, Paris, Sept. 14, 1870, PRO, FO 27/1816.

63. Granville to Bernstorff, London, Sept. 14, 1870, *AD* 1871–1872, II, 575, no. 488. For the full text of Favre's message, see Favre, I, 148.

64. Dréo, pp. 114–118.

65. Newton, I, 318. Malet tells the story of his mission in Edward Malet, *Shifting Scenes, or Memories of Many Men in Many Lands* (London: 1901), pp. 233–270.

66. Lyons to Granville, Paris, Sept. 16, 1870, PRO, FO 27/1816.

67. Malet, pp. 265–269.

68. *Ibid.*, p. 270; Lyons to Granville (private letter), Paris, Sept. 16, 1870, PRO, FO 27/1816.

69. *The War Diary of the Emperor Frederick III, 1870–1871* (London: 1927), p. 121.

70. Favre to Gabriac, Paris, Sept. 13, 1870, MAE, CP (Russie), 244: 284–285.

71. Lyons to Granville, Tours, Sept. 19, 1870, *AD*, 1871–1872, II, 595–598, no. 502.

72. Favre, I, 156.

73. Lyons to Granville, Tours, Sept. 21, 1870, PRO, FO 27/1816.

74. Dréo, pp. 130–132. When Favre returned from his trip Rochefort complained that he had learned of it from a newspaper article, and the rest of the council made the same statement (*ibid.*, pp. 143–144). Maxime Du Camp says that he does not believe that Favre went to Ferrières without consulting the members of the government. He says that if the

trip had been entirely personal and secret it would not have been revealed the day after Favre's departure in *L'Electeur libre,* a newspaper edited by Arthur Picard, brother of the minister of finance (Maxime Du Camp, *Souvenirs d'un demi-siècle* [Paris: 1949], II, 148, fn. 1).

75. Favre, I, 156.

76. The Germans referred to Hendlé as Hell (Busch, *Franco-German War,* I, 157) and Hall (Otto von Bismarck, *Letters to His Wife, from the Seat of War, 1870–1871* [New York: 1903] 58–61, no. 37. Lutz apparently did not go on with Favre's party for there is no later mention of him. Busch reports, before the first Favre-Bismarck meeting, seeing a carriage in which there were three civilians and a Prussian officer (Busch, *Franco–German War,* I, 155). Maxime Du Camp says that Favre was accompanied when he left Paris by Prince Pierre Wittgenstein, military attache of the Russian embassy (Du Camp, II, 148).

77. Bismarck to Favre, Meaux, Sept. 18, 1870, *GW,* VIb, 507–508, no. 1815.

78. Bismarck to Favre, Meaux, Sept. 19, 1870, *ibid.,* p. 508, no. 1816.

79. *AD,* 1871–1872, 604–613, no. 508. Abeken to his wife, Sept. 20, 1870, *Bismarck's Pen: the Life of Heinrich Abeken,* edited by his wife (London: 1911), pp. 285–286.

80. Favre, I, 170.

81. *Ibid.,* p. 169. Although Favre did not specify the amount of money mentioned it would seem that he did in fact name the sum which France eventually paid. Bismarck wrote to his son that the French "believe they can pay 5 milliards [billion] of francs and appeared disposed to that if we leave them Strassburg" (Bismarck to Herbert Bismarck, Ferrières, Sept. 23, 1870, Bismarck, *Letters,* 58–64, no. 37; *GW,* XIV (II), 793, no. 1344; Hans Rothfels (ed.), *Bismarck-Briefe* [Göttingen: 1955], p. 316, no. 226).

82. *AD,* 1871–1872, 604–613, no. 508.

83. Busch, *Franco–German War,* I, 184–185.

84. Favre, I, 121; Dréo, pp. 143–147.

85. *AD,* 1871–1872, II, 610, no. 508.

86. *Ibid.*

87. Favre, I, 180. Bismarck said that Favre wanted a six-week armistice (W. B. Hazen, *The School and the Army in Germany and France: With a Diary of Siege Life at Versailles* [New York: 1872], p. 16).

88. Dréo, p. 145; *AD,* 1871–1872, II, 610, no. 508.

89. *AD,* 1871–1872, II, 610–611, no. 508.

90. Lyons to Granville, Tours, Sept. 27, 1870, PRO, FO 27/1817. In his circular of September 27 Bismarck spoke of Strasbourg, Toul, and Bitsche (*AD,* 1871–1872, II, 661–664, no. 537). Verdy du Vernois speaks of Bismarck having demanded Bitsche (General Julius von Verdy du Vernois, *With the Royal Headquarters in 1870–1871* [London: 1897], p. 166).

91. *AD,* 1871–1872, II, 611, no. 508.

92. Dréo, pp.143–147.

93. Favre, I, 190–191.

94. *AD,* 1871–1872, II, 603, no. 507.

95. Dréo, pp. 150–152. Copies of this account were sent out of Paris by balloon, some of them falling into German hands. Crown Prince Frederick said of the account: "The tenor seems to be fairly accurately reproduced" (Frederick III, p. 135).

96. Deschanel, pp. 62–63.

97. Frederick III, p. 131.

98. Abeken to his wife, Sept. 25, 1870, Abeken, p. 287.

99. Busch, *Franco–Prussian War,* I, 178.

II

Ferrières to Versailles

DURING OCTOBER, 1870 the fears of foreign intervention disturbed Bismarck "day and night," and he realized that the war must be ended as quickly as possible in order to forestall that possibility.[1]

Foreign intervention was, of course, precisely what Favre hoped for and he busily renewed his efforts to secure the aid of the neutral powers. From all he got expressions of sympathy but no concrete offers of assistance. Perhaps Great Britain offered the most serious potential help, and even that could scarcely be called a serious threat to Bismarck. Queen Victoria was aroused to send a telegram to the King of Prussia asking magnanimity for the defeated. It produced from the king an assurance that he would be as generous "as his duty towards his people and army would allow," but he also said that his duty toward Germany would allow him to "do nothing to jeopardise its safety, in the treaties for peace."[2] Far more dangerous than messages of Queen Victoria was the possibility of arousing the British government. Gladstone was repelled by the idea of territorial cessions without the wishes of the populations being consulted, and the prime minister was always inclined to act as his conscience dictated. "It would," he said, "comfort" him to find that the Alsatians were "disposed to be German."[3] At a cabinet meeting on September 30 he proposed that England make "an effort to speak with the other neutral Powers against the transfer of Alsace and Lorraine without reference to the populations."[4] The cabinet rejected the scheme and Granville confessed to being "quite exhausted after the longest fight I ever had against Gladstone."[5] Having downed Gladstone, Granville wrote to Lyons on October 4 that England would not support the use of force by the neutrals to back any "representations" which they might make to Prussia.[6]

Bismarck had less to fear than he might think but, so long as the war continued, the possibility of foreign intervention existed and could become a reality with some untoward incident. Perhaps because of this, forces were at work to bring about a resumption of the negotiations broken at Ferrières, not least among which was Bismarck himself. For example, he apparently made inquiries of Mgr. Dupanloup, Bishop of Orleans, to ask if he would consent to serve as intermediary between Prussian headquarters and the Paris government.[7] But the oddest of Bismarck's attempts to reopen negotiations came in late September and concerned itself with an American general.

When war broke out in the summer of 1870, General Ambrose Burnside was in London negotiating the sale of American railroad bonds.[8] Curious to observe the war, he went to France and eventually arrived at Prussian headquarters where he was introduced to Bismarck by General Phil Sheridan, American observer of the war.[9] The two men got along extremely well, and Bismarck spoke rather freely to the American. He said that, since France would never forgive Germany for defeating her, German policy must be "to diminish the territory of France as much as possible, so as to make her unable, for a long time, to disturb the general peace."[10] Bismarck took advantage of Burnside's presence to ask him to take a message to Paris concerning diplomatic communications with the besieged city.[11] At Burnside's suggestion that he might be of assistance, Bismarck drew up a précis of their conversations concerning peace terms and authorized him to acquaint Favre with it or otherwise use it as he saw fit.[12]

Burnside, accompanied by a Mr. Paul S. Forbes, presented himself to Elihu Washburne, the American minister,[13] and the two Americans spent October 2 and 3 in Paris. During their stay they met both Trochu and Favre. During one of the conversations, Burnside, taking the initiative, asked if he and Forbes might serve as intermediaries between the belligerents to try to bring an end to hostilities. He carefully pointed out that they had "no other mandate than their friendship for France,"[14] but said that he had reason to believe that Prussian headquarters would not reject the idea of an armistice.[15] Favre said that if Bismarck would drop the conditions which he had made at Ferrières, especially that which would place Paris under Prussian guns, he was prepared to sign an armistice. His only desire, he said, was "to consult the nation." He gave Burnside permission to tell Bismarck of their conversations.[16]

When the two Americans reached Versailles, where Prussian headquarters had now moved, they offered "to undertake further negotiations" and expressed themselves freely. They said that Favre now saw clearly that Alsace must be ceded but that the Paris government could agree to it only at the risk of being ousted from office. Therefore he felt the convocation of a constituent assembly was "highly desirable" since, if it expressed a wish for peace, "this might lend support to the Government." They also suggested, rather presumptuously it would seem, that some fortress other than Mont Valerien might be demanded as security for Paris in the event of an armistice.[17]

Thus far Bismarck seems to have taken little active part in the Burnside negotiations. From this point onward, however, his role became considerably more involved. When Burnside and Forbes were on the point of leaving Versailles, Bismarck asked them to remain for a few days so that they could take further proposals into Paris.[18]

On Saturday night, October 8, the Americans again presented themselves at the American legation in Paris. The next morning, at Washburne's house, Burnside told Favre that he had had four interviews with Bismarck, "who was in agreement with the king," and he wished now to report the substance of those four interviews. Bismarck understood the necessity of convoking an assembly, but he demanded certain conditions: an armistice of forty-eight hours to allow the elections and free communications between Paris and Tours for that purpose; free elections in the invaded departments except those of Alsace and Lorraine; exclusion from the armistice of the operations around Metz; no revictualling to be permitted during the armistice.[19] In addition, it was suggested "that a sort of *semi-armistice* might be agreed upon, to extend over a sufficient time to permit the convention to be held; that is to say, there should be no firing; but that the Prussians should be permitted to bring up their guns and provisions and that everything in Paris should remain *in statu quo*."[20] Favre said that he considered these conditions unacceptable but would consult the government and let Burnside know their decision the next morning.[21]

At a cabinet meeting on the evening of October 9 Bismarck's terms were presented to the government,[22] but they were rejected on the ground that they would put the elections at the mercy of the enemy.[23] The following morning, at the foreign ministry, Favre gave Burnside, in writing, the conditions under which France would accept an armistice: two week's armistice with provision for revictualling, and election of deputies from all departments. Burnside said that he would pass these along to Bismarck.[24]

When Burnside returned to Versailles he wrote to Favre to "clarify" their interview of the 10th and to explain that Bismarck felt that the period of "semi-armistice" might be fixed at one month. Again he said that Bismarck had not authorized him to make an offer of this sort but had told him that he could "speak freely," and that Bismarck felt that his conditions would be acceptable to the Prussian government if they were to the French.[25]

Bismarck's role in the Burnside mission is not completely clear. In spite of Burnside's protestations as to his unofficial status it appears that Bismarck did use him as a means of reopening negotiations with the Paris government. Some light on Bismarck's motives is perhaps furnished by Colonel Hoffman of the American legation, who was involved in a minor capacity in the negotiations and who, therefore, talked with Burnside. He says that Bismarck asked Burnside to undertake a "peace mission" into Paris. Bismarck told Burnside that England would probably be given credit if peace were obtained, and that he would rather see the United States get what credit was to be got.[26] On the whole, I see no reason to doubt Bismarck's sincerity in using Burnside to reopen negotiations, and he seemed unable to believe that the matter of revictualling Paris could become a bar to peace. The Government of National Defense, he said, "are not such d----d fools as to stand out on a point like that."[27]

Once again a stalemate had been reached and, for the moment, the center of diplomatic activity shifted to Tours. There Count Chaudordy conducted the business of the French foreign office. Publicly he was as adamant as Favre against a territorial cession, but privately he recognized that France would eventually be forced to such a course of action. "It must appear to rise at the critical time out of the necessities of the hour." He said, however, that the existing government dared not do so since it was pledged to the contrary, but that it stood ready to resign power into the hands of men not so committed.[28] Chaudordy was as anxious as Favre to secure neutral intervention but he was considerably more adept than the foreign minister. And at long last, the efforts of the French seemed about to bear fruit. The British government was under considerable pressure to abandon its position of complete neutrality and to make some effort to end hostilities,[29] and Chaudordy concentrated his efforts on Great Britain, skilfully playing on English sensitivities. He implied to Lyons that England, having taken the lead in organizing the "league of neutrals," had a responsibility to France since that action may have kept her from finding allies. He hinted at a loss of British influence in European affairs and raised the specter of Europe and the Orient dominated by Russia and Prussia. Since he said, "Prussia and France could make concessions to Europe that they would never make to each other," England, alone or in conjunction with the other neutral powers, should ask Prussia and France their conditions for peace. "Then the powers could confer together, declare what are, in their opinion, equitable conditions, and invite the belligerents to accept them."[30]

On October 16 England took the first hesitant steps away from her policy of complete abstention. She approached Russia to see if the two powers could not jointly approach the belligerents with, as suggested peace terms, payment of an indemnity and the dismantling of the fortresses of Metz and Strasbourg.[31] Russia rejected the suggestion, justifying her refusal on Favre's having rebuffed the Burnside terms.[32] Although Chaudordy pressed his case the British cabinet decided to make no further suggestions as to possible peace terms. On October 19 it did, however, recommend to both belligerents that they accept an armistice to permit the convocation of a constituent assembly and to serve as a point of departure for further negotiations,[33] and the other neutrals were asked to lend this action their support.[34]

This move coincided with Thiers's return to Tours from his trip to Europe's capitals in search of support for the French cause. On his arrival in St. Petersburg late in September he had been told that the only help he could expect from Russia would be assistance in opening direct negotiations with Prussian headquarters. It had then been agreed that the czar would, upon request from Tours, obtain permission from Prussia for Thiers to enter Paris to seek authorization to negotiate an armistice.[35] Thiers, a man supremely confident of his own abilities, was convinced that France's chances of ending the war lay in this line of endeavor.

Thus, at the time when England was approaching the belligerents with recommendations of an armistice and was urging the neutrals to do likewise, Russia was encouraging and advocating a renewal of direct Franco-Prussian negotiations.

When Thiers arrived in Tours he knew nothing of England's action.[36] At a meeting of the delegation on October 21 he gave an account of his voyage. His colleagues unanimously authorized him to send a telegram to St. Petersburg accepting the czar's offer of assistance and directed Thiers to prepare to go directly to Paris.[37] At the same time Chaudordy presented England's recommendation of an armistice, news of which had reached Tours that morning. The delegation decided that Thiers should take this note together with its own support, to Paris, and it stipulated that an armistice must last at least twenty-five days and must allow the besieged places to be revictualled.[38] Thiers, perhaps with a shade of sarcasm, compli-

Adolphe Thiers (Picture Collection, New York Public Library)

mented Chaudordy on having achieved "some extraordinary things."[39]

France now had two possibilities which might lead to a reopening of negotiations with Prussia and Thiers was determined to let neither drop. The day after the council meeting he asked the Russian chargé in Tours to request the czar to obtain the promised safe-conduct into Paris.[40] He also asked Lyons for British help in entering Paris and said that if only the fighting could be halted he felt that he would have "a certain authority on the population as well as on the men in power in Paris."[41]

England having taken the initiative in urging an armistice, the Austrian and Italian governments gave their support to the recommendation and Chaudordy told Lord Lyons that the Russian government supported it as well.[42] This was, in fact, a considerable over-statement of the position of the Russian government, which had merely agreed to facilitate direct negotiations between France and Prussia. England did request the safe-conduct and Lord Granville told Bernstorff that the Tours delegation did not propose an armistice, but that they "have every disposition" toward one.[43] Prussia granted the safe-conduct but in effect rejected the British proposal of an armistice, saying that any request must come from the French themselves.[44]

Thiers left Tours on October 28. Upon arrival at Versailles, he had a short interview with Bismarck but, at Thiers's request, they avoided a discussion of political matters.[45] Thiers then proceeded to the contact point at Sèvres, crossed the forward lines about four o'clock in the afternoon, and reached the foreign ministry about five.[46] There he met Favre, related his recent activities and agreed to be present that same evening at ten o'clock at a council meeting which Favre had called.[47]

The meeting that night was held in secret. Thiers brought

news of the fall of Metz and the loss of Bazaine's army, news which "filled everyone with consternation."[48] To offset somewhat this gloomy piece of news he told of a "great success, a kind of intervention of the neutral powers, notably Russia, acting as intermediaries of armistice proposals."[49] It was clear that he did not agree with those who argued for a fight to the finish, for he painted a gloomy picture of France's prospects and said that the departments were "unanimous" in desiring elections for a new assembly. In any event, he said, the important thing was to reopen negotiations.[50] To refuse an armistice proposed by the neutrals would, he said, offend them. An armistice would give the provincial armies a chance to reorganize and Paris could be revictualled; and it would satisfy the country, which wished to begin governing itself once again. He said that the delegation at Tours was in favor of an armistice even though Gambetta was not in favor of using it to call an assembly.[51]

In the discussion which followed, nearly all of the members of the government supported the idea of an armistice, but they insisted on the necessity of revictualling the besieged places.[52] The question was then posed if it should be stipulated that elections must be permitted throughout France. Thiers thought that he could successfully make the participation of Paris a *sine qua non*. As to the participation of Alsace and Lorraine, the majority did not wish to raise any difficulty on this score if it might wreck the possibility of an armistice. Thiers was inclined to be satisfied with using some general expression for the whole of France without singling out any specific provinces, for all felt that the armistice should not prejudge the question of final cessions of territory. Finally, three conditions were laid down for an armistice: an armistice to be granted for the purpose of holding elections; revictualling to be permitted proportionate to the duration of the armistice;

and free elections throughout France. Thiers opposed the suggestion that these conditions should be published, on the ground that negotiations would be made "impossible," for "the Prussians would not allow conditions to be dictated to them publicly."[53] Whereupon, hoping to reassure Paris that the government had not taken the initiative in reopening the negotiations, it was decided to insert a notice in the *Journal officiel,* telling of Thiers's arrival and of the neutrals' adherence to the "common idea" of proposing an armistice for the purpose of convoking a national assembly. It went on to say:

It is well understood that such an armistice must have for conditions revictualling proportionate to its length, and election of the assembly by the entire country.[54]

It is really rather difficult to imagine a better way to have informed the Prussians of their intentions!

The next day, October 31, Thiers received his credentials as negotiator. Disturbances had broken out in Paris because of misunderstanding as to the proposed armistice, and trouble was feared. Lunch was interrupted when messages arrived urging Favre's presence at the Hotel de Ville. As he left it was arranged that if he were not back by two o'clock Thiers should leave for Versailles. Thiers feared that any delay might lead to the revocation of his powers,[55] and when Favre had not returned by two o'clock Thiers left promptly.[56]

When Thiers arrived at Versailles he arranged to see Bismarck the next day, and at noon on November 1 the two men met at Bismarck's house in the rue de Provence. Bismarck showed annoyance at the proposal for an armistice having come from the neutrals, but he did not reject the idea itself. He said that he was as ready to accept an armistice now as he had been at Ferrières but that, since it would favor France, it might be necessary to ask for some military advantage in return for granting it, perhaps one of the forts of Paris or something else of like value. Thiers replied that further negotiations would be useless should Bismarck insist on a Parisian fort as a pledge. He also assured Bismarck that any objections which the Paris and Tours government might have concerning the election of an assembly arose from fears that elections might not be permitted in Paris or in occupied France and that, such fears being removed, all objections would fall. Bismarck said that he was interested only in seeing created a government with which he could deal effectively and he pointed out that he could always deal with the former imperial regime and had, in fact, been in touch with the empress.[57] Despite his show of "the most unmitigated contempt" for Napoleon III, he said that he was willing to use him in France.[58]

The conversation then turned to the question of provisioning Paris during an armistice. Bismarck said that he knew Paris to have provisions sufficient to last until the end of January. It was only a guess but from Thiers's reaction Bismarck inferred that, in fact, there was not that much.[59] Since the quantities of food to be admitted to the city depended on the length of the armistice, that question was taken up next. Thiers agreed with Bismarck that forty-eight hours would suffice for the actual balloting but he felt that much more time would be necessary to permit the convocation of the assembly. He considered twenty-five days the minimum time acceptable and thirty days as a maximum figure. Bismarck seemed to agree to the shorter period, saying that the armistice should be as short as possible to reduce the chance of difficulties arising. When discussion arose as to the meeting place of the assembly Bismarck was not convinced that Paris was the most desirable site and he said that some mention of this problem might well be set out in the armistice conditions.

At this point Thiers was beginning to congratulate himself on having attained his objectives in one meeting with Bismarck. His hopes were jolted when Bismarck said that he would have to ask the opinions of the military staff about all of these points and he felt that they would want some compensations for permitting an armistice. He also raised additional questions concerning the elections.[60]

Bismarck assured Thiers that there would be freedom for the elections, and he was willing to permit them to be held in the occupied territories except for certain border areas, specifically Alsace and German Lorraine. Thiers replied that to exclude those areas was to prejudge questions properly left to the final peace treaty. On this matter, he said, his instructions were positive and he preferred to say nothing about it. Thiers's statement drew from Bismarck the retort that "if it is not to be prejudged against you, it must not be prejudged against us either." The military were, he said, opposed to "electoral agitation" in those areas, and he suggested that nothing concerning the point be inserted in the draft of the armistice so that it would not be prejudged. He said that he had no objection to those areas being represented in the assembly by "notable inhabitants" who would be allowed free passage as well as freedom to express themselves and vote as they might wish without hindrance. Thiers did not insist on this point, feeling that it could be solved.[61] As to the conduct of the armies, it was agreed that they should halt in position as of the day of signing an armistice.[62]

The conversation broke up in mid-afternoon and the two agreed to meet the next afternoon so that the king might have a chance to discuss the proposed armistice with his military advisers.[63] This was the beginning of conversations which took

Bismarck in Versailles (Picture Collection, New York Public Library)

place for the next few days, often at the rate of two a day. Bismarck apparently liked the little Frenchman even though he remained sceptical of Thiers's diplomatic abilities. Thiers was, he said, "an able and likeable man, witty and ingenious," but he was "not fit to make . . . an armistice—hardly fit, indeed, to buy or sell a horse," since he "betrays his feelings" and "lets himself be pumped."[64]

At two o'clock on November 2 Thiers was once again at Bismarck's. The latter was in an irritable mood after having discussed the armistice problems with the king and his military staff. It was agreed, he said, that leading men from Alsace and Lorraine might be designated to represent those regions in the assembly. As to the other points he asked if Thiers had prepared a formal document stating his conditions. Thiers had done so, and Bismarck went over it point by point.

The preamble spoke of the agreement being "in conformance with the desire of the neutral Powers." Bismarck insisted that these words be deleted. Concerning Article I, which dealt with the cessation of hostilities and the convocation of an assembly, Bismarck offered no comment except to say that a date must be fixed for elections so that no time would be wasted during the armistice. Article II stated that the armistice should last for twenty-eight days. Bismarck said that it was to have been twenty-five days and that the longer period was an "inconvenience: it increases the quantity of provisions to be brought into Paris." He did not commit himself on this point, however. As to Article III, which dealt with the meeting place of the assembly, Bismarck said only that it must not meet in Paris. Article IV dealt with the freedom of elections and nothing was said on this point in view of what had already been decided. Bismarck did object to the wording of Article V, which concerned military operations during the armistice, saying that it was too restrictive of the German armies. Instead, he proposed to draw a "line of demarcation outside which the belligerents shall be masters of their movements," and he already had traced a line on a map for this purpose. The sixth and seventh articles provided for revictualling the fortified places and set out in detail the provisions which should be allowed into Paris. Bismarck objected that the amounts stipulated by Thiers would enable Paris to hold out two months longer. It would have to be changed, he said, and he indicated that Paris could be reprovisioned only if a fort were surrendered to the Germans. Thiers replied: "No, provisions and no fort, otherwise no armistice." Bismarck did not insist. Bismarck absolutely refused to consider the eighth and last article, which concerned arbitration by a third party.[65]

Bismarck then took up several matters which Thiers had not included in his memorandum. He wished the Seine estuary to be the limit between the two fleets, a proposal to which Thiers objected since it would abandon the Channel ports to the Germans. Bismarck spoke of the imprisonment by the French of the captains of thirty-five German merchant vessels and of the reprisals which had been levied. At this point the conversation degenerated into mutual accusations of atrocities. At one point Thiers arose as if to go and remained only when Bismarck assured him that he meant no insult to the honor of the French army. Finally the conversation came around once more to the question of the armistice. Bismarck said that "we are agreed upon nearly all points," but said that the Prussian military would not consent to the reprovisioning of Paris, "and without them I am powerless." However, he urged Thiers not to abandon hopes of coming to terms. He would, he said, see the king again and that perhaps an agreement could be reached if Thiers would only reduce his demands concerning revictualling. He promised Thiers a "final answer" at noon on the following day.[66] When Thiers left Bismarck on November 2 he was optimistic about the possibility of an armistice, feeling that the question of the amount of provisions to be allowed into Paris constituted the only block to a satisfactory agreement.[67]

When the two men met at noon on November 3 Thiers was shocked upon being told by Bismarck that a successful revolution in Paris had installed "Red Republicans" in power.[68] At Thiers's request, Bismarck permitted him to send his secretary, M. Cochery, into the city to find out exactly what had happened. Bismarck was as anxious for news as Thiers was and said that negotiations would be broken off if in fact a revolution had succeeded.[69]

That evening, following Cochery's return from Paris, Thiers went to tell Bismarck of the failure of the uprising and to ask the king's decision concerning an armistice. Bismarck said that the military would allow no revictualling except for some "equivalent return." "Give up the revictualling," he said, "or surrender a fort." Thiers replied that this was equivalent to demanding Paris. Bismarck replied that he had begun negotiations fully prepared to make sacrifices but that the Paris troubles and Gambetta's proclamation condemning the surrender of Metz had forced the Germans to abandon any hope of an armistice.[70]

During the night Thiers decided to make a major concession. The following day, November 4, Thiers asked for an interview with Bismarck and said that he was prepared to recommend to the Paris government that elections be held during an armistice without revictualling or even, if necessary, with no armistice at all. Bismarck agreed to permit Cochery to re-enter Paris to arrange a meeting at the outposts between Thiers and the members of the government, at which time Thiers would lay his recommendations before them.

Thiers took the opportunity afforded by this interview to

question Bismarck about Prussia's terms of peace. According to Thiers, Bismarck replied: "To-day we should ask Alsace (Haut-Rhin and Bas-Rhin); as for Lorraine, not a very great slice around Metz." He also said that he would try to persuade the king to return Metz to France if negotiations could begin immediately. Bismarck refused to be specific concerning an indemnity, speaking vaguely in terms of a sum equal to "two French budgets," by which Thiers "guessed" that he was thinking of some two billion francs.[71]

Thiers saw Bismarck again that evening and arranged to see him the next day after his return from Paris. As Thiers left, Bismarck told him that if the Paris government would be disposed to allow elections without an armistice he would allow complete freedom of elections in the occupied departments and would permit free communications between Paris and Tours for all matters concerning the elections.[72]

At nine o'clock on the morning of November 5, Thiers met Favre and General Ducrot, Trochu's deputy, at the Sèvres bridge. The men talked in an abandoned house and Thiers outlined his negotiations with Bismarck. Favre flatly refused to consider an armistice without revictualling but he and Ducrot agreed to the idea of holding elections without an armistice after Thiers told them of his conversation with Bismarck about possible peace terms: "Alsace, part of Lorraine and two milliards [billion]." Favre agreed to lay the proposals before the government and to send a reply to Versailles the next day by Cochery. Thiers returned to Versailles and told Bismarck the inconclusive results of his meeting.[73]

Upon his return to Paris Favre met with the cabinet to tell them of the conversation with Thiers. The cabinet rejected the Prussian offer of a twenty-five day armistice without revictualling. He then put forward the terms of peace. Although Thiers had said that Bismarck would probably ask *two* billion francs, Favre said that Bismarck had asked for Alsace and *three* billion francs. The council rejected this idea as well and said that Thiers should be instructed to break off negotiations immediately and return to Tours. There is no record in the notes of that meeting that Favre ever put forward the question of elections without an armistice.[74]

On Sunday, November 6, Cochery returned to Versailles bearing the government's instructions. When Thiers told him Bismarck expressed regrets but said that he was always ready to permit elections without an armistice. Thiers still had left one hope: inferring from the government's note to him that the question of elections without an armistice had not been squarely put to the council, he arranged for Cochery to stay behind at Versailles so that he might return to Paris to put this question directly to the government.[75]

Thiers left Versailles on the morning of November 7 to return to Tours. Cochery never returned to Paris, for the German military authorities feared that he might carry military information into the capital.[76] This question was, however, raised by Favre at a council meeting on November 8 only to be rejected.[77]

So ended these armistice negotiations. It would seem that there was really a chance to end hostilities at this time. Bismarck had backed down from his demand for a peace rather than an armistice. Thiers himself was convinced that Bismarck sincerely desired peace at the beginning of the negotiations but that by the end he had been overruled by what Thiers called "the military party" at headquarters, a faction which wanted a harsher peace than "the political party" to which he assigned Bismarck. Thiers felt that the Parisian uprising simply lent weight to these arguments.[78]

As to the acceptability of an armistice from the French point of view, Favre felt that to agree to any armistice was dangerous, and to accept an armistice without revictualling might lead to the fall of the government.[79] The government was blockaded in the capital and too subject to its tempers and moods. The uprising of October 31, although followed by a pro-government vote on November 3, had furnished a vivid reminder of the volatile nature of the Parisians. This, plus the policy to which the government was committed may have made the question of armistice or peace out of the realm of possibility.

Trochu is said to have remarked, upon hearing it said that the man in the street wanted peace: "The people in some drawing-rooms want peace; the man in the street wants war."[80] Thiers said: "The Empire ruined us; the Republic keeps us from saving ourselves."[81]

NOTES TO CHAPTER II

1. Otto von Bismarck, *Bismarck, the Man and the Statesman* (New York and London: 1899), II, 120.
2. From the queen's journal, Sept. 25, 1870, *LQV*, II, 71.
3. Gladstone to Granville, Hawarden Castle, Oct. 4, 1870, Ramm, I, 136–137.
4. John Morley, *The Life of William Ewart Gladstone* (New edition; New York: 1932), II, 346.
5. Granville to Lady Granville, Sept. 30, 1870, Fitzmaurice, II, 62.
6. Granville to Lyons, London, Oct. 4, 1870, MAE, CP (Angleterre), 754: 57–63.
7. Abbé Francois Lagrange, *Life of Monseigneur Dupanloup* (London: 1885), II, 389. Also cited in Gabriel Hanotaux, *Contemporary France* (Westminster: 1903–1909), I, 106, fn. 1.
8. Ben. Perley Poore, *Life of Burnside* (Providence: 1882), p. 285.
9. *Ibid.*, Colonel Hoffman, secretary of the American legation at Paris says that Burnside "happened to be at Versailles more from curiosity than any other motive" (Wickham Hoffman, *Camp, Court and Siege: A Narrative of Personal Adventure and Observation During Two Wars* [New York: 1877], p. 196).
10. Poore, p. 288.
11. Dréo, p. 174.
12. Hazen, *School and Army,* pp. 36–37.
13. Hoffman, pp. 197–198; Poore, p. 290.

14. Jules Simon, *Le Gouvernement de la défense nationale* (Paris: 1874), pp. 97–98.

15. Comte d'Hérisson, *Journal d'un officier d'ordonnance, juillet, 1870–fevrier, 1871* (Paris: 1885), p. 167.

16. *Ibid.*, p. 168.

17. Frederick III, pp. 144–146.

18. *Ibid.*, p. 148. See also Hazen, *School and Army,* p. 37.

19. Favre to Burnside, Paris, Oct. 9, 1870, *AD,* 1871–1872, II, 740–741, no. 601.

20. Washburne to State Department, Paris, Oct. 9, 1870, Washburne, *Recollections,* I, 162–163.

21. Favre to Burnside, Paris, Oct. 9, 1870, *AD,* 1871–1872, II, 740–741, no. 601. Washburne to State Department, Paris, Oct. 9, 1870, Washburne, *Recollections,* I, 162–163.

22. Dréo, pp. 196–198. Favre says that he and Trochu revealed the details to the government (Favre, I, 278–279). However, it is doubtful that Trochu talked with the Americans at this first visit. Washburne mentions meetings only on October 9 and 10, but he mentions Trochu only in connection with the second, *after* the report had been made to the government (Washburne, *Recollections,* I, 190–192 and 162–163). Hérisson records being present at a meeting at the foreign ministry at which Trochu was present, but seems inexact as to dates. He also records the two Frenchmen as saying, on October 10, that they must consult the government. But the government had already been consulted the evening before (Hérisson, pp. 168–169).

23. Favre, I, 278–279.

24. *Ibid.*, 279. Hérisson, who served as translator, says that after hearing these conditions, the two Frenchmen asked permission to consult the other members of the government and that, when the conference re-convened Favre gave Burnside a note couched in these terms. This raises the question if there were two government meetings. Dréo records none and I am inclined to believe that Hérisson has confused the dates of the meetings (Hérisson, p. 170). Favre's letter of resumé is in these terms except that it does not refer to any specific two week period for an armistice, merely saying that forty-eight hours was "absolutely illusory," and that any armistice should be prolonged until a solution could be given by the assembly, the armistice to apply to all military operations of the belligerents (*AD,* 1871/1872, II, 740–741, no. 601).

25. Burnside to Favre, Versailles, Oct. 11, 1870, Archives du ministère des affaires étrangères, Paris, MSS, Papiers de M. Jules Favre, pièces diverses importantes relative à la guerre, hereafter cited as MAE, Papiers Favre. On October 16 the *Journal officiel* announced the Burnside mission. The account stressed the personal quality of the attempt at a rapprochement and said that the conversations showed Bismarck's views to be the same as they were at Ferrières (*AD,* 1871–1872, III, 794, no. 625).

26. Hoffman, pp. 196–197.

27. *Ibid.*

28. Lyons to Granville, Tours, Oct. 18, 1870, Anna Augusta W. Ramsay, *Idealism and Foreign Policy* (London: 1925), p. 327.

29. Odo Russell wrote to Granville that "the problem of humane mediation without political interference" might be solved by "addressing a Circular to the Neutral Powers inviting them to join in a collective step." He said that this would throw the burden on Bismarck and Favre for the bombardment of Paris if they should refuse to meet again or should meet without good results (Odo Russell to Granville, Watford, Oct. 16, 1870, Paul Knaplund [ed.], *Letters From the Berlin Embassy* [Vol. II: Annual report of American Historical Association for 1942], [Washington: 1944], pp. 24–25). Also during October Sir Robert Morier suggested that if the neutrals could persuade France to give up Alsace and Strasbourg and Germany to give up Lorraine and Metz some basis of mediation might be found (Wemyss, II, 204–205). In October the *Quarterly Review* carried an article by Lord Salisbury calling for an end to the government's policy of nonintervention ("The terms of peace," *Quarterly Review,* Oct. 1870, CXXIX, 540–556. See also Gwendolen Cecil, *Life of Robert Marquis of Salisbury* [London: 1921–1931], II, 33–37).

30. Sorel, II, 33–35.

31. Granville to Buchanan, London, Oct. 16, 1870, *AD,* 1871–1872, III, 796–797; Ramsay, p. 332. Chaudordy had earlier suggested this as a possible solution (Lyons to Granville, Tours, Oct. 8, 1870, PRO, FO 27/1818; Chaudordy, *Enq. parl., Dépositions,* II, 1–11).

32. Buchanan to Granville, St. Petersburg, Oct. 17, 1870, *British Sessional Papers* (Blue Books), "Further correspondence respecting the war between France and Germany, 1870–1871, Franco-German War No. 1 (1871), C. 444, No. 226, p. 170, hereafter cited as *British Sessional Papers,* "Further correspondence."

33. Granville to Lyons, London, Oct. 20, 1870, MAE, CP (Angleterre), 754: 175; Tissot to Favre, London, Oct. 21, 1870, *ibid.,* fol. 181.

34. Mosbourg to Chaudordy, Vienna, Oct. 22, 1870, MAE, CP (Autriche), 503: 322.

35. Thiers, *Enq. parl., Dépositions,* I, 20–27.

36. Chaudordy, *ibid.,* III, 573–581.

37. Simon, *Défense nationale,* pp. 102–104.

38. Procès-verbal of the session, Tours, Oct. 1870, *AD,* 1871–1872, III, 830–831, no. 646; Simon, *Défense nationale,* p. 104. Gambetta, Crémieux, and Glais-Bizoin were suspicious lest such a move should compromise France (Sorel, II, 43; Valfrey, *Gouvernement,* I, 54–55).

39. Chaudordy, *Enq. parl., Dépositions,* III, 573–581. The rivalry of Thiers and Chaudordy is amusingly reflected in their comments before the parliamentary inquest concerning this incident (see Thiers, *ibid.,* I, 20–27 and Chaudordy, *ibid.,* I, 1–11 and III, 573–581).

40. Lyons to Granville, Tours, Oct. 23, 1870, PRO, FO 27–1819.

41. Lyons to Granville, Tours, Oct. 22, 1870, *ibid.; AD,* 1871–1872, III, 837–839, no. 655.

42. Lyons to Granville, Tours, Oct. 24, 1870, *AD,* 1871–1872, III,

855–856, no. 669. Chaudordy also announced that Austria, Italy, Turkey, and Russia supported England's proposal in a circular (*ibid.*, pp. 842–843, no. 658). Chaudordy also wrote to Gabriac that Gorchakov should be told that England's offer was spontaneous and that France had nothing to do with it. It was, he said, made before Thiers could tell the delegation of his trip. The delegation thought that England and Russia were entirely in agreement. The offer had to be transmitted to Paris and the French government was, he said, grateful to the czar for making that possible (Chaudordy to Gabriac, Tours, Oct. 30, 1870, MAE, CP [Russie], 244: 350). In his memoirs, Thiers says that on October 26 he was shown a telegram by Oukenev, the Russian chargé in which Gorchakov announced the consent of the King of Prussia to the czar's request for a safe-conduct (Louis Adolphe Thiers, *Memoirs, 1870–1873* [London: 1915], p. 64).

43. Granville to Bernstorff, London, Oct. 25, 1870, *British Sessional Papers,* "Further correspondence," p. 172, no. 230; Granville to Lyons, London, Oct. 24, 1870, *AD,* 1871–1872, III, 855, no. 668.

44. Granville to Lyons, London, Oct. 27, 1870, *ibid.*, 189, no. 245.

45. Thiers, *Memoirs,* p. 66; Abeken to his wife, Versailles, Oct. 30, 1870, Abeken, pp. 301–302; Favre, I, 289–290.

46. Thiers, *Memoirs,* p. 67.

47. Favre, I, 290.

48. Thiers, *Memoirs,* p. 68.

49. Jules Ferry, *Enq. parl., Dépositions,* I, 395.

50. Favre, I, 317–319.

51. Thiers, *Memoirs,* p. 69.

52. Thiers, *Enq. parl., Dépositions,* I, 24; Favre, I, 317–19.

53. Thiers, *Memoirs,* pp. 70–71.

54. Note du *Journal officiel, AD,* 1871–1872, III, 899, no. 706; Favre, I, 317–319.

55. Lyons to Granville, Tours, Nov. 10, 1870, PRO, FO 27/1820.

56. Thiers, *Memoirs,* p. 72.

57. *Ibid.*, pp. 73–76. The crown prince noted in his diary: "On Count Bismarck's asking what corresponding advantages it might 'perhaps' be contemplated offering *us,* Thiers expressed great surprise and added that the intention to elect a Constituent Assembly was . . . the concession to be accorded. . . . To the observation that at the very least we must demand the occupation of several of the Paris forts so as to preserve the military *status quo,* he replied indignantly" (Frederick III, pp. 177–178).

58. Lyons to Granville, Nov. 10, 1870, PRO, FO 27/1820.

59. Busch, *Franco-German War,* I, 279 and 280–283.

60. Thiers, *Memoirs,* pp. 77–78; Favre, II, 29–40.

61. Favre, II, 29–40; Thiers, *Memoirs,* pp. 78 and 80; Lyons to Granville, Tours, Nov. 10, 1870, PRO, FO 27/1820.

62. Favre, II, 29–40.

63. Thiers, *Memoirs,* p. 81.

64. Busch, *Franco-German War,* I, 280–283.

65. Busch states that on November 10 he saw a memorandum by Thiers setting forth the French proposals for an armistice. The tenor of the memorandum as set out by Busch corresponds to that set out by Thiers, and it would seem that this is the document to which he refers. Busch makes no mention, incidentally, of the article concerning arbitration by a third party (Moritz Busch, *Bismarck, Some Secret Pages of His History* [New York: 1898], I, 223–224).

66. The account of this meeting is taken almost entirely from Thiers, *Memoirs,* pp. 81–87.

67. Thiers, *Enq. parl., Dépositions,* I, 25.

68. Lyons to Granville, Tours, Nov. 10, 1870, PRO, FO 27/1820.

69. Thiers, *Memoirs,* p. 88.

70. *Ibid.,* pp. 90–91; Favre, II, 38.

71. This account is taken from Thiers, *Memoirs,* pp. 91–93. Valfrey (*Gouvernement,* II, 32, fn. 1) quotes the following story from A. Boucher, *Récits de l'invasion. Journal d'un bourgeois d'Orléans pendant l'occupation prussienne* (Orleans: 1871); at the home of the Bishop of Orleans, Thiers said that Bismarck had said to him: "If Paris wishes to force us to take it, we will stay here until hunger reduces it to surrender. We will not use bombardment; but we will be more demanding, we will ask five milliards [billion], all Lorraine and all Alsace." "And if we treat today," asked Thiers. "We will claim," answers M. Bismarck, "only two milliards. We will leave you Metz; you will give us behind that city German Lorraine; you will keep the larger part of the Haut-Rhin; you will give up Strassburg and the rest of Alsace. This is the peace that I offer you; I will have trouble persuading the king, but I will finish by convincing him." Valfrey says that he always found Thiers less precise on these details each time that his words had any official character.

72. Favre, II, 39.

73. Thiers, *Memoirs,* pp. 95–98.

74. Dréo, pp. 282–285.

75. Thiers, *Memoirs,* pp. 98–99.

76. *Ibid.,* pp. 100–101.

77. Dréo, p. 293.

78. Lyons to Granville, Tours, Nov. 10, 1870, PRO, FO 27–1820.

79. Favre, II, 86.

80. D. W. Brogan, *France Under the Republic* (New York: N.D.), p. 45.

81. *Ibid.*

III

A Time of Tensions

BETWEEN THIERS'S RETURN to Tours in November and the signing of the armistice in January little that was new was offered in the diplomatic contest between Germany and the Paris government. Neither side ever publicly retreated from the positions taken at Ferrières and Versailles on any major point nor was there ever again any real chance of involving the neutrals in the war.

Bismarck clearly left the way open for a renewal of negotiations for an armistice with elections or for elections without an armistice. The matter caused a "violent quarrel" between Thiers and Chaudordy. The latter maintained that elections would be impossible without an armistice and Thiers urged that elections be held without an armistice. Exasperated, Thiers cried out: "They will at least be much more free under the Prussians than under Gambetta's Prefects."[1] The French government admitted that it might be willing to reduce the duration of an armistice as well as the amount of provisions to be allowed to enter the besieged cities,[2] but it refused to consider elections without an armistice or an armistice without revictualling.

On December 14 Bismarck told a British diplomat that

peace might well be delayed "for many months" in the absence of "any legal Body of men in France to represent the national will."[3] Certainly the chaotic conditions of French politics were complicating Bismarck's efforts to end the war on terms favorable to Prussia by negotiating with a government sufficiently stable to guarantee their performance. The rich profusion of past and present French régimes gave Bismarck, at least in theory, several groups with which to deal. Bonapartists, Republicans, Legitimists, and Orleanists were all scrambling for power during the winter of 1870 and at one time or another Bismarck dealt with them all. The two Royalist factions held the least attractions for him. He felt that an Orleanist restoration would almost certainly launch France on an aggressive foreign policy. Even before the fall of the empire he instructed Busch to write a piece for the German press concerning the hopes of the Orleans princes. In no uncertain terms it warned that the Orleanists sought to regain the throne "by a display of energy, and would endeavour to retain it by yielding to the lusts of Chauvinism, the thirst for glory and the ambition to patronise the whole world which are such conspicuous French characteristics. . . . Napoleon's fall seems to be near, but has not yet taken place. . . . A peace concluded with an Orleans restored to the throne of France, would doubtless be a less genuine peace than one effected with Napoleon, who has at least accumulated glory enough."[4] Late in September one of the Legitimist princes visited Bismarck at Ferrières to plead the merits of a Bourbon restoration.[5] And as late as mid-November Bismarck said that "Henry V would be as acceptable as any other, provided he had an understanding with Orleans, and got the backing of the French people."[6]

Such ideas seem to have been considered only rarely, however. Practically, Bismarck's choice was between the imperial régime and the Government of National Defense. He would have preferred to deal with the Bonapartists but, whatever his own attitude toward republicanism, Bismarck was sufficiently realistic not to let his personal inclinations stand in the way of his goals. Early in October he publicly denied that the republican institutions of France constituted any danger to Germany.[7] And indeed he told Busch that when "a negotiator from Gambetta" had asked if he would recognize the republic he had replied "not merely a Republic, but if you like a Gambetta Dynasty, only that dynasty must give us a secure and advantageous peace."[8] That was Bismarck's goal, and to achieve his "secure and advantageous peace" he was prepared to deal with any and all French factions which presented themselves. As a result, he conducted negotiations—often simultaneously—with Bonapartists and republicans alike.

When Napoleon III surrendered at Sedan Bismarck was hopeful that his surrender meant the end of the war and he indicated that his conditions would be easier if such were the case.[9] He also expressed the hope that the imperial régime would be able to survive the surrender.[10] Unfortunately for his purposes, Napoleon made it clear that he was surrendering only for himself and not for France. He refused to sign any peace preliminaries and referred Bismarck instead to the government of the empress-regent in Paris.[11] Bismarck did not write off so easily the possibility of coming to terms with the Empire, however. Even after the revolution in Paris had installed the Government of National Defense he went to great lengths to make it clear that Germany still recognized the imperial regime as the only government authorized to enter into peace negotiations.[12] Napoleon was given the best of treatment, so good in fact that there was publicly voiced criticism of the less than Spartan captivity to which he was consigned. Bismarck could see no point in killing by harsh treatment the goose which might lay the much desired golden egg of a peace treaty and he defended Napoleon's elegant captivity at Wilhelmshöhe as being in Germany's interest, piously explaining that it was not for Germany to stand in judgment on the defeated emperor.[13] Bismarck carefully took the stand that the form of France's future government was immaterial,[14] and he received Favre at Ferrières, but he also kept open his contacts with Napoleon.[15]

The most important of Bismarck's negotiations with the Bonapartists during September and October revolved around the strange Regnier affair. Early in September, after the arrival in England of the Empress Eugenie, she received a letter from a man named Regnier proposing a plan whereby she should return to France, call together the French parliament at Metz under the protection of Marshal Bazaine's army, and make peace with the Germans.[16] Regnier followed the letter by appearing in person and requesting an audience with the regent. Eugenie apparently thought that he was an agent of the Germans and refused to see him even though some members of her suite did see him and, far from finding the lunatic they had expected, were impressed with the man's sincerity.[17] Eugenie persisted in her refusal to see him, however, and she also refused to give him a message for delivery at Wilhelmshöhe, where Regnier said he was going. Regnier was not so easily dismissed. With the help of Augustin Filon, tutor to the Prince Imperial, he contrived to secure an innocuous postcard message from the prince to his father.[18] Armed with this, Regnier then left for the continent. Eugenie was annoyed with Filon and there was considerable concern among her suite as to what use Regnier would make of the boy's message.[19] The empress telegraphed to warn Napoleon not to receive Regnier, "*un inconnu.*"[20]

However, Regnier went not to Wilhelmshöhe but to German headquarters, arriving at Ferrières at the time of Bismarck's interview with Favre. He seems to have had no trouble getting an interview with Bismarck, and in the course of two conversations he unfolded his scheme and suggested that instead of going to see Napoleon he should go instead to Metz to try to persuade Marshal Bazaine to support his scheme for an imperial restoration.[21] Bismarck later said that he was puzzled by Regnier's relationship with the empress and had decided that he might be a hair dresser or tradesman who, having fallen from Eugenie's favor, was trying desperately to regain her good graces by being of service to her. He also said that he had not taken Regnier too seriously.[22] Perhaps not, but the fact remains that Bismarck did see him and did go along with his scheme. It may have been because information reaching headquarters indicated that Bazaine and a large part of his besieged army were hostile to the government in Paris.[23] But whatever the reason Regnier did receive permission to see Bazaine and he entered Metz on September 23. He produced the postcard from England and pleaded with Bazaine to send an officer to Eugenie to persuade her to come to terms with Bismarck. Somewhat reluctantly, Bazaine agreed to send General Bourbaki to England to see the empress.[24] Bourbaki left Metz with Regnier but the two parted company. Regnier announced that he was returning to Bismarck and that in a few days he would bring Eugenie a draft treaty for her signature.[25]

Bismarck was probably eager to have Regnier return from Metz for since his departure still another element had been added to the already complex situation. On September 22 Napoleon had sent a letter to Bismarck which, while saying nothing about peace negotiations, did raise the question of an armistice for Bazaine's army so as to save it for the preservation of order once a peace treaty had been signed.[26] When

Regnier returned to headquarters, however, Bismarck realized that he was no nearer a solution of his problems than he had been before. Although Regnier claimed authority to negotiate in Bazaine's name he was so vague as to Bazaine's terms that a wire from Bismarck brought the reply that Bazaine was ready for surrender negotiations only if he were allowed free exit with his troops and also the news that he had no authority for the surrender of the fortress of Metz itself. Bismarck was totally uninterested in a scheme which would not only not give the fortress of Metz to the Germans but would also run the risk of delivering the army of Metz into the hands of the republicans. He proceeded to order Regnier to leave headquarters and replied to Napoleon that he could not consider an armistice with Bazaine without knowing his future political stand.[27]

Bismarck might have continued to deal with Regnier even after Bazaine's rebuff had Bourbaki's mission succeeded. But although Eugenie sympathized with Bourbaki's motives in leaving Metz, she accused him of having abandoned his post and she notified the Prussian government that Regnier had no authority whatever to negotiate in her name.[28] Regnier was to appear once more, this time while Bourbaki was trying unsuccessfully to arrange his return to Metz. Eugenie finally agreed to receive him. Regnier, who was furious that Bourbaki had claimed not to know Bismarck's peace terms, sketched out the terms which he claimed to have from Bismarck himself: the army of Metz to be granted an armistice with the honors of war and the right of reprovisioning; it would then hold a neutral zone where the parliament would be called to ratify the terms of the peace which the regent would be expected to sign. And the terms of the peace? They "would be painful but not disastrous, it would cost France much money and some districts of Alsace." Eugenie heard him out but refused the entire scheme.[29]

Napoleon had heard the news of Bourbaki's arrival in London with satisfaction.[30] He was displeased, therefore, that Eugenie had refused to deal with him. In a letter of October 6 he told her that he would certainly never sign a disastrous peace and he warned that it must never appear that they were placing the interests of the dynasty ahead of those of the national defense. At the same time, he felt that Bazaine's army was their only real hope and he said that she should use Bismarck's good will to "keep in touch with the marshal and to await events."[31]

Under constant pressure from her advisors to come to terms with the Germans, Eugenie finally decided to make an effort to find out what Bismarck's peace terms might be. To that end she proposed to send an emissary to German headquarters and, through Napoleon, she requested permission for Théophile Gautier, *fils,* to be allowed to proceed to Versailles.[32] Napoleon secured the passport which she requested but he was displeased when he heard that she had written to King William I. The letter would only embarrass the king, he said, a practice "unwise with someone from whom one wants something." He was even more strongly opposed when he heard that the empress was considering going to Metz and he stressed the necessity of letting events in France seem to arise spontaneously and not result from intrigue by the Bonapartists.[33] Gautier arrived at Versailles on October 23 but he found that in the two weeks since he had left England events had taken an unforeseen turn.

In mid-October Marshal Bazaine had taken the initiative in contacting German headquarters with a view to withdrawing his army from Metz to some place in French territory where he could convoke the assembly which could in turn reconstitute the French government in any form which would be representative of the feelings of the country. For that purpose he sent General Boyer to Versailles.[34] Bismarck had already heard from Bernstorff that Eugenie was weakening in her determination not to negotiate, and this new opportunity must have seemed heaven-sent.[35] He received Boyer cordially. He disclaimed any intention of dictating the future form of France's government but he also indicated that he would prefer to deal with the imperialists than with the republicans. He had, however, certain specific conditions which must be met before Bazaine's army could be permitted to leave Metz: Bazaine must make a public declaration of support for the regency; Eugenie must issue a proclamation to the French people calling for their support and must be prepared to sign whatever peace terms he might propose; and a French parliament based on new elections must be convened to ratify her acceptance of his terms. If these conditions—essentially a revival of the Regnier terms—were met he was prepared to permit Bazaine to leave Metz with the honors of war. He refused, however, to divulge what his ultimate conditions of peace might be.[36]

At Metz a council was called by Bazaine to consider Bismarck's terms. It refused to issue a declaration of support of the regent on the grounds that the army should not meddle in politics but it also authorized Boyer to get in touch with Eugenie concerning Bismarck's offer. Boyer left for England, arriving there on October 22. He urged Eugenie to sign a peace treaty with Bismarck and assured her of army support should she do so. He could, of course, shed no light on Bismarck's peace terms. By now Eugenie was prepared to go to France under Bazaine's protection but she insisted on knowing Bismarck's peace terms before she would do so. Her advisors brought enormous pressure to bear on her to accept Bismarck's terms and she was in "a dreadful state of mind."[37] She refused to be stampeded, however, and she dispatched messages to Bismarck and King William asking what terms she would be expected to sign and also demanding a two week armistice with reprovisioning for Bazaine's army. While waiting for replies to her messages she arranged a meeting in London with Count Bernstorff. He could not or would not shed any light on Bismarck's demands except to say that they would involve some cession of territory. He did urge her to deal with Bismarck and said that she could probably expect more lenient terms than Bismarck was prepared to give to any other party or faction. Her insistence on knowing Bismarck's terms plus the fact that Bazaine's declaration of support for the empire was not forthcoming brought these negotiations to a halt as quickly as they had begun.[38]

It was these negotiations which were under way when Gautier arrived at Versailles. And although it was quickly apparent to Bismarck that the London negotiations were not going to succeed he nevertheless listened to Gautier's proposals. He offered Bismarck a treaty whereby France would demilitarize Strasbourg and its environs, establishing it as a free city, pay an indemnity of two billion francs, and surrender Cochin China. When Bismarck refused these terms Gautier offered—subject to Eugenie's approval—to create a buffer state of Alsace, the inhabitants of which would vote at the end of five years whether they would remain independent, return to France, or go to Germany. These terms, too, were refused, and these negotiations ended when Metz fell on October 27.[39]

Eugenie made one last desperate attempt to prevent the fall of Metz when, on October 25, she offered to designate Bazaine "Lieutenant-General of the Empire" with power to sign a peace treaty. In the absence of a statement from Bazaine that he would support the empire Bismarck rejected this scheme as he had rejected the others.[40]

It should be noted that the breakdown of these negotiations came when Bismarck already knew that Thiers was on his way to Versailles and this may have made him more willing to end fruitless negotiations in favor of those which offered more promise. When the negotiations with Thiers collapsed also, Bismarck faced a stalemate in his search for some French faction to deal with. In spite of earlier failures, he was not prepared to drop the possibility of an imperial restoration and he continued to negotiate with the Bonapartists. One of the difficulties facing him was that the Bonapartists themselves were now divided into several factions, each favoring a different scheme for ending the war. The captive Napoleon III displayed the same lassitude and inability to reach a decision which had characterized the last years of his reign, and with the absence of any strong leadership from him, his followers were hopelessly divided. Out of this tangled web three proposals emerged. Each of them caught Bismarck's fancy at one time or another and each failed for different reasons.

The first plan was the one which Napoleon himself espoused. This was to by-pass the old assembly altogether in favor of a new assembly chosen from the membership of the old *conseils généraux* of the Empire. He argued that the old assembly had been discredited and that it would stir up the country dangerously to try to hold new elections. The councils, on the other hand, he considered to be representative of the feelings of France and hence competent to decide the issue of continued war or peace. And as to the future form of France's government, he felt them to be sufficiently loyal to the Empire as to give it a chance of restoration and sufficiently conservative to keep out of power men such as Gambetta and Favre. All of these were arguments which appealed to Bismarck and he espoused the idea.[41] Implicit in this plan were certain questions such as who had the legal right to summon any such assembly, and Bismarck asked Napoleon to send him someone versed in French law to discuss the matter with him. Napoleon hesitated and did not finally settle on Count Clary as the right man for the mission until early in January, and by that time the plan had suffered a fatal blow because on December 25, apparently fearing some such move, Gambetta dissolved the councils.[42]

The second scheme came from lesser lights in the Bonapartist camp. Ever since Eugenie had rejected Bismarck's proposals at the time of Boyer's mission there had been dissatisfaction among some of the colony of imperialist exiles in England, particularly on the part of Persigny. Early in December Persigny and Count Palikao unfolded to Count Bernstorff a scheme whereby the old Corps Legislatif and Senate would be convoked by Palikao at Orleans to choose a legal government for France and to make peace with Germany. They did not approve of Napoleon's plan and were confident that the old assembly would come out for a restoration of the empire. Since at the moment Napoleon's search for an emissary to Bismarck had not been successful Bismarck adopted this new scheme. Then, inexplicably, Persigny and Palikao hesitated, arguing that for their plan to be feasible the republic had to be soundly defeated and the time was not yet ripe. The Bonapartist lethargy seems to have afflicted them because they never raised the question again.[43]

The third proposal, which originated with Eugenie, began with the least chance of success and came closest to succeeding. In mid-December an intimate advisor to Eugenie, Clement Duvernois, reported to Bernstorff that the empress was prepared to negotiate peace preliminaries with Bismarck on the basis of territorial cessions no larger than Nice and

Savoy. She was prepared to return to France and to call a plebiscite to ratify the preliminaries and, at the same time, to decide the question of the continuation of the dynasty.[44] Bismarck rejected this plan for a variety of reasons not the least of which was that Eugenie clearly expected to get easier terms than he was prepared to give to the republic.[45] Napoleon, too, disapproved of Eugenie's scheme. At the moment he still hoped that his own scheme would succeed and he also warned her of the possible indignities to which she might be subject should she return to France unbidden by any popular call.[46] By early January Eugenie had dropped all of her conditions. Clement Duvernois said that she was now prepared to negotiate with Bismarck provided only that the Germans recognize her as regent and give her a chance to establish herself in France. Since Paris seemed about to fall, the time seemed propitious for settling both the question of a peace treaty and that of the political future of France. Bismarck agreed to receive Clement Duvernois at Versailles to discuss these questions.[47]

Having made this decision Bismarck marshaled every conceivable argument to convince the king that it was in Germany's interests to come to terms with the Bonapartists and to help facilitate an imperial restoration.[48] But just when Bismarck thought his goal in sight it disappeared like a mirage. Clement Duvernois, traveling under the name of "Duparc," left London on January 16. But instead of going directly to Versailles he went first to Wilhelmshöhe to consult with the emperor and then to Brussels to consult with the Bonapartist colony in that city. As a result he did not arrive at Versailles until January 28 and then he found Bismarck on the point of closing negotiations with Favre for ending the war. The Bonapartists had procrastinated for the last time.[49] Bismarck did talk to "Duparc" even though the negotiations with Favre ended successfully. Moreover, he kept up his contacts with the Bonapartists. This is not to say that Bismarck did not negotiate in good faith with the Paris government, but until he should have completed all negotiations with them he was apparently holding the possibility of a Bonapartist restoration over the head of France, like the sword of Damocles.[50]

The end of 1870 and the beginning of 1871 was a particularly busy and tense time for Bismarck. He was immersed in the negotiations surrounding the establishment of the new German Empire, involved in the diplomacy surrounding the opening in London of the Black Sea Conference, and trying to find a faction in France with which he could deal. He had a prodigious capacity for work but even his limits must have been stretched to the breaking point, and during those weeks he was often irritable and out of sorts. Opposition tended to anger him under the best of conditions and during these weeks he as often complained of his enemies at German headquarters as he did of his French antagonists. For example, the negotiations with the Bonapartists had not enjoyed wholehearted support at headquarters. Some of the officers had nothing but contempt for France and objected to any negotiations—whether with Bonapartists or republicans—until France should have been thoroughly beaten. Moltke was of this view and the Grand Duke of Baden felt that his influence with the king was so great that the king might well have rejected an imperial restoration even if Bismarck's negotiations had succeeded.[51] Indeed, it was precisely because of this military influence that Bismarck had brought all of his powers of persuasion to bear on the king in January when it looked as though Clement Duvernois's arrival at Versailles would bring his negotiations with the imperialists to a successful conclusion. Bismarck resented the intrusion of the military into a field which he considered essentially political and hence within his own domain. He complained that his work was made more difficult by them: "They snatch it unto themselves, spoil it, and I am the one who is responsible for it all afterward."[52]

Bismarck's annoyance with the military over this matter was merely symptomatic of a dangerous and growing hostility between the chancellor and the Prussian generals. The quarrel was of long standing.

This rift between the Prussian civil and military officials began during the Austro-Prussian war of 1866. The war had begun with harmony between Bismarck and the military but before it ended there was bitterness on the part of the generals over what they considered Bismarck's interference in purely military matters. Bismarck had no stomach for a deeper Prussian involvement in Austria and he used all of his influence with the king to prevent a march on Vienna and to limit the Prussian peace terms. It was only natural that hard feelings should arise over such jurisdictional quarrels, and even Bismarck said that "the weight of influence which the King allowed me in 1866 was certainly contrary to military traditions."[53]

But worse was to come. When the war with France began the high command set out to prevent Bismarck from intruding on its territory. Not only did he receive little cooperation in such comparatively unimportant matters as securing living accommodations but, insofar as possible, he was told nothing about the course of military operations.[54] The first serious differences of opinion between Bismarck and the military came at the time of the battle of Sedan. That battle, resulting as it did in the downfall of the Bonapartist regime, had important political as well as military repercussions. Bismarck felt that the German armies should suspend their offensive until the political situation in France should be clarified.[55] Moltke had other ideas, however, and he made it abundantly clear that the terms of surrender would be the same whether Napoleon III surrendered for himself or for France.[56] And he persuaded the king to adopt his point of view and to pursue the French until they were destroyed. From that time Bismarck was never invited to attend a war council.[57] Relations steadily got worse. Bismarck accused the military—and with reason—of placing obstacles in the way of his negotiations with Bazaine to gain his support of the regent.[58] Not until mid-October did Bismarck succeed in receiving copies of telegrams sent by German headquarters to the press and even then this concession was grudgingly granted and poorly handled.[59]

Moltke did not share Bismarck's fear of foreign intervention and he and most of the other military leaders bitterly resented what they considered Bismarck's interference in military matters. By the end of October relations beween Bismarck and Moltke were positively acrimonious.[60] Bismarck thought that the king listened too much to the generals in political matters.[61] He complained of his treatment at the generals' hands: "Why don't the military inform me of all that is important? In 1866 it was different. At that time I was called in on all discussions. And that is as it ought to be. My business demands that: for one thing, I must be informed about military events in order to conclude peace at the right time."[62]

The issue which brought this dissension to the danger point was the question of the bombardment of Paris. On the surface this, too, would seem to have been solely a military matter and so the generals considered it. To Bismarck, however, matters of larger policy were at stake. He had always feared foreign intervention and hoped for a quick end to the war to forestall that possibility. As the war dragged on into the winter of 1870 peace seemed not to be in sight. Although the military initiative still lay with the German armies the French forces showed signs of making a recovery. On November 9 the French Army of the Loire, composed of raw recruits, won a genuine victory at the battle of Coulmiers. However transitory this success might be, it lent weight to Gambetta's demand for war *à outrance* and weakened Thiers's contention that an armistice was absolutely essential. To make matters worse, there was always the possibility—albeit a remote one—that the Black Sea Conference might turn its attention in the direction of the war in France.

For all of these reasons Bismarck was anxious to have Paris bombarded, hoping to end the wearisome siege as quickly as possible. He was supported by Roon, but he was bitterly opposed by Moltke and most of the other high military figures. They were unconvinced of the threat of foreign military intervention, were certain that starvation would eventually reduce Paris, and felt that there was nothing to be gained from a bombardment until it could be mounted with maximum strength and force so as to have the maximum effect. In an effort to carry his argument with the king Bismarck used every trick and strategem to whip up public support in Germany for his position. His attempts understandably met with growing hostility from the so-called "anti-bombardiers." Typical of their feelings is the statement of General Blumenthal that "to yield up one's convictions to the judgment of unscientific and unjustifiable interference would be an unpardonable sign of weakness."[63] Bismarck complained bitterly that neither the king nor Moltke gave him any information and that they treated him rudely.[64] The bombardment did not really begin in earnest until early January.

This quarrel was an unfortunate one because it exacerbated feelings at headquarters to a dangerous degree. It was particularly unfortunate in that the results of the bombardment, when it finally did come, were so inconclusive. For by the time that it began there were already signs that Paris was on the verge of starvation and its surrender appeared imminent in any case.

NOTES TO CHAPTER III

1. Lyons to Granville, Tours, Nov. 14, 1870, Newton, I, 338. It seems that Favre was wavering on this point as well. On November 19 he wrote to Gambetta that he had argued in council for elections without an armistice, but had given way before the argument that resistance would be impossible if an assembly were called (Favre to Gambetta, Paris, Nov. 19, 1870, *AD,* 1871–1872, III, 1018, no. 779). He had raised the question of holding elections without an armistice at the meeting of the council on November 10. The debate on this point lasted for four days (Dréo, pp. 301–317).

2. Favre to Chaudordy, Paris, Nov. 15, 1870, Favre, II, 50; Chaudordy to Gabriac, Tours, Nov. 17, 1870, MAE, CP (Russie), 244: 381; Lyons to Granville, Tours, Nov. 24, 1870, PRO, FO 27/1820.

3. Odo Russell to Granville, Versailles, Dec. 14, 1870, Knaplund, pp. 28–29.

4. Busch, *Our Chancellor,* II, fn., pp. 89–90.

5. Hazen, *School and Army,* p. 11.

6. Bismarck to Arnim, Nov. 12, 1870, quoted in Lillian Parker Wallace, *The Papacy and European Diplomacy, 1869–1878* (Chapel Hill: 1948), p. 138.

7. Sorel, II, 18.

8. Busch, *Franco-German War,* I, 265–266.

9. Ducrot, p. 61.

10. Michael Howard, *The Franco-Prussian War: the German Invasion of France, 1870–1871* (New York: 1961), p. 223, fn. 4.

11. Herbert Geuss, *Bismarck und Napoleon III: ein Beitrag zur Geschichte der preussich-französischen Beziehungen, 1851–1871* (Cologne: 1959), p. 280.

12. Busch, *Bismarck,* I, 172.

13. *Ibid.,* pp. 186–188; Geuss, p. 282; Raymond, p. 164; Bismarck to Count H. Bismarck, Ferrières, Sept. 23, 1870, Bismarck, *Letters to His Wife,* pp. 58–61, no. 37. When Napoleon III was on his way into captivity Bismarck was remarkably unconcerned about the possibility that he might break his word and escape (Busch, *Bismarck,* I, 159).

14. Bismarck to Bernstorff, Meaux, Sept. 17, 1870, *GW,* VIb, 503–504, no. 1812; Busch, *Bismarck,* I, 197.

15. During September and October a man named Hellwitz was back and forth between Kassel and German headquarters although the actual purpose of his missions is unknown (Geuss, pp. 282–283).

16. Comte Fleury, ed. *Memoirs of the Empress Eugenie* (New York and London: 1920), II, 529; Thomas Wiltberger Evans, *Memoirs: the*

Second French Empire (New York: 1905), p. 432; Robert Sencourt, *The Life of the Empress Eugenie* (New York: 1931), p. 293; Augustin Filon, *Recollections of the Empress Eugenie* (Paris: 1920), pp. 170 ff.

17. Filon, p. 176; Fleury, II, 529.

18. Filon, p. 180; Fleury, II, 530.

19. Filon, p. 181.

20. General de Castelnau, "Sedan et Wilhelmshöhe," *Revue de Paris,* Nov. 1, 1929, XXXVI, #6, 177.

21. Evans, p. 433.

22. Castelnau, *loc. cit.,* p. 200.

23. Verdy du Vernois, p. 168.

24. Bazaine's testimony, *Enq. parl., Dépositions,* IV, 199; Fleury, II, 534–535; Evans, pp. 535–536.

25. Filon, p. 186.

26. Castelnau, *loc. cit.,* pp. 170–173; Geuss, p. 286.

27. Filon, p. 193; Geuss, pp. 286–287.

28. Filon, p. 188. See also Cadorna to Visconti Venosta, London, Oct. 17, 1870, Italy, Ministero degli Affari Esteri, *I documenti diplomatici italiani* (Rome: 1952–), Ser. 8, I, 230–231, no. 278, hereafter cited as *DDI*.

29. Filon, pp. 189–190.

30. Castelnau, *loc. cit.,* p. 179.

31. Napoleon III to Eugenie, Wilhelmshöhe, Oct. 6, 1870, "Lettres à l'Imperatrice Eugenie (1870/71)," *Revue des deux mondes,* 7 per., Vol. 59, 1930, pp. 11–12.

32. Castelnau, *loc. cit.,* p. 181.

33. Napoleon III to Eugenie, Wilhelmshöhe, Oct. 20, 1870, "Lettres à l'Imperatrice Eugenie," *loc. cit.,* p. 13–15.

34. Tissot to Favre, London, Oct. 27, 1870, MAE CP (Angleterre), 754: 218–221; Bazaine's testimony, *Enq. parl., Dépositions,* IV, 210–211.

35. Geuss, p. 288.

36. Bazaine's testimony, *Enq. parl., Dépositions,* IV, 211–212; Tissot to Favre, London, Oct. 27, 1870, MAE, CP (Angleterre), 754: 218–221; Boyer's testimony, *Enq. parl., Dépositions,* IV, 248; Evans, pp. 439–441; Fleury, II, 542–545; Filon, pp. 202–217; Geuss, pp. 290–291.

37. Granville to Lady Granville, October 23, 1870, Fitzmaurice, II, 66.

38. The story of the Boyer negotiations is drawn from Evans, pp.438–444; Fleury, II, 542–550; Sencourt, pp. 296–297; Marshal le Boeuf's testimony, *Enq. parl., Dépositions,* I, 65–66; General Boyer's testimony, *Enq. parl., ibid.,* IV, 248–257; Marshal Bazaine's testimony, *ibid.,* pp. 210–222; Filon, pp. 202–219; Geuss, pp. 289–293; Karl Ringhoffer, *The Bernstorff papers* (London and New York: 1908), II, 282–285. When Eugenie was 93 years old she said that Bismarck had demanded that she, "claiming my powers as Regent . . . was to have ordered Marshal Bazaine to issue a manifesto declaring that the army of the Rhine intended to remain faithful to its oath, to make itself the champion of the Napoleonic Dynasty, and to rally around me." Then she was to order Bazaine to surrender Metz to the Germans and to join

her with the army at Calais or Rouen where she would "summon the Chambers, reconstitute the government, and negotiate peace" (Maurice Paleologue, *The tragic Empress* [New York and London: 1928], pp. 236–238).

39. Fleury, II, 554–556; Filon, pp. 219–222; Geuss, p. 293. Sencourt (p. 297) says that Strasbourg, with an undetermined part of Alsace, was to be surrendered. See also Paul Matter, *Bismarck et son temps* (Paris: 1906–1912), III, 148–149.

40. Geuss, p. 294; Eugenie to Bismarck, N.D., Ringhoffer, II, 285; Cadorna to Visconti Venosta, London, Oct. 26, 1870, *DDI,* Ser. 2, I, 320–322, no. 379.

41. Geuss, pp. 298–299; Napoleon III to Eugenie, Wilhelmshöhe, Nov. 19, 1870 and Dec. 21, 1870, "Lettres à l'Imperatrice Eugenie," *loc. cit.,* pp. 19–20 and 20–24. Du Camp says that the idea of basing the new assembly on the "conseils généraux" was conceived by the French financier Edmond Archdeacon who told it to Clement Laurier and Adrien de Germiny when they were in London negotiating a loan for the French government from the House of Morgan. According to this story a prince of Mecklenburg approved of the plan and undertook to get Bismarck's approval of it (Du Camp, II, 185–187).

42. Castelnau, *loc. cit.,* pp. 192–195; Geuss, p. 299 and p. 201; Du Camp, II, 186–187. As late as January 17 Bismarck continued to revert to the scheme (Busch, *Bismarck,* I, 476).

43. Geuss, pp. 299–300 and 302; Busch, *Bismarck,* I, 424 and 428–429. Persigny also intimated that the ambitious Prince Napoleon had a plan for ending the war under his own authority, but Bismarck refused to receive him since he had little following in France (Busch, *Bismarck,* I, 439–440 and 443).

44. Geuss, pp. 300–301; Busch, *Bismarck,* I, 417; Odo Russell to Granville, Versailles, Dec. 18, 1870, Fitzmaurice, II, 74.

45. Geuss, p. 301; Odo Russell to Lord Granville, Versailles, Dec. 18, 1870, Knaplund, pp. 29–35.

46. Napoleon III to Eugenie, Wilhelmshöhe, Dec. 21, 1870, "Lettres à l'Imperatrice Eugenie," *loc. cit.,* pp. 20–24.

47. Geuss, pp. 302–303; Busch, *Franco-Prussian War,* II, 203–204; Hermann Oncken, *Grossherzog Friedrich I von Baden und die deutsche Politik von 1854–1871* (Stuttgart: 1927) II, 314.

48. Geuss, pp. 303–306.

49. *Ibid.,* pp. 307–308; Castelnau, *loc. cit.,* p. 195.

50. Geuss, pp. 308–311; Waldersee, p. 94; Bismarck to Fabrice, April 18, 1871, Berlin, PEA, I, 31–34. There is also some evidence that in January 1871 Bismarck was considering a scheme to advance the Prince Imperial to the French throne (Raymond, p. 317).

51. Oncken, II, 167.

52. Bismarck to his wife, Versailles, Oct. 20–23, 1870, Bismarck, *Letters to His Wife,* p. 73. On this subject of the quarrels between Bismarck and the military see also Alfred Vagts, *Defense and Diplomacy:*

the Soldier and the Conduct of Foreign Relations (New York: 1956), pp. 442–444.

53. Bismarck, *Memoirs,* II, 104.

54. *Ibid.;* Craig, pp. 204–205; Vagts, pp. 442–444.

55. Bismarck to Herbert Bismarck, Rheims, Sept. 7, 1870, Bismarck, *Letters to His Wife,* pp. 48–51, no. 32.

56. Ducrot, pp. 61–62; Howard, p. 222.

57. Friedrich von Holstein, *Memoirs and Political Observation* (Cambridge, Eng.: 1955), p. 82.

58. Craig, pp. 207–208; Howard, pp. 271–272 and 278–279.

59. Craig, p. 204.

60. *Ibid.,* pp. 208–209.

61. Diary entry, Nov. 9, 1870, Oncken, II, 160.

62. Bismarck to Waldersee, Nov. 16, 1870, Vagts, p. 442.

63. Albrecht von Blumenthal, ed. *Journals of Field-Marshal Count von Blumenthal for 1866 and 1870–71* (London: 1903) p. 222. The story can be found in Blumenthal, pp. 197–250; Craig, pp. 209–211; Hollyday, pp. 82–84; Verdy du Vernois, p. 160 and pp. 234–236; Vagts, p. 443; and Howard, pp. 352–357.

64. Blumenthal, p. 240.

IV

Armistice

On January 17 the Paris government discussed the question of surrender. There was some disagreement as to their competence to negotiate for all of France and the consensus was that negotiations, when they became necessary, should deal only with the surrender of Paris so as not to commit the full government to any pre-determined course of action.[1] Three days later the mayor of Paris not only rejected the idea of surrender but, more importantly for the government, refused absolutely to accept the responsibility of negotiations with the Germans.[2] This threw squarely on the Paris government the responsibility of negotiating the surrender of Paris and all that it might entail. On January 21 Favre assured Gambetta that "we shall sign no preliminaries of peace."[3]

Conditions in Paris were becoming daily more desperate and when the bread supply was sufficient for only two days Favre determined to bring hostilities to an end. On the morning of January 23 he wrote to Bismarck to ask for an interview.[4] His colleagues granted him "general powers" to negotiate and, having received a favorable reply from Bismarck, he presented himself at the Sèvres bridge contact point at six o'clock in the evening. On the far side of the river Favre and his companions were met by German officers who took them to Versailles by carriage.[5]

Shortly after eight o'clock Favre met Bismarck at the latter's quarters. Favre announced that he had come to resume negotiations where they had been broken off at Ferrières. He also said that he was authorized to speak only for Paris and asked what conditions of surrender the city could expect.[6] Bismarck told Favre that he arrived "too late." He had, he said, an "embarrassment of choice" with which to deal and he indicated that he was already engaged in "far advanced" negotiations with Napoleon III. Nor was this his only alternative to negotiating with the Paris government because he was in touch with a commission of the legislative body.[7] Favre protested that an imperial restoration would lead to civil war and that the legislature lacked authority. Why, he asked, would Bismarck not prefer to deal with a freely elected assembly? Bismarck replied that the destruction in some of the departments as well as what he called Gambetta's *"régime du terreur"* made highly unlikely the convocation of a freely elected, truly representative assembly.[8]

Favre then pressed Bismarck for his conditions if Paris were to surrender. He was particularly anxious concerning the future of the Paris garrison and the national guard and Prussian plans for entering Paris. Bismarck said that no agreement on these points had yet been reached between the emperor, Moltke and himself. According to the laws of war, he said, the garrison should be taken prisoner but the difficulty of moving them to Germany would lead him to consent to keeping them prisoners in Paris. He insisted that the national guard be disarmed and said that not until that time would any provisions be permitted in the city. He said that he was prepared to forego the entry of Prussian troops into the city if he could get control of the Paris forts but the emperor and the military party wished an entry. As a compromise, he proposed that the city be occupied only as far as the Champs Elysées in return for which he was prepared to allow sixty battalions of the national guard to retain their arms. Favre protested the impossibility of governing a city half occupied and half free and asked that Paris be either totally occupied or totally unoccupied. In the latter case he conceded that the forts should be occupied but asked that the city be permitted to re-provision. He further proposed that the city pay a contribution of war and that an armistice be agreed to immediately so that elections might be held to choose an assembly to meet at Bordeaux to decide on war or peace. Bismarck asked Favre to put his ideas in writing to present to Emperor William. Favre objected that these were private ideas and might later be unacceptable. Upon Bismarck's assurance that they would be for himself alone Favre wrote them down. The conversation ended some two and one-half hours after it had begun.[9]

Favre proposed to remain at Versailles so that his trip might remain secret and, since he could not risk going to a hotel, Bismarck put an apartment at his disposal. They agreed to meet again the next day at one o'clock by which time Bismarck hoped to have obtained the emperor's permission to negotiate with Favre.[10]

Bismarck saw the emperor that same night and again on the following morning, January 24. At the second meeting there was a full council of war before which he laid Favre's offer to conclude an armistice, with Paris giving up its arms and surrendering its forts.[11] The occasion of Paris's surrender was the cause of the latest clash between Bismarck and the military party. There had never been any real relaxation of tensions following the quarrel over bombardment and an attempt by the crown prince to reconcile the differences between Moltke and Bismarck had only made their relations worse.[12] Moltke and Bismarck both presented to the emperor their plans for the future conduct of the war. Both men wanted to secure the surrender of Paris, of course, but their real differences concerned what should come after that. Bismarck, still professing to fear foreign intervention, wanted to link the surrender of Paris with the conclusion of the war: Moltke considered that Paris's capitulation would be merely preliminary to yet another stage in the conflict, a stage which would see French resistance absolutely crushed. In this quarrel William supported Bismarck and authorized him to begin armistice negotiations when the opportunity should arise.[13] There the situation stood when the council of January 24 was held. The generals still did not wish to halt military operations,[14] but when Bismarck met Favre later he was able to tell him that he could now open negotiations for an armistice.

Their conversation turned to Favre's suggestions of the previous evening. Bismarck voiced some concern as to whether the delegation, now moved to Bordeaux, would honor a convention signed by the Paris government, but he offered no objection in principle to an armistice and the convoking of an assembly. After some argument concerning the length of an armistice the two men finally agreed on three weeks with the right of renewal. Other points were not so easily settled. Bismarck said that German public opinion would insist on the entry of German troops into Paris. When Favre protested that negotiations might as well be broken off if this were insisted on Bismarck agreed to lay the matter before the emperor again. On the question of the national guard, Favre insisted that they be permitted to retain their arms. Concerning the Paris garrison, it was easily agreed that they should not be taken to Germany. Favre now argued against their imprisonment even in France. Instead, he asked that they be allowed to remain in Paris pending a final solution, going free if peace were concluded and becoming prisoners only if hostilities should be resumed.[15]

Favre returned to Paris on the afternoon of January 24. That night and the following morning he and his colleagues considered Bismarck's proposals. They approved Bordeaux as the site of the assembly meetings and they decided that it was unnecessary to say anything about elections in Alsace and Lorraine. They supported Favre in his demand that German troops not enter Paris during the armistice and they urged the desirability of surrendering to the Germans only a portion of the Parisian forts. Trochu and Vinoy further suggested that Favre ask for three divisions of ten thousand men each in the regular army to help maintain order in the city. Favre's powers were signed "subject to [*sauf*] ratification of conventions which might be agreed to by M. Jules Favre."[16] Favre left for Versailles that same afternoon.

That very day Bismarck's hand had been strengthened when Emperor William issued two orders directing that the chancellor was to be kept informed of all military operations and also instructing the military that they were to enter into no communications with the French until the emperor should have decided that the matter was not within Bismarck's jurisdiction.[17] Bismarck had finally won his point and on January 25 and 26 he and Favre proceeded to settle most of the outstanding issues.

Favre asked what indemnity Paris would be expected to pay: Bismarck replied that he considered one billion francs a proper amount and that any other sum would be insulting to so rich a city. The government authorized Favre to go as high as one-half billion francs. Bismarck apparently reconsidered insulting Paris for he and Favre finally agreed on the sum of two hundred million francs.[18] Favre refused to consider an additional sum of three hundred million francs chargeable to the war indemnity.[19] Bismarck reluctantly agreed to let the national guard keep its arms but said that the Prussian military would agree to leaving armed, in addition to the guard, only one division of regulars.[20] He was able to grant one of Favre's most insistent demands when he announced that he had persuaded the emperor not to insist on the occupation of Paris.[21] He warned, however, that this reluctantly granted concession was only for the period of the armistice and did not necessarily apply to the final peace treaty.[22] There was a stalemate concerning the fate of Belfort: Favre refused to surrender it and Bismarck refused to extend the armistice to it.[23] Favre also refused to grant Bismarck's request that the armistice not be applicable to Garibaldi, who was fighting in the French armies.[24] Bismarck asked that all of the city's fortresses be surrendered, although Favre asked that Vincennes be excepted since it was a state prison.[25] Bismarck also demanded that all of the cannon of the fortifications be thrown into the moat of the forts.[26]

By January 26 virtually all the major items of an armistice had been agreed on and there remained only military details to be discussed. However, for these points Bismarck, who complained that Favre had difficulty understanding military matters, asked that he bring a military man when he returned to Versailles.[27] Just as Favre was leaving the two men agreed on a mutual cease fire to begin at midnight. Bismarck agreed to Favre's request that the French be permitted to fire the last shot.[28]

At the negotiations of the 27th Favre was accompanied by General Beaufort d'Hautpoul. Bismarck announced that he would read aloud the stipulations agreed to since negotiations began, after which each would be discussed and adopted in turn. It was agreed that the armistice would last twenty-one days. A line was to be drawn between the armies neither of which would come within ten kilometers of it. Since the Germans refused to withdraw to the right bank of the Loire River the line was drawn from Angers in the west to Quarre-les-Tombes in the east. Beyond Quarre-les-Tombes the Prussians proposed to leave the drawing of the line in abeyance until the military situation there should be clarified, and Bismarck proposed that discussion on this point be postponed until the following day. It was agreed that the Somme should be the border between the armies in the north and it was stipulated that Le Havre, together with a 24 kilometer radius, should be excluded from the area of occupation. For the naval forces, the meridian of Dunkirk was agreed to as the armistice line.

Bismarck agreed that the new French assembly might convene at Bourges if the French wished it, since as Favre pointed out, it was more centrally located than Bordeaux. General Beaufort objected to the Prussian demand for control of all the Paris forts as well as the gates to the city and he protested the detention of the Paris garrison in the camps of Saint Maur and Gennevilliers. Favre objected to Moltke's demand that a half-million rifles be handed over, saying that this would mean the virtual disarmament of the national guard. Beaufort insisted that the Prussians occupy the suburban towns only where they were virtually dependencies of the occupied forts. He convinced Moltke that Vincennes would be of little use to the Prussians. He also persuaded Moltke to agree to dismounting the guns of the fortifications instead of throwing them into the moats, the gun carriages to be delivered to the Prussians.[29] Thus the arguments went, tedious hours spent on endless details.

When Favre returned to Paris to tell the council of that day's negotiations it was clear that a final armistice would soon be reached. The government finally broke its silence and announced in the *Journal officiel* that negotiations had been going on, giving the general outlines of what had been agreed on. Paris generally remained calm,[30] in spite of some grumbling on the part of elements in the national guard.

On January 28 Favre was once more at Versailles. This time he was accompanied by General Valdan. The appointment of General Beaufort had been a disaster from the beginning. The Prussians were convinced that he was drunk[31] and his behavior, regardless of the cause, was sufficiently eccentric to humiliate Favre[32] and to cause Bismarck to indicate that his presence at the negotiations was no longer welcome.[33] When Favre and Valdan met Bismarck the discussion dealt primarily with the regulation of military details. Valdan failed to get Prussian approval for two divisions of French regulars to remain armed but he did get final approval of the fortress of Vincennes to remain in French possession.[34] Finally the only point to be settled concerned the eastward extension of the armistice line. Since Favre still refused to surrender Belfort and since the state of the fighting on the eastern front was unknown, it was agreed that Belfort and the departments of Doubs, Jura, and Côte d'Or would be excluded from the armistice.[35] When the time came to sign the armistice it was found that Favre had neglected to provide himself with a seal for the authentication of his signature on the instrument. Consequently, at the signing on the evening of January 28 Favre used a ring which he wore and which he had received from Felice Orsini in 1858.[36]

The armistice was to be put into effect within three days. Immediately after the signing Favre sent a telegram to Gambetta telling him of the armistice and of the final choice of Bordeaux for the meeting of the assembly. But Favre made no mention of the delay of three days before the armistice would go into effect, nor did he specify the exceptions to the general application of the armistice. This brought him under bitter criticism when the French armies of the east halted and suffered a catastrophic defeat which was ended only by their retreat into Switzerland, where they were interned.[37]

At dinner, after the armistice had been signed, Favre was dejected and quiet.[38] As he left Bismarck he thanked the chancellor for his kindness—and then proceeded to make a sign as though cutting his own throat.[39]

One can well understand the feelings which the Paris government must have had upon learning that the war was at last over: a mixture of relief and joy, of apprehension and fear. All in all, the terms of the armistice were not prohibitively crushing. Favre had, for the moment, saved Belfort, and he had not had to pay as much as he was prepared to pay for Paris's war indemnity. In retrospect we can see that it was a blunder to leave the national guard armed. Even Bismarck had predicted that the French would have cause to regret the decision. But the government had wanted it and gained the point.

The government now had to worry about the reception which Paris and France would give to the armistice. They had, too, to begin the task of creating a regular government which could negotiate a permanent peace with the newly proclaimed German Empire. The problems which faced France were enormous and would have been difficult for even a more experienced group of men leading a united nation.

NOTES TO CHAPTER IV

1. Dréo, pp. 530–538.
2. *Ibid.*, p. 553.
3. Favre to Gambetta, Paris, Jan. 21, 1871, Valfrey, *Gouvernement*, III, 45; Deschanel, p. 106. In his memoirs Favre says that when he went to Prussian headquarters he was determined to seek only an armistice for Paris and not for the rest of France since the Paris government had no authority to speak for it (Favre, II, 371–372). Gambetta said that he was

told "at the moment when one negotiated with M. Bismarck, that one would treat only for Paris" (Gambetta, *Enq. parl., Dépositions,* I, 555).

4. Favre, II, 737–378.

5. Favre, *Enq. parl., Dépositions,* I, 358–359; Favre, II, 378–380. Favre was accompanied by his son-in-law, M. Martinez del Rio, who served as his secretary, and by Captain d'Hérisson d'Irisson. Favre says that Hérisson stayed with him throughout the negotiations. However, on this occasion the captain seems not to have gone, remaining behind at Sèvres until Favre returned from Versailles on January 24, at which time says Hérisson, Favre told him of his first two interviews with Bismarck. Hérisson says that he wrote down the story as Favre told it to him and that it differed "considerably" from that "which he pretends, in his book, to have dictated the day after and that he has now published" (Hérisson, pp. 330–333). Holstein, who was present, mentions the American consul-general Read as having been there although he says that Read "maintained almost complete silence" (Holstein, p. 80).

6. Favre, II, 380–382. Hérisson says that Bismarck announced to Favre that the situation had changed since Ferrières and that if France continued to hold to the formula of no territorial cessions whatsoever, further negotiations would be fruitless (Hérisson, p. 331).

7. Favre, *Enq. parl., Dépositions,* I, 342; Favre, II, 380–389. Hérisson says that Bismarck pointed to a door behind which he said was an agent of the emperor (Hérisson, pp. 330–333).

8. Favre, II, 380–389.

9. *Ibid.,* Favre said that the Prussians wrote down everything, even things still under discussion and not yet agreed to and that Bismarck wanted everything in writing (Favre, *Enq. parl., Dépositions,* I, 361).

10. Favre, II, 380–389.

11. Frederick III, pp. 281–282; Abeken to his wife, Versailles, Jan. 24, 1871, Abeken, p. 337.

12. Vagts, p. 443; Hollyday, pp. 85–86.

13. Craig, pp. 212–213.

14. O. Lorenz, *Kaiser Wilhelm und die Begründung des Reichs,* p. 512, quoted in Matter, III, 236. Moltke's proposals for Paris would have amounted to unconditional surrender. He would have demanded the occupation not only of the forts of the city but of all Paris. In addition, he would have had all colors and weapons handed over to the Germans. He would have permitted the officers to be free on parole, but the entire Paris garrison, some 250,000 men, he would have had transported to Germany as prisoners of war. The only part of this scheme which Bismarck accepted was the occupation of the forts of the city (Arnold Oskar Meyer, *Bismarck, der Mensch und der Staatsmann* [Leipzig: 1944], p. 433, quoted in Vagts, p. 487, fn. 32).

15. Favre, II, 390–398; Favre, *Enq. parl., Dépositions,* I, 360. Favre says that in this conversation of the 24th he and Bismarck agreed on all principal points. Hérisson says that Bismarck gave Favre, apparently on the 24th, a projected convention which provided: an armistice of twenty-one days; disarmament of the army, which would remain prisoner of

war at Paris; sixty battalions of the national guard to remain armed for the maintenance of order, the rest and the "corps francs" to be dissolved; the army to surrender its arms and flags, the officers to keep their swords; the armistice to extend to all parts of France and a line to be traced between the two armies; Paris to pay an indemnity and to hand over its forts to the Germans; the Germans not to enter the walls during the period of armistice; cannon on the walls of Paris to be thrown into the moat; elections to be held for an assembly (Hérisson, pp. 333–334).

16. Dréo, pp. 592–598.

17. Craig, pp. 213–215; Vagts, p. 444.

18. Hérisson, p. 334; Favre, II, 399. Gaston May says that what Bismarck really said to Favre, according to Cresson, prefect of police of Paris, was: "The city of Paris is a girl rich enough and well enough kept to pay her ransom" (Gaston May, *Le traité de Francfort* [Paris: 1909], p. 24).

19. Favre, II, 399.

20. *Ibid.,* pp. 390–398.

21. *Ibid.;* Frederick III, pp. 283–285.

22. Favre, II, 398.

23. *Ibid.,* pp. 402–403.

24. Hérisson, p. 346.

25. Frederick III, pp. 283–284.

26. Dréo, pp. 602–606.

27. Busch, *Bismarck,* I, 374.

28. Favre, II, 404.

29. Beaufort, *Enq. parl., Dépositions,* III, 163–176. This information, annexed to Beaufort's testimony, is from "Negotiations of January 27, 1871" by one Lt. Calvel, who was present at the session with the Prussians. At a session of the Paris government on January 27 Favre told of the Prussian decision to allow the cannon to remain if the carriages were confiscated (Dréo, pp. 609–614). I have accepted this statement, which supports the Beaufort-Calvel account, over that of Hérisson. He says (Hérisson, pp. 368–374) that it was he who was assigned to take the signed armistice convention to Bismarck and that he did a "little additional negotiation." He says that he told Bismarck that the convention was signed but that he was to turn it over only after some slight changes had been made, otherwise he was to await Favre's arrival. He says that Bismarck was annoyed and surprised but, after seeing the emperor, he agreed to dismantle the cannon of the fortification, accept the line of investment around Paris as set out by the French and, as an absolute *sine qua non,* allow the Paris garrison to keep its battle flags.

30. Favre, II, 405–406.

31. Frederick III, p. 285.

32. Busch, *Franco-German War,* II, 264.

33. Hérisson, pp. 349–350.

34. Valdan, *Enq. parl., Dépositions,* III, 177–185. Hérisson tells the story that the German maps showed Vincennes surrounded by forests and for this reason Moltke insisted on keeping it. Valdan had no map with

which to combat this error but "happily" Hérisson had one which had been given to all officers on the general staff, and with this he was able to convince Moltke and save the day for France (Hérisson, pp. 357–361).

35. Favre, *Enq. parl., Dépositions,* I, 363–365.

36. Bismarck told Favre that the emperor so admired the bravery of Paris that he wished to honor the defenders of the city by giving to the convention the name of "armistice" rather than "capitulation" (Favre, III, 4–5). May says that this was a mere euphemism which the French wanted and which the Germans were only too willing to oblige since they found that it was easy for Favre to "delude himself and to be contented with appearances" (May, pp. 20–22). For the story of the signet ring see Lt. Col. Rousset, *L'armistice de 1871* (Paris: 1927), p. 44; also see Valdan, *Enq. parl., Dépositions,* III, 179.

37. The situation surrounding this omission is confused. Favre told the parliamentary committee (*Dépositions,* I, 365–367) that he understood that the armistice would extend to the east with only the line between the opposing armies there to be decided later. This, he said, was the way he thought that Bismarck understood it and that they had meant no exceptions to the general application of the armistice. He said that when he sent the telegram to Gambetta he was in a troubled state and did not know that the armistice would be delayed, thinking that it would go into effect immediately for Paris and three days later for the provinces. He also said that it was the task of Valdan to set out the actual delimitation of the armies in the east. Before the same committee, Pelletan, who was apparently in at the discussions, said that as he recalled Bismarck said to Favre that "a line of neutrality will be traced for the other armies, but since you do not want to give Belfort, operations will continue in the east" (*Dépositions,* I, 461–472). Rousset points out that Bismarck had to countersign the telegram and should have known the contents; yet he did not point out the omission to Favre (Rousset, p. 44). He raises the question if this lapse was intentional on Bismarck's part. Favre says that the Paris government was ignorant of affairs in the provinces, having received only two dispatches between January 1 and the signing of the armistice, and those were on January 16 and 19 (Favre, III, 13).

38. Busch, *Franco-German War,* II, 270.

39. Abeken to his wife, Versailles, Jan. 28, 1871, Abeken, pp. 339–340.

V

Aftermath of the Armistice: Elections

IN THE DAYS IMMEDIATELY following the signing of the armistice, the division of the French government between Paris and Bordeaux made a bad situation even more difficult since the split became ideological as well as geographical once the fighting had ended. The Paris-Bordeaux controversy not only complicated Franco-German relations but it also revealed how easily France could have plunged into civil war.

The controversy had its origin in the confusion surrounding the application of the armistice in eastern France. The Bordeaux delegation had so little information about the negotiations at Versailles that Favre's telegram of the 28th had produced the impression that a final peace treaty had been signed.[1] However, determined to carry out Favre's instructions, within hours they had ordered a general suspension of hostilities.[2] Understandably, they were astonished to learn that Belfort and the eastern departments were not included in the armistice. Matters were made worse when the delegation decreed exclusion from the new assembly of all officials and official candidates of the imperial regime. This was directly contrary to an electoral decree promulgated by the Paris government on January 29, by the terms of which the new assembly should be chosen by universal manhood suffrage.[3] Gambetta also publicly lashed out at the "criminal carelessness" of the armistice provisions and accused the Germans of wanting to use an assembly "in a state of panic" to gain from France "a shameful peace."[4]

The Germans were deeply suspicious of Gambetta's influence and Bismarck was quick to remind Favre of his fears that truly free elections were impossible under the circumstances.[5] This potentially dangerous situation ended anticlimactically when, on February 5, the Paris government annulled Gambetta's decree of ineligibility. The following day Gambetta resigned rather than take the advice of some of his followers to establish himself as the dictator of France.[6]

This quarrel beween Paris and Bordeaux was played out against a background of hectic activity at Versailles. Favre spent most of his time at German headquarters, and although Bismarck complained of the inexperience of the French, relations between the two men were generally good,[7] and they and their subordinates reached agreement on a series of conventions regulating matters arising out of and implementing the armistice.[8]

Those days were not easy for anyone, least of all for Bismarck. He insisted on doing much of the routine work himself.[9] There were those at headquarters who grumbled that the armistice terms were too lenient on France[10] but Bismarck, who could be extraordinarily gracious when he wished to be, apparently was satisfied and went out of his way to placate Moltke and the military party which had wanted a truly harsh armistice.[11]

In the midst of the feverish activity the French elections were held without incident. Article II of the armistice convention had specified that the purpose of the armistice was to enable an assembly to be chosen to pass on the question of peace or continued war. For several reasons, however, it would be an overstatement to say that this issue was always clearly stated to an electorate eager and alert to discover the candidates' programs. In the first place, France was in a state of disorganization and, in places, of near chaos. Over one-quarter of the departments were occupied. In those departments postal communications were forbidden and the Germans posted electoral notices and decrees.[12] Second, a divided French government gave little or no leadership. The voters were urged simply to "choose men of good reputation and independent character."[13] In such a situation leadership should logically have come from the political parties, but formal party organization scarcely existed. Third, the situation was further confused by the use of the *scrutin de liste,* which made it possible for party lines to be crossed and for men of widely divergent political beliefs to be nominated and elected on the same list. In such circumstances it is remarkable that the elections of 1871 were held with as little confusion as there was.

There was no formal machinery for choosing the candidates. In each department self-appointed committees drew up the lists, sometimes without consulting the candidates. The result was that republicans and royalists often appeared on the same ticket while prominent figures such as Thiers were named in several departments. Beyond the question of peace and war it was hard to tell for what principles some candidates stood, and it was not always possible to know on that score. Candidates were not required to issue any sort of platform and few did so outside Paris.[14] In some parts of France the lists of candidates did, however, carry the simple designation "Peace" or "War."[15]

The assembly which was elected was heavily royalist in make-up. The republican faction was about evenly divided between "war" republicans and "peace" republicans. The Bonapartists were the repudiated party, only some thirty deputies being elected who openly supported the imperial régime.[16] A violent partisan quarrel was later to develop as to whether this assembly had a mandate to assume constituent functions. In this election France may or may not have spoken about her political future, but she certainly spoke in favor of peace with Germany when she rejected resoundingly the Bonapartists and the Gambettists, the factions associated in her mind with beginning the war and wanting to continue it. Certainly the assembly felt itself to have a mandate for peace when it ratified the preliminary peace treaty in March by a vote of 546 to 107 with 23 abstentions.

Still another fact clearly emerged from the election: the ascendancy of Thiers, who was elected from twenty-six departments. Thiers himself was quite aware of the probable significance of the vote and he spoke with the air of a man likely to play a leading role in events. His chances of heading the new government were helped by the fact that the first order of business would be the negotiation of peace, an onerous task which no faction or party would gladly undertake and the mishandling of which could have disastrous political results.[17] In spite of this Thiers was anxious to have negotiations open as soon as possible and he took pains to see that Bismarck was made aware of the conservative nature of the new assembly.[18]

The assembly was to meet in Bordeaux's Grand Théatre, which was hastily converted to its new function. Only about two hundred and fifty of the delegates had arrived in Bordeaux in time for the first session on February 12 and it lasted only about three-quarters of an hour.[19] At the session of February 13 Favre submitted the resignation of the Government of National Defense but announced that it would remain in office until a new government could be established. Then he asked permission of the assembly to return to Paris for a few days.[20]

When the assembly next met, on February 17, Keller, speaking on behalf of a group which included the delegates from Alsace and Lorraine as well as some of the Gambettists, proposed a declaration for the action of the assembly. He asked that the assembly go on record against the separation of Alsace and Lorraine from France. Indeed, he denied that France *could* divest herself of the populations involved without their prior consent. To do so would be to imperil "the continuity of her national existence." "We give you our hand. Don't refuse us yours."[21]

Under the dramatic circumstances of the moment such an impassioned plea must have had an enormous impact. However, not only would it have been useless to have adopted such a resolution but it would also have tied the hands of the French negotiators at the peace table. Thiers, therefore, took the lead in opposing its adoption, urging that the negotiators be left a free hand and pleading that this matter be disposed of without delay. There seemed no doubt in his mind whatever as to who would be negotiating for France: "I could not accept a mandate that I would be unable to carry out as an honest man and as a good citizen."[22]

The assembly recessed to permit a committee to examine Keller's motion. When they reconvened the committee, with only one dissenting vote, proposed a substitute resolution to the effect that the assembly, while sympathizing with Keller's feelings, intended to rely "on the wisdom and the patriotism of the negotiators." The substitute motion was overwhelmingly approved.

After disposing of this business the assembly chose Thiers to head the government and bestowed on him the title of "*chef du pouvoir exécutif,*" a title not at all to his liking.[23]

On February 19 Thiers presented his cabinet to the assembly. There was some surprise at some of his choices, particularly his retention of Favre as foreign minister.[24] The objections remained largely unvoiced, however, and the assembly passed to other matters.

Favre asked the assembly to name a commission which would "associate parliamentary action with that of the executive power as much as possible" in the ensuing peace negotiations. He said that this was not intended in any way to compromise the freedom of action of the assembly but was intended instead to bolster the "moral authority" of the negotiators. He asked that the assembly consider this matter immediately since he and Thiers wished to leave for Paris as soon as possible. The proposal was accepted in principle in spite of some voiced objections that there had been insufficient debate on so important a point. Thiers followed Favre to ask the assembly to suspend public sessions during the peace negotiations lest some proposal made in debate inadvertently hinder the negotiations.[25] Later in the day when the assembly met to name the members of the commission requested by Favre, Gambetta returned to the question of their role in the peace negotiations. He expressed concern lest their participation later serve to compromise the assembly's freedom of discussion and debate and he wished the assembly's sovereignty to be specifically reserved. Jules Simon, on behalf of Thiers, assured Gambetta that the government would assume full responsibility for the negotiations and had no intention of compromising the assembly.[26]

Armed with the authority that he wished, Thiers, accompanied by Favre, left Bordeaux on the night of February 19. They arrived in Paris on the evening of Monday, February 20. Thiers went promptly to the ministry of foreign affairs and sent word to Bismarck that he would visit Versailles the next day.[27]

NOTES TO CHAPTER V

1. Lyons to Granville, Bordeaux, Jan. 31, 1871, PRO, FO 27/1855.

2. Charles de Freycinet, *Souvenirs, 1848–1893* (Paris: 1912–1913) I, 236–238.

3. Frank H. Brabant, *The Beginning of the Third Republic in France* (London: 1940), pp. 31, 39, 43.

4. *Ibid.*, pp. 44–45.

5. Bismarck to Favre, Feb. 3, 1871, *ibid.*, p. 56.

6. *Annual Register,* New series (London: 1862–), 1871, Part I, 165–166; Favre, III, 27–32.

7. Bismarck wrote: "These people understand business so little that I have to help them in their work" (To his wife, Versailles, Feb. 1, 1871, Bismarck, *Letters,* p. 115, no. LXX).

8. The most important of the agreements, by date and subject, are: (1) January 30: convention relative to reestablishment of railway service for the revictualling of Paris (A. Villefort [ed.], *Recueil des traités, conventions, lois, décrèts et autres actes relatifs à la paix avec l'Allemagne* [Paris: 1872–1879], I, 397–399. A résumé of the terms of the armistice will be found in Sir E. Hertslet, *The map of Europe by treaty* [London]: 1875–1891), III, 1905–1906, no. 434); (2) January 31: convention of demarcation between the German armies and the French army of the north (Villefort, I, 9–11); (3) February 2: convention for reestablishment of telegraphic communication for the duration of the armistice (*ibid.*, pp. 13–14); (4) February 3: convention for reestablishment of postal communications in the occupied areas (*ibid.*, pp. 14–16); (5) February 5: additional convention for demarcation between the armies in the north. Annex to the convention of January 31 (*ibid.*, pp.16–17); (6) February 11: convention relative to evacuation of French and German sick and wounded (*ibid.*, p. 18); (7) February 15: convention extending the armistice to the eastern departments and surrendering Belfort with the honors of war (*ibid.*, pp. 19–20).

9. On two occasions Abeken wrote to his wife of Bismarck's personal attention to detail in all matters concerning the armistice (Versailles, Jan. 30, 1871, Abeken, pp. 340–341 and Jan. 31, 1871, *ibid.*, pp. 341–342).

10. Busch, *Franco-German War,* II, 314; Blumenthal, p. 294.

11. Stosch said that a better relationship was established between Bismarck and Moltke over the negotiations. "Bismarck tried to curb his earlier rudeness and was, during these days, endlessly obliging and amiable. The old proverb has again been proved true: 'Idleness is the root of all evil.' The waiting has lasted too long" (Albrecht von Stosch,

Denkwürdigkeiten des Generals und Admirals Albrecht von Stosch ersten Chefs von Admiralität [Stuttgart and Leipzig: 1904] p. 228).

12. Brabant, p, 63.

13. Decree of February 2, 1871, *ibid.*

14. R. A. Winnacker, "The French election of 1871," *Papers of the Michigan Academy of Science, Arts, and Letters,* XXII (1936), 477–483. See also Hanotaux, I, 31. Brabant says that "only in a few places (Paris, for instance) were formal addresses drawn up by the candidates" (Brabant, p. 70).

15. Brabant, p. 70.

16. For a general discussion of the election and interpretation as to its meanings see the works cited by Hanotaux, Brabant, and Winnacker.

17. Lyons to Granville, Bordeaux, Feb. 10, 1871, PRO, FO 27/1856.

18. Lyons to Granville, Bordeaux, Feb. 12, 1871, *ibid.*

19. Dréo, p. 678. See also Anatole Claveau, *Souvenirs politiques et parlementaires d'un témoin, 1865–1873* (Paris: 1913–1914), II, 6–7.

20. France. *Annales de l'assemblée nationale. Compte rendu in extenso des séances* (Paris: 1871–), I, 4.

21. *Ibid.*, pp. 61–62.

22. *Ibid.*, pp. 62–63. Favre is said to have remarked during the committee discussions that Prussia had not yet asked the cession of Alsace and Lorraine and that she might be content with the neutralization of those areas (Mazade, *La guerre de France* quoted in Sorel, II, 220, fn. 2). If Favre did say this it is utterly incomprehensible how he could have believed it in the light of Bismarck's repeated demands.

23. *Annales,* I, 64; Favre II, 520, Pièces justificatives, no. 24. When Thiers heard of his title he said: "Chief of the Executive! If I am called 'chef' people will think I am a cook. I want to be President" (Paul Bosq, *Souvenirs de l'assemblée nationale,* p. 23, quoted in Brabant, p. 94).

24. Duc de Broglie, *Mémoires, Revue des deux mondes,* Feb. 1, 1929, p. 564. The members of this government were: Dufaure (justice), Favre (foreign affairs), Picard (interior), Simon (public instruction and cults), De Larcy (public works), Lambrecht (agriculture and commerce), Le Flô (war), Admiral Pothuau (navy), and Pouyer-Quertier (finance).

25. *Annales,* I, 75–76 and 78.

26. The members of the commission were Benoist d'Azy, Teisserenc de Bort, de Merode, Deseilligny, Victor Lanfranc, Laurenceau, Lesperaut, Saint-Marc Girardin, Barthelemy Saint-Hilaire, General d'Aurelle de Paladines, Admirals La Roncière le Noury and Saisset, Pouyer-Quertier, Vitet, and Batbie (*ibid.*, p. 79–80).

27. Favre, III, 89–90.

VI

Peace Preliminaries

When Thiers arrived at Versailles on February 21 the most pressing matter was obtaining an extension of the armistice. It had already been twice extended from its original termination date of February 19, and it was now to expire on February 24. During the negotiations for the earlier extensions Bismarck's skilful manoeuvering had caused Trochu to remark that Bismarck's method was *"de demander un boeuf pour avoir un oeuf."*[1] It was not a bad appraisal of his method, and he used it again. Although Bismarck was quite prepared to extend the armistice until the first of March[2] he categorically refused Thiers's request for an extension. When Thiers protested that it was utterly impossible to conclude a peace treaty in forty-eight hours Bismarck fully agreed. He suggested that forty-eight hours was, however, quite enough time in which to conclude a preliminary treaty dealing with all basic questions in dispute, and he cut short Thiers's objections by saying that the emperor had specifically commanded him "not to prolong the armistice and to fix the preliminaries between now and Thursday."[3]

The discussion then turned to the entry of German troops into Paris. Thiers warned that it would be a "catastrophe" but Bismarck said that the honor of the German armies must be considered and, as an alternative to a symbolic entry into the city, he suggested a German occupation of the center of the city at least until the peace treaty should be ratified. Thiers considered this scheme even more dangerous than the first and he requested permission to lay his case before the emperor.

The two men next discussed peace conditions. Thiers expressed the hope that they would be no more severe than those asked in November. Bismarck said that he had already asked for Alsace and parts of Lorraine, and these he proposed to keep. Furthermore, he intended to keep Metz as a security measure although he did not support the minister of war, who wanted to take Nancy as well. He said that additional German losses since November required him to ask for monetary compensation of six billion francs instead of four billion. Thiers protested that such a sum could not be raised and he pleaded for more time to discuss peace terms. Bismarck went to see the emperor and returned to say that the emperor would receive Thiers the next day and that the armistice would be extended until midnight, Sunday, February 26.[4]

When Thiers left Bismarck he was deeply disturbed. Had he known, Bismarck was by no means absolutely determined to have Metz, as he had said, although the question of German acquisition of that city was hotly debated at headquarters. Moltke and the military leaders considered the city and its fortresses indispensable for the future defense of Germany against France[5] and as early as August, 1870, Bismarck had indicated that he intended to demand Metz.[6] This did not indicate, however, any eagerness on Bismarck's part to have the city for he felt that the population of Metz might prove to be unassimilable into Germany and hence a source of weakness. In November he had given Thiers reason to hope that Metz might be returned to France. Before the February negotiations began Bismarck openly expressed doubt that the French could be forced to surrender Metz and he brought pressure to bear on the emperor to persuade him to give up the city, questioning the claim of the military that they had to have it.[7] The very day that Bismarck first met Thiers he spoke to his staff concerning his reluctance to take Metz and he indicated that he would prefer to leave the city to France and build a new fortress for Germany if he could get a greater war indemnity.[8] Bismarck felt the matter to be so important that he thought that the future of the negotiations and even of war or peace might hinge on the fate of Metz.[9] The pro-Metz faction at headquarters felt deeply about the matter and feared that the emperor might surrender to the anti-Metz faction.[10]

On February 22 Thiers went alone to Versailles. He had secured audiences with both the emperor and with the crown prince and he proposed to win more favorable terms for France if he could. His first audience was with Emperor William. Bismarck had warned Thiers not to press the old man too closely and Thiers largely confined himself to pleading for William's generosity toward France. The only specific issue on which he dwelt was that of the entry into Paris but he was unable to dissuade William from this gesture to the honor of his armies.[11]

Thiers then was received by the crown prince and he turned on Frederick the full force of his powers of persuasion. However, he had no more success than he had had with the emperor. Frederick supported the German entry into Paris[12] and he refused to go into details concerning peace terms, referring Thiers to Bismarck in such matters.[13]

Following the interview with the crown prince, Thiers once more met with Bismarck. It was a stormy day and the conversation "gave rise to hot discussions." Quickly they reached a stalemate on the question of Metz and seemed to be deadlocked as well on the question of the war indemnity. Thiers annoyed Bismarck by saying that a war indemnity of six billion francs "would turn the war indemnity into a mere financial speculation." Bismarck stubbornly maintained his stand and said that he was not free to change the figure without further instructions. He ended the interview by saying that when he had received such instructions from Berlin he would send two envoys to deal with Thiers.[14]

On February 23 there were no conversations at Versailles. Instead Bismarck sent to Paris the two financial envoys of whom he had spoken. The bankers, Messrs. Henckel and Bleichröder, informed Thiers that they were not authorized to discuss the amount of the indemnity but could only deal with means of facilitating its payment. Thiers told them that the first basis of an indemnity was justice—to repay war expenses—but not to make a profit for the benefit of the conqueror. The Germans said that Prussia's expenses had been great and spoke of adding to those expenses aid for widows and orphans. Thiers said that France could not contract a debt which would be impossible to pay. Instead, he said that Prussia should occupy France and "she will see if she can get six billion from it."[15]

That evening the full parliamentary commission met to hear Thiers's description of the negotiations thus far. He warned that Metz was lost and told them his fears concerning the future of Belfort and the eastern frontier. The commission agreed with Thiers that the six billion franc indemnity was excessive, but "with one accord" they agreed that France had no alternative but to sign the peace whatever its terms. They rejected the offers of the Prussian bankers to help handle the financing of the war indemnity, preferring instead that France handle it alone, and they expressed confidence in Thiers's handling of the negotiations.[16]

When Thiers returned to German headquarters on February 24 Favre went with him and stayed with him during the remaining days of the negotiations. They were in a bad frame of mind when they left Paris for they had heard from the Swiss minister that Bismarck was perfectly willing to begin hostilities if his terms were not accepted.[17] The first order of business was the future of Metz. Bismarck warned that he had opposed Roon's plan to take two-thirds of Lorraine but that France must give up Metz. "In Germany," he said, "they accuse me of losing the battles Count Moltke has won." "Do not ask me for impossibilities." Thiers had already written off Metz as lost and he was not prepared to push the issue.[18]

They considered the matter of the war indemnity next. Bismarck said that although Berlin still insisted on the need for including war expenses, widows' and orphans' pensions, funds for maintaining prisoners, and the share of the south German states, he was now authorized to set five billion francs as the minimum acceptable sum. Thiers accepted it, delighted to save one billion francs.[19]

The next question was that of the future of Belfort. Bismarck was personally no more anxious to have Belfort than he was to have Metz[20] and he had already decided that he could use the demand for Belfort to overcome French resistance to surrendering Metz.[21] Needless to say, he did not tip his hand to Thiers, and Thiers was later to say that the negotiations concerning Belfort were a "struggle" which he would remember as long as he lived. Thiers categorically refused to give up both Metz and Belfort. Bismarck told Thiers that it was "quite impossible" for any part of Alsace to remain in French hands. Thiers offered to sign a peace treaty immediately if Bismarck would give back Belfort, otherwise he would sign nothing.

Bismarck finally agreed to lay the matter before the emperor but he warned that it would be hopeless unless Moltke were won over. As it happened, both the emperor and Moltke were away from their quarters just then and it was necessary to await their return in order to settle this question of Belfort.[22] When the emperor returned he indicated his willingness to surrender Belfort if Moltke approved. The emperor did express, however, his wish to keep for Germany the battlefields and cemeteries of Vionville, Ste. Marie aux Chênes and St. Privat.[23] When Moltke returned to headquarters Bismarck discussed the matter of Belfort with him and when he rejoined Thiers he was able to report that Moltke had agreed to return Belfort to France. Bismarck left the room again and returned to propose an alternative plan: "Which will you have, Belfort or the abandonment of our entry into Paris?"[24] He said that he was prepared to renounce the German entry into Paris if Thiers would give up his demand for Belfort.[25] The issue was thus squarely up to Thiers and without hesitation he chose to keep Belfort. Once more Bismarck left the room and when he returned he brought "the definite concession of Belfort on condition that we will give up four little villages on the confines of Lorraine where eight to ten thousand Prussians are buried."[26] Thiers agreed to the exchange and Belfort was saved for France.

The negotiations had been long and arduous and at times had become acrimonious. Thiers and Favre were not noted for their taciturnity and they repeatedly harangued Bismarck until he wearily asked them to answer "with simple counter-proposals." "You know that we will start shooting on Monday if we aren't through here by then. That language you would certainly understand. We have been sitting here today for seven hours already and are not finished yet. My health cannot stand such things."[27]

The French negotiators did not leave Versailles until 9:30 that night. Upon their return to Paris they met with the parliamentary commission until after midnight, relating the course of the negotiations. The commission extended its thanks to Thiers and Favre for their work.[28]

February 25 was for Thiers the "bitterest day in my life" since the peace preliminaries were to be signed on that day. However, that was deferred. Thiers felt that the draft treaty was poorly drawn,[29] and the day was spent in argument and seemingly interminable discussions from one o'clock until nine in the evening. Bismarck complained to his staff that Thiers was ignorant of the geography of his own country,[30] and he accused Thiers of reopening questions which had already been settled. Bismarck absolutely refused to accept Thiers's contention that the ceded territories should bear a portion of the French public debt, and he accused the French of dragging out the negotiations and of wanting to start the war again in the hopes of getting the support of "your good friends the English." Again Bismarck suggested that his bankers be accepted as intermediaries in the matter of paying the war indemnity and again Thiers refused to hear of it. Bismarck finally became so annoyed that he called his terms an "ultimatum" and announced that he would speak no more French, a step which he had taken before when he wished to express his displeasure.[31]

Favre and Thiers left for Paris about ten o'clock in the evening. They had reached agreement with Bismarck on most of the terms of two documents, an extension of the armistice until March 12 and the preliminary peace treaty itself. It was to be a preliminary treaty only, since early in the negotiations, Thiers and Bismarck had agreed that in the interests of a speedy conclusion of hostilities, the task of preparing a final peace treaty should be turned over to plenipotentiaries meeting in Brussels. The preliminary treaty was to be signed the following day.[32]

The signing was scheduled to take place at one o'clock in the afternoon of February 26 but it was delayed for some three hours. When the time came to sign, the question naturally arose as to the status of Prussia's south German allies. Thiers felt that separate conventions should be signed with Bavaria, Württemberg and Baden but Bismarck would not hear of it. Instead, the delegates from those states signed the single document without comment, their secondary status thus being reflected at this moment of German triumph.[33]

The preamble said that the treaty of February 26 was "to serve as preliminary basis for the definitive peace to be concluded eventually." It was in ten articles.

Article I designated in rough outline the new frontier, leaving to a commission the task of tracing the boundary in detail. East of that line France surrendered all lands to Germany. Two villages in the department of the Moselle were ceded to Germany as well, and Belfort was to remain French.

Article II bound France to pay to Germany five billion francs, "at least" one billion during 1871 and the rest within the space of three years from the ratification of the preliminaries.

Article III provided for the beginning of the evacuation of France after the ratification of the preliminaries: immediately after, the city of Paris and the forts on the left bank of the Seine, then the departments to the left of the Loire river in "the shortest period possible." The French army was to withdraw behind the Loire until after the signing of a definitive peace, with the exception of the Paris garrison, which was limited to forty thousand men, and the garrisons indispensable to the safety of the fortified cities. It was provided that the departments between the right bank of the Seine and the eastern frontier should be gradually evacuated "after the ratification of the definitive treaty of peace and the payment of the first half-billion" of the war indemnity: it was specified which departments should be evacuated after successive payments of the indemnity. The article concluded:

His Majesty the Emperor will be disposed to substitute a financial guarantee for the territorial guarantee consisting of the partial occupation of French territory, if it is offered by the French government according to conditions recognized by His Majesty the Emperor and King as sufficient for the interests of Germany.

Article IV provided that German troops should abstain from levying requisitions on the occupied departments, but the support of the occupation troops was to be an obligation of the French government.

Article V dealt with the rights of the inhabitants in the territories ceded to Germany. It provided that their commercial and legal rights should be regulated "as favorably as possible" in the final peace treaty. They would be allowed a period during which they would enjoy "private facilities for the circulation of their products." The German government agreed not to raise any obstacle to those wishing to emigrate from those territories, nor to take any measure hindering their persons or their property.

Article VI provided for the exchange of prisoners of war.

Article VII set Brussels as the site of the negotiations for the definitive treaty of peace "to be concluded on the basis of the present preliminaries," and said that they were to take place "immediately after the ratification" of the preliminaries.

Article VIII provided that the administration of the occupied departments should be returned to the French authorities after ratification of the definitive peace treaty, but subject to the orders of the occupation authorities relating to the safety, support, and distribution of troops.

Article IX stated that the preliminary treaty should give to the German military authority no authority over any parts of France not already occupied.

Article X, provided that the preliminary treaty should be submitted immediately for ratification by the emperor and by the French national assembly. The treaty was dated at Versailles, February 26, 1871. Bismarck signed for Prussia and Thiers and Favre for France.

In an additional paragraph, the representatives of Bavaria, Württemberg and Baden "adhered" to the treaty, "having taken part in the present war as allies of Prussia, and now being part of the German Empire."[34]

Two other agreements were signed this same day. The first was an "additional convention." The first article extended the armistice to March 12. The second article repealed Article IV of the armistice by which the entry of German troops into Paris was forbidden. This convention provided that German troops not to exceed thirty thousand in number should occupy that portion of Paris between the Seine, the rue du Faubourg St. Honoré, and the Avenue des Ternes. Article III provided that German authorities might continue to levy taxes in the occupied departments, but they might no longer levy contributions in specie, a practice which had been followed during the war. A fourth article reserved to both parties the right to denounce the armistice upon three days' notice at any time after March 3.[35]

There was another agreement negotiated by Generals Valdan and Moltke which carried out Article II of the "additional convention" relative to the occupation of Paris by German troops. It arranged the billeting of the troops and provided that the occupation forces should be allowed to visit the Louvre and the Invalides, provided they were unarmed and conducted there by their officers.[36]

The next day a proclamation was issued announcing the prolongation of the armistice at the cost of a partial occupation of the capital. The Parisians were told that the future of the city and of France depended on their behavior. German troops would enter the city at ten o'clock on the morning of March 1 and would evacuate it immediately after ratification of the peace preliminaries by the national assembly.[37] It was a situation full of unpleasant possibilities, of course, and Favre was terrified lest some "act of madness" occur to precipitate trouble in the occupied city.[38]

Favre was not alone in hoping for a quick ratification of the preliminary treaty. Although Germany was victorious Bismarck feared that French rejection of the treaty would open the door to foreign intervention, a worry which never completely left him.[39] Thiers was as anxious to end the war as either of the other men and his reasons are highly revealing. They were succinctly stated in the phrase "each hour costs us millions."[40] Whatever his true feelings, Thiers repeatedly gave the impression that he was more concerned about France's loss of money than of territory, operating on the theory that money lost was gone forever but that a lost province could always be regained. He once told the parliamentary committee which accompanied him to Paris: "Do not let us exaggerate what is asked of France at this moment, it is only a small portion!" To which a member of the committee replied: "There are cases where cutting away a small portion of a man leaves him no longer a man."[41]

When Thiers arrived in Bordeaux on February 28 he was determined to speed ratification of the treaty in any way possible. Going directly from the train to the assembly, he asked the assembly to declare urgency and to approve the resolution: "The national assembly, submitting to the consequences of facts of which it is not the author, approves the peace preliminaries."[42]

Thiers then left it to Barthelemy Saint-Hilaire to read the terms of the treaty to the assembly. He read the financial provisions of the treaty in full but he read the full territorial provisions only after the Left objected to his proposals to summarize them.[43] Following the reading, the assembly debated the question of urgency and immediate consideration of the treaty. In general the extreme Left wished examination of the treaty deferred until the next day while the Right wanted it considered that very evening. Eloquently Thiers defended his call for urgency. The fate of France, he said, took precedence over the assembly and the political parties which stood behind its members. By acting promptly the assembly could perhaps spare Paris a "great sorrow." The negotiators had, he said, "with despair and even with tears" carefully examined each treaty provision and had done their best to save for France "its territory and riches." "But for you . . . there are only three or four questions whose solution is in all spirits and all hearts." He asked that no one abstain from voting. His plea was made to an assembly most of which was as anxious as he to end the war and the point was easily carried. The assembly voted to consider the treaty in committee that same evening and to meet in public session at noon the following day.[44]

When the assembly met on March 1 Victor Lanfranc read the report of the committee which had accompanied the negotiators to Paris. Whatever differences of opinion may have existed between Thiers and the committee were not revealed in Lanfranc's report. He said that the negotiations had been conducted under close supervision of the committee and that the treaty had been signed only after the committee had given its "unanimous advice" to do so. Therefore, on behalf of the committee, he urged the assembly to adopt the treaty in the form in which Thiers had submitted it. In spite of losses, "the honor of France is saved in this cruel treaty."[45]

The question was then opened for debate. Edgar Quinet spoke against the treaty. He said that "all negotiations would be impossible if one admitted in advance . . . that peace is the only refuge for France." He argued that Prussia wanted to see an assembly chosen by universal manhood suffrage give approval to the dismemberment of France. In this way feudal Germany would revenge herself on France's democratic institutions by "making of them the instrument of our ruin." To sign this treaty would be to deliver France to the Germans. He would not sign a treaty which was no peace at all but "perpetual war under the mask of peace."[46]

Bamberger, a deputy from the Moselle, called the treaty a "sentence of death." "One man only . . . should sign it: that man is Napoleon III."[47] This remark set off a furious verbal battle between supporters and opponents of the former Imperial régime. The treaty was lost sight of as the charges were hurled about. The affair was brought to a close only when the assembly had adopted a motion declaring Napoleon III responsible for the "ruin, invasion, and dismemberment of France" and deposing the dynasty.[48]

When order was at last restored Bamberger, on behalf of the deputies of the Moselle and Lorraine, warned that acceptance of the treaty would "break the first condition of stability of the republican government: that is the union which must exist between the parts of a nation."[49] Victor Hugo—a living symbol of opposition to the imperial régime—then rose to deliver a plea against the treaty. Paris, "as majestic as Rome and as stoical as Sparta," had given its mandate "to vote against the dismemberment of the fatherland." One possible good he did see coming from the treaty. One day, he predicted, a France bent on revenge would rise up to seize "the whole left bank of the Rhine." France would then call the German people to join her in forming a United States of Europe and drive out the German emperor in gratitude for Germany having driven out Napoleon III.[50] Hugo's word clearly had little effect on those not already of his opinion for he was constantly interrupted and audible conversations were not controlled by the presiding officer.[51] Louis Blanc followed Hugo in the debate. He stigmatized the peace as worse than war "since to ruin it would add shame." "The choice to make is between war for honor and peace at the price of honor."[52]

General Changarnier answered Blanc. He admitted that the terms were hard but said that no better could be obtained. France, he said, was paying for the crimes committed against Germany by Napoleon I.[53]

Deputy Buffet rose to announce on behalf of some of the members from the Vosges that they would abstain from voting. They recognized the necessity of ratifying the treaty but since part of their department would become German under the terms of the treaty they feared lest an affirmative vote on their part be construed as giving the approval of their constituents to the transfer.[54] Thiers assured Buffet that the reasons for such an abstention were completely understandable. He said that he would never have signed the peace had he not felt that continued resistance was impossible. He asked that he not be forced to give the reasons for his conviction. "My silence is a sacrifice that I make to the security and the future of my country."[55]

This veiled remark was immediately seized upon by a deputy named Brunet. He begged the assembly to establish a committee to examine the question if continued resistance was impossible. He predicted that it would be found that France

The Germans enter Paris, March 1, 1871. (Picture Collection, New York Public Library)

could still fight on and he called on the assembly to "declare general war" rather than to submit to this treaty.[56] A series of fervent speeches on the Left supported Brunet's idea. In response to Thiers's cry, "Give us the means," a deputy named Tirard called out "The *levée en masse*."[57] Thiers made a final appeal after which cloture was voted. The treaty was ratified overwhelmingly: 546 to 107, with 23 abstentions. When the results were announced the delegates from the departments of Moselle, Bas- and Haut-Rhin declared that the treaty was null and void and proceeded to leave the assembly.[58]

While this debate was proceeding at Bordeaux the German troops made their triumphal entry into Paris. Under ideal weather conditions the troops paraded before William I at the race course of Longchamps in the Bois de Boulogne, after which they entered the city across the Pont and Avenue de Neuilly, through the Porte Maillot and under the Arc de Triomphe. Paris was virtually a dead city and there were no untoward incidents.[59] Bismarck too entered the city and went as far as the arch. He did not go through it, however, since the emperor had deferred his formal entry until March 3.[60]

At eleven o'clock that same night, at the foreign office, Favre received a telegram from Bordeaux announcing the ratification of the preliminaries. Since he could not get through the Prussian lines until the following morning he sent a telegram to Versailles to inform Bismarck of the ratification and to request immediate evacuation of Paris. Early the next morning a telegram was sent to Favre requesting written confirmation of the news from Bordeaux, but before it could reach him he appeared in person at Versailles.[61] Bismarck was still asleep and had left word that he was not to be disturbed. Favre returned to Paris but appeared again that afternoon at German headquarters, armed this time with the official ratification documents, which had been sent from Bordeaux by special messenger. Bismarck received him graciously enough but he perhaps betrayed his feelings when he said that "if we had foreseen that your chamber would be able to examine and ratify the treaty in twenty-four hours we would have made other dispositions." Finding the French papers in order Bismarck handed over the imperial ratification. Orders were given to begin the evacuation of Paris at eight o'clock the following morning, March 3.[62]

There was keen disappointment at German headquarters over the absence of a full-scale entry into Paris. The emperor was particularly annoyed at not being able to enter Paris at the head of his troops. The Germans, he said, "were as good as being chased out of Paris." There were some who wanted the Guards to enter the city but Moltke and Roon insisted on the literal observance of the agreement.[63]

Thiers, too, was determined to carry out the terms of the treaty and he instructed Favre to stop trying to embroil the neutrals in France's behalf, for he felt that such activities would only end in a rebuff from the neutrals and a delay in the German evacuation of France.[64] To obtain a permanent peace treaty and to secure the evacuation of France as quickly as possible now became the guiding principles of Thiers's foreign policy.

NOTES TO CHAPTER VI

1. Dréo, p. 679.
2. Bismarck to Manteuffel, Versailles, Feb. 19, 1871, *GW,* Vib, 704, no. 2047.
3. Thiers, *Memoirs,* p. 103–105. The account of these negotiations is drawn heavily from the account in Thier's memoirs (pp. 102–116).
4. *Ibid.,* pp. 105/108.
5. Hartshorne, pp. 220–221.
6. *Ibid.,* p. 229.
7. *Ibid.,* pp. 229–231.
8. Busch, *Franco-German War,* II, 341.

9. Frederick III, pp. 308–309.

10. Stosch, p. 235; Abeken to his wife, Hartshorne, p. 232.

11. Abeken, pp. 346–347.

12. Thiers, *Memoirs,* p. 109.

13. Frederick III, pp. 309–312; "Both men expressed the wish for peace but referred him to Count Bismarck for all details of the negotiations" (Stosch, p. 235).

14. Thiers, *Memoirs,* pp. 108–110; Bismarck told Busch that Thiers was prepared to pay an indemnity of fifteen hundred million francs (Busch, *Franco-German War,* II, 341–342).

15. Favre to Broglie, Paris, Feb. 24, 1871, MAE, CP (Angleterre), 755: 280–282.

16. Thiers, *Memoirs,* pp. 110–111; Favre, III, 96–97.

17. Thiers, *Memoirs,* p. 112.

18. *Ibid.*

19. *Ibid.,* p. 113. Sorel accepts Bismarck's own figures at face value, for he says: "If one takes into account the losses sustained since that time [September] one sees that the chancellor did not exaggerate too much when he asserted that the demands of the government were lower than those of the nation." He says that "the greed of learned German statisticians" exceeded that of Prussia (Sorel, II, 238).

On the other hand, a confidante of the Empress of Germany says that the financial experts consulted by Bismarck felt that the war indemnity would cripple France for years (Princess Catherine Radziwill, *Germany Under Three Emperors* [London: 1917], p. 205). Waldersee says that Bismarck's advisers, "with the exception of Count Henckel, all were in favour of a sum under 5 milliards [billion]" but that it had been agreed to ask seven billion with the intention of coming down to five billion. In finally setting the amount of the indemnity, he says, Bismarck wanted a sum "high enough to damage France but not high enough to seem to the country impossible or to force it into a condition of despair" (Waldersee, p. 110).

20. Busch, *Franco-German War,* II, 341.

21. Hartshorne, p. 232.

22. Thiers, *Memoirs,* pp. 113–114.

23. Abeken, p. 347.

24. Thiers, *Memoirs,* p. 115.

25. Favre, III, 104–106.

26. Thiers, *Memoirs,* pp. 114–115.

27. Stosch, p. 237; *GW,* VII, 505–506, no. 391.

28. Thiers, *Memoirs,* p. 115; Favre to Broglie, Feb. 25, 1871, MAE, CP (Angleterre), 755: 286.

29. Thiers, *Memoirs,* pp. 115–116.

30. Abeken to his wife, Versailles, Feb. 25, 1871, Abeken, pp.349–350.

31. Favre, III, 112–114.

32. *Ibid.,* pp. 95–96 and 107. Favre had rejected the suggestion of Berlin as the meeting place of the final peace negotiations.

33. *Ibid.,* pp. 118–119.

34. The text of the treaty can be found in Hertslet, III, 1912–1918. See also France. *Documents diplomatiques français, 1871–1914* (Paris: 1929–1961), Ser. I, I, 1–5, no. 1, hereafter cited as *DDF;* A. Mendelssohn-Bartholdy and others, *Die grosse Politik der europäischen Kabinette* (Berlin: 1922–1926), I, 3–6, no. 1, hereafter cited as *GP; Politique extérieure de l'Allemagne* (Paris: 1927), I, 17–20, no. 12, hereafter cited as *PEA.*

35. *Convention additionelle,* Villefort, I, 27–28.

36. Villefort, I, 29–30.

37. *Ibid.,* II, 256–258, no. 22.

38. Favre to Simon, Paris, Feb. 26, 1871, Jules Simon, *Le gouvernement de M. Thiers* (Paris: 1878), I, 133.

39. Busch, *Our Chancellor* II, 75–76.

40. Thiers to Simon, Paris, Feb. 25, 1871, Simon, *Thiers,* I, 124–125.

41. *Memoirs of the Count de Falloux* (London: 1888), II, 340–341. Falloux says that although he did not serve in the assembly he was in close touch with members of that body. See also Du Camp, II, 259: Du Camp quotes Thiers to this effect and says that others received such confidences as well.

42. *Annales,* I, 88.

43. *Ibid.,* pp. 89–91.

44. *Ibid.,* pp. 94–96.

45. *Ibid.,* pp. 98–99. The debates on ratification are also included in full in Villefort, II, 11–81. Brabant (pp. 122–131) also deals with the debates at some length.

46. *Annales,* I, 100–101.

47. *Ibid.,* p. 102.

48. *Ibid.,* pp. 104–105.

49. *Ibid.,* p. 106.

50. *Ibid.,* pp. 106–109.

51. Claveau, II, 37.

52. *Annales,* I, 110–113.

53. *Ibid.,* p. 113.

54. *Ibid.,* pp. 113–115.

55. *Ibid.,* p. 115.

56. *Ibid.,* pp. 115–117.

57. *Ibid.,* p. 120.

58. *Ibid.,* pp. 122–124.

59. Frederick III, pp. 319–322; Favre, III, 150–151.

60. Bismarck to his wife, Versailles, Mar. 5, 1871, Bismarck, *Letters,* pp. 123–125, no. LXXVIII; *GW,* XIV/II, 816, no. 1410; Rothfels, pp. 371–372, no. 237.

61. Abeken to his wife, Versailles, Mar. 3, 1871, Abeken, pp. 356–357.

62. Favre, III, 154–158.

63. Frederick III, pp. 322–325. Abeken wrote of "the mortification here at the hurried evacuation in Paris" (Abeken to his wife, Versailles, Mar. 6, 1871, Abeken, p. 358).

64. Thiers to Favre, Bordeaux, Mar. 10, 1871, MAE, Papiers Favre. Thiers asked Lyons for his opinion of bringing the question of Franco-German relations before the London conference considering the Black Sea question. Lyons discouraged this and said that he felt that Thiers had asked his opinion only "to relieve his conscience" (Lyons to Granville, Bordeaux, Mar. 6, 1871, Newton, I, 374–375).

VII

The Brussels Negotiations

In the days after the ratification of the peace preliminaries there were many problems to be regulated in order to establish relations between the French and the German army of occupation. These were worked out in long and arduous negotiations which resulted in a series of conventions concerning details arising from and pertaining to the occupation.[1]

Despite such conventions there were constant sources of irritation which gave rise to mutual accusations and recriminations between the German and French authorities. In view of the problems involved it was essential that a man of real ability be chosen as military governor of France when Bismarck returned in early March. He named such a man in the person of General von Fabrice, former minister of war of Saxony. He maintained his headquarters first at Rouen and then at Soisy. The French government attached Lieutenant Colonel Delahaye to Fabrice's headquarters as their permanent representative but Favre also was a familiar figure there as was Pouyer-Quertier, French minister of finance.

The peace preliminaries had named Brussels as the site of negotiations for the final peace treaty. It was a custom of international usage for peace negotiations to be held in a neutral country in order to place victor and vanquished on at least a theoretical footing of equality.[2] Baron d'Anethan, Belgian foreign minister, professed to be flattered at the choice of Brussels and offered the facilities of the Belgian foreign office for the use of the negotiators.[3]

To represent Germany at the negotiations Bismarck named Balan, minister to Belgium, and Harry von Arnim, Prussian minister to the Holy See. The French sent to represent them Baron Baude, minister plenipotentiary at Athens, and M. Goulard, a member of the national assembly.[4] France also sent two *ad hoc* commissioners, M. de Clerq and General Doutrelaine, whose functions were to assist at all conferences and to clarify various questions in private meetings. Doutrelaine was a prisoner of war at Coblenz and was released at Bismarck's order so that he might participate in the Brussels talks.[5]

During the negotiations there also sat at Brussels a military commission charged with drawing the new frontier between France and Germany. The Germans on this commission were General von Strantz, Hauchecorne and Herzog. Doutrelaine and Colonel Laussedat represented France but found that Baude and Goulard virtually ignored their work and recommendations.[6]

On March 14 and 15 two crown councils were held at Berlin to discuss the instructions for the German representatives at Brussels. Arnim was present at both. Bismarck had a complete draft treaty to guide his diplomats and the council went over it article by article. At the end of the second council the ministers of Bavaria, Württemberg, and Baden countersigned the council reports but they made no material contributions to the discussions. It was agreed that this same procedure would be followed with relation to the final peace treaty.[7] Thus Bismarck mapped out every step to be followed by Balan and Arnim. Arnim left Berlin thoroughly briefed and instructed to make no final commitments without looking to Bismarck for instructions.[8] Bismarck was taking no chances of losing control of the Brussels negotiations and subsequent experience with Arnim was to prove the wisdom of his precautions.

The French were not so well organized. Thiers arrived at Versailles, the new seat of government, only on March 14. That very week Paris rose in revolt against the government. Thus, at the very moment when the French government should have been free to concentrate on the coming negotiations it was distracted by rebellion at home. To make matters worse, Thiers had only relatively inexperienced men from which to choose his negotiators[9] and they went to Brussels with only the sketchiest preparations and instructions.[10] Baron Baude, the first of the French representatives to leave for Brussels, arrived there on March 18 without credentials, instructions, or any specific proposals to present to the Germans, Arnim arrived on March 21 armed with the carefully prepared draft treaty and ready to open negotiations.[11]

When Baude wrote requesting instructions Favre told him to delay the opening of negotiations for forty-eight hours. He had mislaid certain important papers at the foreign office when the revolt began and he proposed to send them to Brussels by Goulard. He said that he was sending a *"projet de protocole"* and he suggested that Baude secure a copy of the German treaty so that a counter-proposal might be drawn up.[12] In contrast with the well organized draft which the Germans were prepared to present, Favre's instructions proved to consist largely of long-winded discussions of issues which might arise. He presented only the most general considerations to guide his representatives in their conversations with the Germans.[13]

While Baude waited for the arrival of Goulard and the

promised instructions he broached unofficially to Arnim the subject of the negotiations. Since he had no proposals to present he refrained from asking Arnim for a copy of the German treaty, but he did ask him about the principal points contained therein. Arnim revealed them and Baude sent them to Paris to facilitate work on the French proposals. Arnim also proposed that in the interests of speed the Brussels negotiations be limited to "fixing as precisely as possible . . . general principles," the details of which could then be referred to "special conventions which would have the same force and value as if they were textually inserted in the treaty."[14]

Goulard finally arrived in Brussels on March 26 and on March 27 the two teams of diplomats met to consider procedural matters. Baude informed the Germans that he had specific instructions to insist on regular protocols for the formal sessions. The Germans protested that while this might be necessary in a multi-state congress, in a bilateral negotiation relations would only be aggravated by setting every word on paper. Officials in Paris or Berlin, removed from the scene, could easily take offense at some unfortunate word or expression long after the negotiators had forgotten it. They agreed, subject to approval from Versailles, to draw up a protocol only when they had reached agreement on specific articles. They also decided to maintain absolute secrecy concerning the progress of negotiations. The Germans then presented to the French some of the articles of their draft treaty but declined as yet to deliver all of their proposals.[15]

The following day, March 28, the plenipotentiaries of both sides met in a salon of the Belgian foreign ministry for the formal opening of the negotiations and for an exchange of credentials.[16] At this opening session there occurred an incident which revealed a latent division in the German ranks. The *procès verbal* of this first session spoke of the plenipotentiaries of France and of the "German Empire" but made no mention of the representatives of the states constituting that empire. Quadt and Uxkull, representatives of Bavaria and Württemberg respectively, insisted that they too should be mentioned since they held credentials as representatives of their own kingdoms. A quarrel developed among the Germans and the French carefully avoided mixing in it.[17] The incident brought into the open an antagonism which had been developing for several days and which had been the cause of much correspondence between Brussels and Berlin. Balan and Arnim wanted to keep the south German delegates in the background[18] and they urged their colleagues not to let the French see the differences of opinion among the Germans. The south Germans served notice that they expected to be kept informed of the course of the negotiations, a demand which Balan and Arnim assured Bismarck they intended to fulfil with discretion.[19]

The second formal meeting of the conference was set for Monday, April 3. Before then, however, a series of informal discussions were held. By March 31 the French had been given all of the German treaty proposals,[20] but the French government showed no disposition to accept them without debate. Indeed it quickly became apparent that serious differences existed between the two sides. Fundamentally the difficulty stemmed from differing views as to the relationship between the preliminary and final peace treaties. Basically the Germans felt that the preliminaries had established certain agreements and principles the details of which would be discussed and settled quickly at Brussels. To the French the emphasis in the earlier treaty lay on the word "preliminary" and they considered it precisely that: a springboard for negotiations on questions by no means decided beyond argument. They were prepared to argue points which the

Germans considered settled. The endless haggling was by no means to Bismarck's taste and his dispatches to Brussels and to Fabrice at Soisy constantly demanded speed.

These difficulties were aggravated by the dangerous uprising in Paris. The German government showed anxiety lest the apparent inability of the French to suppress the Commune endanger payment of the war indemnity. Bismarck purported to doubt the good will of the French government and he constantly threatened to increase the size of the war indemnity should Germany be forced to raise the size of the occupation army to cope with the explosive situation.[21] Balan told the French negotiators that "considering the state of France," the "too extended prolongation" of the negotiations could be considered as a return to a state of war and he suggested that they convert the German draft treaty into a final treaty quickly.[22]

To make matters worse, Bismarck was not entirely pleased with the conduct of his own representatives at Brussels. He felt that they were too inclined to fuss over unimportant formalities of wording and that they were much too stiff in their relationship with their counterparts.[23] One can imagine Bismarck's reaction when, involved in really important problems, he received a dispatch from Balan and Arnim requesting the assignment to them of a police agent because of the presence in Brussels of so many French "intriguers" and Bonapartists.[24] Bismarck wryly answered that while he had no doubts that the French in Brussels were given to intrigue he really failed to see how such intrigues could have any important bearing on the peace negotiations.[25]

Bismarck's patience had grown thin within a few days of the opening of the negotiations and he was threatening to present his treaty as an ultimatum and to move the discussions to Berlin.[26] But, in spite of his mounting irritation, Bismarck was not the man to give way recklessly to anger. Early in the negotiations Baude had raised the issue of attaching part of the French debt to the territories ceded to Germany. In reporting this to Bismarck Arnim said that he intended to tell Baude that the negotiations would be broken off unless this demand were dropped.[27] Bismarck was quick to tell Arnim not to threaten a total rupture of negotiations.[28] He wanted no irrevocable decisions until "all points of difference have been shown," and, until he had the full French counterproposals he did not wish to be forced into a situation requiring an ultimatum. Besides, at the moment, he was not at all certain that the emperor would approve such a drastic course of action.[29]

The negotiations had scarcely begun at Brussels when Bismarck decided to use Fabrice's headquarters as an alternate channel of communications with the French government in an attempt to reconcile the differences and frustrations which had arisen at Brussels. At the beginning of April Favre visited Fabrice at Rouen. The general urged Favre to do nothing to irritate Bismarck further. He said that the chancellor was under real pressure in Berlin from the military, who had never forgiven him for the failure of the army to enter Paris properly at the end of the war, and from the financiers, who were on watch against French failure to pay exactly the sums due Germany. Favre assured Fabrice of his good faith. He offered to convert the peace preliminaries to a definitive treaty "except for adding to it the delimitation of Belfort," leaving questions of detail to subsequent agreement between the two governments.[30]

Thus within two weeks of the opening of the Brussels negotiations little substantial progress had been achieved toward a definitive peace treaty and major differences had arisen concerning every principal issue under discussion. Out of the numerous proposals and counterproposals certain issues had rapidly emerged as the major stumbling blocks to a quick settlement.

1. *Frontier changes.* The peace preliminaries had set out in great detail the new frontier between France and Germany. By Article I of that treaty an international commission was to trace these boundaries on the actual terrain. As a result of the Belfort question one alteration had been provided: Germany was to have the villages of the Marie-aux-Chênes and Vionville while France was to retain Belfort "with a radius which shall be hereafter determined." This last proviso was to open the door to a bitter diplomatic struggle.

Although Favre realized that there was little chance of any appreciable change in the frontier as set out in the preliminaries he insisted that Baude and Goulard raise the question of the Belfort radius early in the negotiations at Brussels.[31] He drew extensively on religious, historical, and linguistic evidence to justify the French demand for an area larger than that dictated by military considerations alone.[32] Baude and Goulard felt that the fact that the Germans had not at first submitted any article dealing with this question indicated the intention of proposing some modifications in the terms of the preliminaries and they urged Favre not to raise the question until the Germans had shown their hand.[33]

The fact that a German member of the boundary commission, Wilhelm Hauchecorne, was also the Director of the Mining Academy in Berlin raises some interesting questions about the motives of the Germans in setting the new boundary with France. Much has been made of the fact that the boundary imposed on France took the bulk of the high grade French iron ores. This raises the question if this was a deliberate policy of Bismarck and the German authorities. It would appear that economic factors played a distinctly secondary place in German thinking and that strategic considerations were the main factors which determined the drawing of the boundary.

In August 1870 when German governments were established for Alsace and Lorraine five *arrondissements* were specifically detached from Lorraine and added to the government of Alsace: Sarreguemines, Thionville and Metz in the department of Moselle and Sarrebourg and Château-Salins in the department of Meurthe. These areas, plus the two Alsatian departments of Upper and Lower Rhine, constituted the area which Germany proposed to annex. By detaching these areas from the territory to be annexed Germany gave up much of the known ore field in the department of Meurthe around Nancy and a significant part of that in the department of Moselle around Longwy. Conversely, had Germany decided to take *all* of the area of Lorraine she would have gained the *entire* proven ore fields of Lorraine as well as other reserves of high phosphorus ores whose value was a matter of debate.

Why were these particular boundaries chosen? Had Metz not been included it could be inferred that linguistic factors were of predominant importance. The inclusion of Metz seems to rule out language as the primary factor. For strategic reasons the military insisted on having the boundary follow a line from Thionville to Metz. By so doing they acquired for Germany important ore reserves. That this was an incidental factor, however, may be deduced from the fact that by *not d*rawing the line slightly west of Thionville they *lost* more valuable reserves than they *gained*. Moreover the minister of war, von Roon, wanted Nancy to strengthen yet further the frontier. Bismarck, whose view was of necessity as much political as military, was not prepared to hold out for Nancy and, as we have seen, had serious doubts about the wisdom of acquiring even Metz. The military, which considered Nancy of less strategic significance than Metz, held out for the latter but gave up Nancy and in so doing lost valuable ore areas for Germany.

Certainly ignorance on the part of the German civil and military leaders need not have been the reason for this seeming indifference to economic considerations. Almost from the beginning of the war the German press had freely discussed the matter of territorial annexations and the Prussian government had made no secret of the approximate areas which it proposed to annex. As early as December 2 Bismarck had instructed the Prussian ministry to examine all private suggestions about peace terms and to draw them up in the form of treaty articles for his inspection.[34] Men who were familiar with such economic matters could certainly have brought them to the attention of the proper authorities with a good chance of having their arguments being considered. And, perhaps of greater significance is the fact that Wilhelm Hauchecorne—the same Hauchecorne who now served on the boundary commission at Brussels—had prepared a report in August, 1870, concerning French mineral deposits and that this report did reach highly placed German authorities who were in a position to bring it to the attention of Bismarck. There is no evidence that the report was utilized or even seen by the German negotiators but it *could* have been and the fact remains that the information which it contained could easily have been discovered had the civil and military authorities wished to do so. It seems clear that they did not. Far more stress was placed on the size of the area around Metz than around Thionville yet the ore deposits around Thionville were far more valuable than those around Metz.[35]

The fact that the preliminary peace had not defined the scope of the Belfort radius gave Favre the chance to negotiate for as much territory as possible. But it also gave the Germans another chance to get more of the ore-bearing areas and

Hauchecorne was the one man to make the most of the opportunity. It was in this matter of Belfort that Baude and Goulard urged Favre to let the Germans make the first move. In fact the Germans did have a plan to offer. They were prepared to interpret the radius of Belfort strictly in a military sense of seven and one-half kilometers[36] and to limit the French to that unless they received compensations in the form of territory west of Thionville in the north, including the communes of Moyeuvre and Hayange. Bismarck said that he was prepared to make the exchange in order to discourage smuggling.[37] Doutrelaine felt that this was a specious argument designed to conceal some more devious reason and he pointed out to Favre that the cessions which Germany asked would virtually sever communications between France and Luxembourg and that the region contained important mineral reserves which France could ill afford to lose. Favre did reject the proposed exchange.[38]

We do know that Hauchecorne and the other commissioners at Brussels called Bismarck's attention to the fact that valuable ore reserves did lie in the region west of Thionville and recommended that Germany try to acquire these areas even though they also lay in French-speaking territory.[39] In view of his subsequent actions concerning this exchange it seems clear that Bismarck was not engaging in any chicanery nor indeed that he was even convinced of the vital importance of this particular frontier change. In any event, Doutrelaine argued eloquently against surrendering Moyeuvre and Hayange. While he acknowledged that Germany should expect compensation for a larger radius for Belfort, he suggested that it be found elsewhere in the negotiations, at one point specifying Longwy, but nothing came of this suggestion.[40] He found an ally in an odd place. Moltke felt that the military value of the iron works of Hayange and Moyeuvre was slight but he suggested as an alternative compensation for Germany a larger radius for Metz in order to gain control of certain battlefields in that area.[41]

Through all of the discussion the Germans steadfastly held to their original position that Belfort's radius could only be established within the military definition of that term unless France was prepared to make the necessary cessions in the north.

2. *The war indemnity and the French national debt*. From the beginning of the negotiations Favre felt that the financial clauses of the preliminaries offered the best opportunity to ease France's burden by diplomatic means. He was prepared to claim as deductions from the indemnity such items as the two hundred million franc indemnity levied on Paris,[42] communal and private claims rising out of German requisitions, and those resulting from German depredations on French forests.[43] Baude and Goulard realized the practical difficulties of forcing such issues into the negotiations regardless of their merits, and they felt that the most which could be expected was the insertion in the treaty of a clause establishing a commission to consider such matters.[44] They urged Favre not to raise claims which would be difficult to support and they finally did win his approval to state the entire matter of the French claims in principle in the treaty, leaving the details to be worked out later.[45]

In his initial instructions to Baude and Goulard Favre had raised another issue closely connected with that of reduction of the war indemnity. He said that he intended to rely on an "incontestable principle of natural law" whereby "territory which passes under a new domination carries with it the charges with which it is burdened, and the new sovereign is not justified in declining them." With the ceded territories, he said, Germany must accept "a proportional part of the general debt of France," and he anticipated that this sum would amount to "several hundreds of millions." He also imagined that Bismarck would readily accept this principle.[46]

Favre was completely mistaken in this belief. The matter had come up in the crown council of March 14. Bismarck said that although this question had not been explicitly discussed during the February negotiations he had hinted that, if France would accept a war indemnity of six billion francs, Alsace-Lorraine might be included in a settlement of the state debt. However, when the indemnity was set at five billion francs there was no such reservation. Therefore no article on this subject was included in the draft treaty which was being prepared.[47]

When the French raised the question at Brussels they insisted that the proposed German terms by which France surrendered to Germany all *rights* in the ceded territories, were incomplete since nothing was said about the corresponding *obligations,* which were recognized in international and in private law. Only the French counterproposal made this clear.[48] The Germans categorically refused this claim on the grounds that the ceded territories were free of their share of the French public debt by virtue of the reduction of the war indemnity from six to five billion francs.[49] No compromise seemed possible on these two stubbornly held positions.

3. *Rights of peoples in Alsace-Lorraine.* Before the Brussels conference began Favre told his representatives that France must insist on a reservation in the minutes of the conference which would recognize the rights of the populations of Alsace and Lorraine to be consulted in the change of sovereignty which affected them so intimately.[50] Baude and Goulard urged him not to inject this disruptive issue into the conversations and Thiers and Favre did abandon this stand abruptly in early April.[51]

A closely related issue, one which had far more substantive importance, concerned the means whereby the people in the ceded territories might change their nationality.

The Germans proposed a period of one year during which "French subjects resident in the ceded territories" should have the right to emigrate to France. Those not using this right should remain German subjects. The period of one year would be extended to two for natives of the ceded territories absent from French territory at the time of ratification of the treaty. The French, on the other hand, proposed a period of six years during which "individuals in the ceded territories presently domiciled there" could preserve their French citizenship and the right of moving their domicile by making a declaration to that effect to the proper authorities. The French would also have retained for minors this option of nationality until the end of the year during which they should attain their majority.

Arnim absolutely refused to consider the six-year period demanded by the French, and Uxkull pointed out that France had been satisfied with a period of one year at the time that she annexed Savoy and Nice. It was perhaps not a wise comparison because the French were quick to point out that a plebiscite *had* been held in that case to consult the wishes of the people and that one year had appeared ample time for the few Savoyards and Nicois who wished to change their place of residence to do so. Balan went so far as to suggest a compromise which would stipulate one year for the right of option and a longer period for removing property but he said that the matter would have to be referred to Berlin.[52] The Germans felt that it was impossible to allow the French request for the option for minors since it would be "morally impossible" for Germany to accept fifteen or twenty years of uncertainty as to the status of such people.[53] To Favre Baude and

Goulard acknowledged the justice of this argument,[54] but they fought hard for their basic plan.

France contended that the "right of emigration" called for by the German plan proceeded on the assumption that the inhabitants of the ceded territories were already German and that it would result in unfair expulsions whereas the French proposal, which they called the "right of choice," would respect individual rights and would allow a free choice of political régimes without the necessity of any displacement. The Germans hotly denied the charge and pointed out that any French subjects who would accept the German police laws governing foreigners could remain.[55]

4. *Method of payment of the war indemnity.* Article W of the German peace proposals called for payment of the war indemnity entirely in precious metals at Berlin, the last three billion to be paid in nine equal installments from March 1872 to March 1874.

France considered these terms an "unjustifiable aggravation" of the terms of the preliminaries both because of the stipulation of Berlin as the place of payment and because of the proposed plan of payment. They contended that they should be allowed to pay at Paris since the debt was incurred in France. This was, they said, a rule well recognized in international usage and by the "precedents of 1815 which are not unknown to Germany," an obvious reference to the indemnity levied on France after the Napoleonic wars.[56] As for the method of payment, France proposed to pay two billion of the indemnity in precious metals and the remainder in securities.[57] France also wanted the three billion in securities to be considered not as a promise to pay but as payment itself and, therefore, to be followed by evacuation of the occupied portion of France.[58] This proposal prompted Arnim to say that "even a Frenchman will admit that at the present time it is not possible to speak seriously of French securities without waking the suspicion of tactless irony."[59]

In mid-April a German finance official went to Brussels to discuss these matters with the French. In the course of his conversations he stated it as his personal opinion that the German insistence on payment in specie was intended only to exclude payment in bank notes or paper money but not all forms of negotiable instruments.[60] The French seized on this as a concession by the Germans and steadfastly resisted Arnim's attempts to get the discussions back onto a basis of payment entirely in precious metals. Arnim suggested that the French accept a simple restatement of the peace preliminaries, which merely acknowledged the obligation and said that it must be paid within three years. The French refused, insisting that the method of payment was the very core of the matter. Arnim finally did concede that the German government would receive notes of fixed duration *(traites à échéance fixe)*. He said that the internal situation in France made it absolutely impossible for Germany to accept bonds.[61]

5. *Renewal of treaties between France and Germany and the Alsatian customs agreement*. At the crown council of March 14 Bismarck said that France must be prepared to make concessions concerning customs duties with regard to Germany. The German proposal called for a blanket renewal of former treaties with France but Bismarck realized that Thiers, a known protectionist, might be unwilling to grant this. Therefore, he warned his negotiators not to show "excessive zeal" in trying to renew the treaties and he specifically said that this point should not be made a condition precedent for a peace settlement. He was not prepared to start a customs war with France but he felt that this issue might be found useful in gaining other concessions from France.[62]

Favre knew that the Germans wanted a renewal of the

commercial treaties, especially the 1862 commercial treaty between France and the Zollverein. He was prepared to grant a renewal on a provisional basis only and he instructed Baude and Goulard that they should make it quite clear that they were doing Germany a favor in consenting to renewal at all since it was favorable to Germany and since many French industries would approve a French refusal to renew the treaty.[63] To bolster his arguments he added that France must save at least four hundred million francs annually to meet her obligations and most of that sum could only be raised by increasing the tariff rates. In fact, he said, France would probably denounce her commercial treaty with England in order to raise the tariffs.[64]

Baude and Goulard felt that in Germany's desire for a renewal of the treaties France had the only weapon of any value with which she might wring concessions from Germany. They told Arnim that the Berlin government might well consider the relationship between tariff renewal and the financial charges levied against France.[65] They refused to grant Germany "most favored nation" status and said that France wished to denounce all of her treaties.[66] At the same time they said that they were prepared to reinstate noneconomic and nonfiscal treaties.[67]

While Baude and Goulard were taking this firm stand at Brussels Favre, who had also recognized that the German demand might be used to gain some concession for France, weakened his own negotiators' stand by telling Fabrice that he *was* willing to renew the commercial treaties on a temporary basis even though he did say that Germany would later be put on a par with other nations.[68] Baude and Goulard bitterly opposed even a provisional renewal of the commercial treaty, "the only question on which our adversaries are in our power, just as we are in theirs on all the others."[69]

Bismarck did not want to break off negotiations over this point but he was prepared to press this advantage. He instructed Arnim to insist on an extension of the treaties so long as France's other treaties of a similar nature remained in force, and he insisted that Germany be accorded "most favored nation" status.[70]

A related issue was raised by Article V of the German treaty proposals which was designed to give to Alsace and Lorraine a privileged position vis-à-vis French customs, at least during the transitional period. There was not much difference in principle here for Favre was prepared to give special consideration to the products of the lost territories. His motives were not entirely altruistic. Certainly he wanted to help Alsace and Lorraine but he also wished to avoid a serious dislocation of the French industrial system which would suddenly be cut off from the rich Alsatian and Lorraine markets.[71] On April 9 Pouyer-Quertier and delegates from the two provinces signed an agreement providing for reciprocal free entry of goods until the definitive peace should make other arrangements.[72] In spite of this promising beginning Arnim wrote to Bismarck on April 21 that as yet he had been unable to get from the French a hard and fast agreement as to details.[73] This matter was later to assume major proportions.

6. *Freedom of the seas and restitution of confiscated merchant vessels.* The Germans demanded freedom from seizure in time of war of enemy merchant ships and cargoes. Favre had anticipated this demand and he was probably correct when he said that Prussia made much of this principle only because her merchantmen had been helpless against the French fleet. For the idea to be useful, he said, it would have to be part of the general law of nations and that would be possible only if all of the great powers would sign an agreement to that effect. He was prepared to espouse such a prin-

ciple only if France gained some compensation in the assessment of the war indemnity.[74]

A corollary to this question was the controversy involving the fate of merchant vessels captured at sea during the war. The Germans proposed that all seized vessels and cargoes be returned to their owners or in lieu of restoration their value at the moment of capture. The French wished only to restore vessels and cargoes not yet adjudged by a prize court. Baude refused Arnim's demand for an immediate return of all ships in French ports not yet judged. To do so would, he said, give Germany advantages from a treaty not yet signed.[75]

An amusing sidelight on this question is revealed in the minutes of the German crown council of March 14. At that meeting Delbrück suggested setting lower premiums on these claims for, should it become necessary for the Reichstag to compensate German nationals in the event that France refused to do so, the lower valuation would be to the advantage of the German government.[76]

7. *The Eastern railways.* One of the most bitterly disputed points concerned that portion of the eastern railways' *(Chemin de fer de l'est)* properties which lay in the territories ceded to Germany.

This issue arose at the very outset of the negotiations when the French delegates, representing the creditors of the railroad company, insisted that the rights of such creditors must be respected in any peace treaty. Bismarck's attitude toward this was succinctly put: "It's none of their business." He was not interested in considering the matter in any peace treaty.[77] The German proposal began by cancelling all concessions granted to the railway by the French government. It agreed to "try" to arrive at agreement with the owners on the price of an indemnity but it also said that, in the event of failure to reach any agreement, the German government reserved the right to expropriate the railroad outright. Bismarck wished this done so that France could not later lodge a protest on behalf of her nationals.[78]

The French proposal specified that Germany accepted all rights and obligations to which the French government had been liable. Thus the obligation of indemnification would be transferred from the French to the German government. It also proposed that, should Germany wish to acquire full rights in the railroad, the indemnity price should be settled by a mixed commission composed of representatives of France, Germany, and the railroad company.

To the French the German proposition was based on an unacceptable premise. They said that by the treaty of February 26 Germany acquired only the rights which *France* held with regard to the company but that the *private* obligations of the company would have to be settled separately. If this proved to be too slow for Germany, they proposed a way to speed the matter up: France could pay Germany, guarantee her against all claims, and deduct the amount from the indemnity of war levied against France.[79] We do not have Bismarck's reaction to this particular plan but it is not difficult to imagine. We do, however, know that he announced himself prepared to accept an assumption by France of all expenses of the arrangement with the railroad in settlement of additional occupation expenses to Prussia.[80]

Bismarck was clearly growing impatient over this problem and he said that he wanted it stated in the treaty that the railroad would be expropriated against the payment of an indemnity and for that there was no need for the consent of the French government. He stressed again that Germany could expropriate without paying any indemnity at all and she was permitting it to be mentioned in the treaty only to furnish France with a basis for later refusing to mix in the affairs of the company should it try to drag France into the company's business in Germany.[81] Germany would regulate this affair by virtue of her "sovereign right."[82] And there the situation rested at the end of April.

The hard feelings which were apparent at the beginning of April grew steadily worse as the month wore on and as it became apparent that stalemate was resulting from virtually all important phases of the negotiations. As tempers grew short and nerves raw virtually anything furnished cause for friction.

Early in April Favre had two interviews with Fabrice during which he raised the question of moving negotiations from Brussels to St. Denis. He also indicated his wish to meet personally with Bismarck in the interests of ironing out existing difficulties.[83] Bismarck was not completely averse to meeting Favre. He felt that it could be useful but for the moment he wanted to delay such a meeting until all principal questions had been settled at Brussels.[84] But as the negotiations at Brussels dragged on with little apparent settlement being reached, Bismarck's annoyance grew. Balan and Arnim repeatedly wrote discouragingly about the progress of negotiations and suggesting that the French were deliberately using obstructionist tactics on orders from Versailles. Less than a month after negotiations began they suggested that Bismarck himself intervene to break the deadlock.[85] Finally Bismarck advised them to hold no more formal conferences with the French until private conferences should have produced some definite French stand on the German proposals.[86]

In a dispatch of April 18 Bismarck told Fabrice his thoughts in no uncertain terms. In February he had supposed that the peace would be signed in "6 to 8 weeks" and that the French government would be sufficiently stable by that time to carry out the conditions of the peace treaty. Germany had begun a unilateral observance of the preliminaries whereas France had done nothing which could equal Germany's diminution of her own guarantees. He affirmed his confidence in the loyalty of the present French government even though events in France made him question the future of that government. German interests might best be served by a direct attack on Paris but such action had not been taken because of consideration for the wishes of the French government. "It would be hard to find," he said, that the French government had given anything in return. In his conversation with Fabrice, Favre had said that he was prepared to sign a treaty stating agreement on general principles, leaving details to be worked out later. Bismarck pointed out the obvious fact that such a procedure would only call for still a *third* treaty. He was impatient with what he considered the reluctance of the French government to take decisive action against the Commune and he warned that further delays might cause the indemnities established in February to be increased to cover the added expenses which Germany had incurred because of the slow course of negotiations and the conditions which prevailed in France.[87]

Although Fabrice was considerably more sanguine about the intentions of the French government and tried to convince Bismarck of this, relations between the two sides deteriorated badly by the third week in April. On April 23 there took place a conversation between Arnim and Baude which sheds some light on the thinking of the chief negotiators.

Arnim began by telling Baude that his tactic of fighting every proposal was courageous but unrealistic. Baude replied that France had to fight to protect herself and her former subjects and that her negotiators were answerable to the national assembly for their actions, a situation which did not face Bismarck. Arnim conceded that there was some truth to this but he also said that Baude should realize "a truth which leaps into view."

Well, if I were French I would say that I have to deal with a will of iron which disposes of the most effective power that the world has ever seen. Forget that it is a question of a man, but suppose that you find yourself opposite an elemental but intelligent force, and that you are lost if, in attracting it to yourself, you fall again by its action. Instead of hunting for a lightning rod, you argue with the thunderbolt.

Baude's reply was equally blunt.

I know perfectly well that our arguments do not have the slightest effect on Monsieur de Bismarck. However, one should remember that one day we could have a Bismarck and you some imbeciles and that you would be very surprised if one wished to pay you according to your system.

Arnim told him that they were, however, dealing with the present and that Baude should realize that France, by her attitude, had succeeded in awakening a "triple mistrust in your good will, in your ability and in your power." He said that France could prove her good will by reaching an agreement and reducing to "one or two questions" those points on which she felt she must resist Germany's demands. By so doing she could gain support where now she was only stirring up hatred, and support "would be worth more than the millions which grieve you."

At Arnim's urging Baude agreed to try to make this clear to Thiers, but he also urged patience with France and warned that German intervention in France would be a mistake even from the point of view of German interests.[88]

Finally Bismarck notified Fabrice to tell the French government that unless their representatives at Brussels were ready to reach an agreement he was prepared to break off negotiations altogether.[89] He also warned that France could expect no help in suppressing the Commune if she persisted in her policy of resisting publicly every proposal of the German government.[90] At the same time he made public his feelings in a speech delivered to the Reichstag. In it he included all of his recent complaints and said that although he hesitated to interfere in France's domestic affairs for fear of driving together the warring factions, he reserved full freedom of action to do so if he felt that German interests were endangered.[91] Three days after the Reichstag speech Bismarck sent a strongly worded letter to Fabrice stating that the signing of a peace treaty was, by the terms of the preliminaries, an absolute condition precedent to withdrawal of German troops from France even if France should pay the first half-billion francs of the war indemnity before that time. If the French had any doubts on this score, if indeed they should refuse a public statement recognizing this principle and declaring their intention of faithfully carrying out the peace, "it would then be expedient to resume war operations." He was, he said, prepared to recommend such action to the emperor.[92]

Bismarck's speech and the threats which surrounded it caused consternation among the French. Thiers placed the blame for the deadlock at Brussels squarely on Bismarck: "The natural disposition of Prince Bismarck made him a man difficult to get on with, in fact what was vulgarly called in France a '*mauvais coucher.*'"[93] In his dispatches to Baude and Goulard, Favre gave the impression of a harried and really bitter man. He obviously felt that Bismarck's anger was not entirely feigned and that it was menacing. He contended that the plight of the French government was due to Bismarck's obstinacy in having German troops enter Paris and in disarming the Paris garrison. France, he said, had bought the right to be believed and he railed against Bismarck for his suspicions and for even suggesting that the government might come to terms with the Commune. Germany could have peace if she would convert the preliminaries to a permanent treaty.[94] This last offer he repeated again to Fabrice,[95] and on April 28 he told Fabrice that he wished to see Bismarck personally.[96] He said that he was "at the end of his rope."[97]

Bismarck's threat to break off negotiations seemed to have a salutary effect, however brief, on breaking the deadlock at Brussels. Baude asked that formal sessions be resumed. Although Arnim refused to do so he wrote to Bismarck that real progress had been made in private discussions in decreasing the points of difference and he was optimistic for the future of the negotiations.[98] Two days later, however, Arnim proposed that France be presented with an ultimatum requiring payment of the war indemnity in gold and silver within a period of three years, liquidation of the Alsace-Lorraine debt question, and acknowledgement of Germany's right to expropriate the eastern railway. Should this ultimatum meet the "expected resistance" then Germany should propose "an ultimatissimum which will make the conditions of payment a bit easier but France will accept other responsibilities not discussed in the preliminary peace." The bait which his "ultimatissimum" was to offer was to be payment of the five billion francs over a four, and eventually a five, year period. In return France should renounce her debt-sharing scheme for Alsace-Lorraine, allow Germany to take over the eastern railway for a payment of seventy million thalers, grant Germany a preferential commercial treaty, and allow favors for agricultural and industrial products from Alsace and Lorraine.[99]

Arnim's move was a desperation one and by the end of April it was obvious that the negotiations had reached a virtual impasse.

NOTES TO CHAPTER VII

1. On March 4 and 6 two conventions were signed regulating the evacuation of the forts on the left bank of the Seine and the occupation of Versailles by the French army. On March 10 a convention was signed at Reims re-establishing postal service in the occupied departments (Villefort, I, 31–40).

2. May, p. 41.

3. Balan to Bismarck, Brussels, Mar. 12, 1871, PRO London, microfilm, Germany, Hauptarchiv d. Auswärt. Amt., Frankreich, No. 72, 2–3: 33, hereafter cited as GA (i.e. German Archives).

4. Thiers to Favre, Bordeaux, Mar. 5, 1871, Gaston Bouniols, *Thiers au pouvoir, 1871–1875* (Paris: 1921), pp. 23–32; Jules Valfrey, *Histoire du traité de Francfort et de la libération du territoire français* (Paris: 1874–1875), I, 13, fn. 1. Baude was also French minister to Belgium (Favre to Tachard, Paris, Mar. 7, 1871, MAE, CP [Belgique], 61: 105).

5. Bismarck to Favre, Berlin, Mar. 21, 1871, Paris, Bibliothèque nationale, MSS, Papiers Thiers, LI (nouvelles acquisitions françaises 20651), 166, hereafter cited as BN, Papiers Thiers.

6. Aimé Laussedat, *La délimitation de la frontière franco-allemande* (Paris: 1901), pp. 26–27. May lists as other members of this commission Renard, an engineer and Bouvier, a captain of engineers (May, p. 41, fn. 1).

7. The minutes of these crown councils are in GA, Frankreich, no. 72, 2–3: 29–32 and 48–50.

8. Bismarck to the emperor, Berlin, Mar. 17, 1871, *ibid.*, fol. 68.

9. May, pp. 44–45.

10. Both Valfrey (*Traité,* I, 17–18) and May (pp. 44–45) say that Goulard and Baude received no instructions during their stay in Brussels. On March 16 Favre wrote that he and Thiers would consult with the French plenipotentiaries the next day (Favre to Broglie, Mar. 16, 1871, MAE, CP [Angleterre], 756: 97–98).

11. Baude to Favre, Brussels, Mar. 21, 1871, MAE, CP (Belgique), 61: 114.

12. Favre to Baude, Versailles, Mar. 22, 1871, MAE, MD (Allemagne), 156: 6. This citation is to a collection in the French archives entitled "Conferences de Bruxelles." It is largely composed of copies of documents found also in the Correspondence politique but occasionally there is found in it material not duplicated elsewhere.

13. Favre to French plenipotentiaries at Brussels, Versailles, Mar. 22, 1871, MAE, CP (Belgique), 61: 125–139.

14. Baude to Favre, Brussels, Mar. 24, 1871, *ibid.*, fols. 153–155.

15. "Compte rendu" of the meeting, Hans Goldschmidt, *Bismarck und die Friedensunterhändler 1871. Die deutsch-französischen Friedensverhandlungen zu Brüssel und Frankfurt März-Dez. 1871* (Berlin: 1929), pp. 40–42, no. 10; Goulard and Baude to Favre, Brussels, Mar. 28,

1871, MAE, CP (Belgique), 61: 162–164. Favre agreed to abandon his demand for regular protocols but asked that he be given an "exact and detailed account of each of your conferences" (Favre to Baude and Goulard, Versailles, Mar. 30, 1871, *ibid.*, fols. 171–173).

16. Goulard and Baude to Favre, Brussels, Mar. 28, 1871, MAE, *ibid.*, fols. 166–168. Text of procès-verbal, MAE, MD (Allemagne), 156: 57.

17. "Compte rendu" of the meeting, Goldschmidt, pp. 43–44, no. 11.

18. Balan and Arnim to Bismarck, Brussels, Mar. 29, 1871, *ibid.*, pp. 46–47, no. 13.

19. Balan and Arnim to Bismarck, Brussels, Mar. 30, 1871, GA, Frankreich, no. 72, 4–5: 66.

20. Bismarck to Balan and Arnim, Berlin, Mar. 31, 1871, *ibid.*, pp. 49–52, no. 17. The text of the German proposals is found in the French foreign office archives (MAE, MD [Allemagne], 156: 74–95). A "Projet de traité: contrepropositions françaises" dated April 1871 is found in MAE, CP (Belgique), 61: 186–211.

21. Bismarck to Balan and Arnim, Berlin, Mar. 3, 1871, Goldschmidt, pp. 49–52, no. 17.

22. Baude to Favre, Brussels, April 1, 1871, MAE, CP (Belgique), 61: 212.

23. Bismarck to Balan and Arnim, Berlin, Mar. 31, 1871, Goldschmidt, p. 49, no. 16 and pp. 49–52, no. 17.

24. Balan and Arnim to Bismarck, Brussels, Mar. 23, 1871, *ibid.*, p. 35, no. 7.

25. Bismarck to Balan and Arnim, Berlin, Mar. 3, 1871, *ibid.*, pp. 49–52, no. 17.

26. Bismarck to Balan and Arnim, Berlin, April 1, 1871, *ibid.*, pp. 53–54, no. 18.

27. Arnim to the foreign office, Brussels, April 2, 1871, *ibid.*, pp. 57–58, no. 22.

28. Bismarck to Arnim, Berlin, April 2, 1871, *ibid.*, p. 58, no. 23.

29. Bismarck to Balan and Arnim, Berlin, April 2, 1871, *ibid.*, pp. 59–61, no. 25.

30. Favre, III, 312–313.

31. Favre to Baude and Goulard, Versailles, Mar. 22, 1871, MAE, CP (Belgique), 61: 125–139.

32. Favre to Baude, Versailles, Mar. 23, 1871, *ibid.*, fol. 142. Accompanying note concerning Belfort, *ibid.*, fols. 143–148. In a later dispatch Favre argued that in setting the radius of Belfort France was concerned to keep open communications with Switzerland. He said that France and Switzerland demanded that the right of transit be guaranteed in the peace treaty (Favre to Baude and Goulard, Versailles, Mar. 27, 1871, *ibid.*, fols. 160–161).

33. Goulard and Baude to Favre, Brussels, Mar. 31, 1871, *ibid.*, fols. 178–181.

34. Goldschmidt, p. 11, no. 1 and pp. 11–12, no. 2.

35. Much of this material dealing with the boundary location and

the considerations affecting it is taken from Hartshorne's excellent article, "The Franco-German boundary of 1871," *passim.*

36. Baude to Favre, Brussels, April 18, 1871, MAE, CP (Belgique), 61: 319.

37. Bismarck to Balan and Arnim, Berlin, Mar. 31, 1871, Goldschmidt, pp. 49–52, no. 17.

38. Baude and Goulard to Favre, Brussels, April 4, 1871, MAE, CP (Belgique), 61: 223–224; Doutrelaine to Baude and Goulard, *ibid.*, fols. 225–226; Favre to Baude, Versailles, April 13, 1871, *ibid.*, fols. 266–268.

39. Report of Strantz, Hauchecorne, and Herzog, Brussels, April 19, 1871, Goldschmidt, pp. 77–79, no. 40.

40. Annexes to dispatch Baude to Favre, Brussels, April 18, 1871, MAE, CP (Belgique), 61: fols. 328–343. A German account of these meetings is contained in the report of the German commissioners (Goldschmidt, pp. 77–79, no. 40).

41. Molkte to Bismarck, Berlin, April 25, 1871, G.A., Frankreich, no. 72, 6–7: 95. The economic worth of the iron works at Moyeuvre and Hayange would seem to have been considerably greater than Moltke realized. Clapham lists the Wendel works at these two towns among the leading French steel mills (John H. Clapham, *Economic Development of France and Germany, 1815–1914* [3rd ed.; Cambridge, England: 1928], pp. 236–237).

42. Favre to Baude and Goulard, Versailles, Mar. 22, 1871, MAE, CP (Belgique), 61: 125–139.

43. Baude to Favre, Brussels, April 5, 1871, *ibid.*, fols, 229–230; Baude and Goulard to Favre, Brussels, April 14, 1871, *ibid.*, fols. 312–313.

44. *Ibid.*

45. Favre to Baude and Goulard, Versailles, April 19, 1871, MAE, MD (Allemagne), 158: 65–69.

46. Favre to Baude and Goulard, Versailles, Mar. 22, 1871, MAE, CP (Belgique), 61: 125–139. In a proposed treaty article the sum was figured "in round sums at 741 million francs" (Conférence de Bruxelles, Traité de Paix, Avant projet française, MAE, MD [Allemagne], 156: 162–174).

47. Crown council of March 14: minutes, GA, Frankreich, no. 72, 2–3: 29–32.

48. Meeting of April 5, 1871: minutes, MAE, CP (Belgique), 61: 237–240. Count Uxkull told de Clerq that he felt this principle could be assumed since other clauses spoke of charges (Note on meeting of April 24, 1871, *ibid.*, fols. 401–412).

49. Baude to Favre, Brussels, April 3, 1871, *ibid.*, fol. 214; Arnim to the foreign office, Brussels, April 2, 1871, Goldschmidt, pp. 58–59, no. 24.

50. Favre to Baude and Goulard, Versailles, Mar. 22, 1871, MAE, CP (Belgique), 61: 125–139.

51. Traité de paix entre la France et l'Allemagne: analyse des conférence de Bruxelles et de Francfort, MAE, MD (Allemagne), 172: 232–239.

52. "Compte rendu" of meeting of April 8, annexed to report of April 9, MAE, CP (Belgique), 61 : 248–250.

53. Account of meeting of April 24, 1871, *ibid.,* fols. 401–412.

54. Baude and Goulard to Favre, Brussels, April 28, 1871, *ibid.,* fols. 401–412.

55. *Ibid.,* also account of meeting of April 24, 1871, *ibid.,* fols. 401–412.

56. Report of meeting of April 14, 1871, *ibid.,* fols. 294–300.

57. Balan and Arnim to Bismarck, Brussels, Mar. 30, 1871, Goldschmidt, p. 48, no. 14.

58. Arnim to Bismarck, Brussels, April 21, 1871, *PEA,* I, 35–37, no. 17.

59. Balan and Arnim to Bismarck, Brussels, April 23, 1871, Goldschmidt, pp. 89–92, no. 48.

60. Report of meeting of April 14, 1871, MAE, CP (Belgique), 61 : 294–300.

61. Baude and Goulard to Favre, Brussels, April 26, 1871, *ibid.,* fols. 418–420.

62. Crown council of March 14, 1871 : minutes, GA, Frankreich, no. 72, 2–3 : 29–32.

63. Favre to Baude and Goulard, Versailles, Mar. 22, 1871, MAE, CP (Belgique), 61 : 125–139.

64. Fabrice to Bismarck, Rouen, April 8, 1871, *PEA,* I, 26–30, no. 14.

65. Baude and Goulard to Favre, Brussels, April 18, 1871, MAE, CP (Belgique), 61 : 321–327.

66. Arnim to Bismarck, Brussels, April 21, 1871, *PEA,* I, 35–37, no. 17.

67. Note on conference between de Clerq and Uxkull, Brussels, April 24, 1871, MAE, CP (Belgique), 61 : 401–412.

68. Fabrice to Bismarck, Soisy, April 23, 1871, Goldschmidt, p. 95, no. 52.

69. Baude and Goulard to Favre, Brussels, April 29, 1871, MAE, CP (Belgique), 61 : 456–459.

70. Bismarck to Arnim, Berlin, April 25, 1871, *PEA,* I, 44, no. 20.

71. Favre to Baude and Goulard, Versailles, Mar. 22, 1871, MAE, CP (Belgique), 61 : 125–139.

72. *DDF,* I, 26, fn. 2.

73. Arnim to Bismarck, Brussels, April 21, 1871, *PEA,* I, 35–37, no. 17.

74. Favre to Baude and Goulard, Versailles, Mar. 22, 1871, MAE, CP (Belgique), 61 : 125–139.

75. Baude to Favre, Brussels, April 10, 1871, *ibid.,* fols. 258–259.

76. Crown council of March 14, 1871 : minutes, GA, Frankreich, no. 72, 2–3 : 29–32.

77. Bismarck to Fabrice, Berlin, April 1, 1871, Goldschmidt, pp. 55–56, no. 19.

78. Crown council of March 14, 1871 : minutes, GA, Frankreich, no. 72, 2–3 : 29–32.

79. Baude and Goulard to Favre, Brussels, April 21, 1871, MAE, CP (Belgique), 61 : 377–380.

80. Bismarck to Fabrice, Berlin, April 18, 1871, *PEA,* I, 31–34, no. 16; Favre, III, 331–332.

81. Bismarck to Fabrice, Berlin, April 24, 1871, *PEA,* I, 39–43, no. 19.

82. Bismarck to Arnim, Berlin, April 25, 1871, *ibid.*, p. 44, no. 20.

83. Fabrice to Bismarck, Rouen, April 9, 1871, GA, Frankreich, no. 72, 5–6: 47.

84. Bismarck to Fabrice, Berlin, April 8, 1871, Goldschmidt, p. 65, no. 31.

85. Arnim to Bismarck, Brussels, April 11, 1871, Goldschmidt, pp. 68–69, no. 34; Balan and Arnim to Bismarck, Brussels, April 12, 1871, *ibid.*, pp. 70–72, no. 36.

86. Arnim to Bismarck, Brussels, April 14, 1871, Goldschmidt, p. 73, no. 38.

87. Bismarck to Fabrice, Berlin, April 18, 1871, *PEA,* I, 31–34, no. 16.

88. Resumé of conversation between Arnim and Baude, Brussels, April 23, 1871, GA, Frankreich, no. 72, 6–7: 97–100.

89. Bismarck to Fabrice, Berlin, April 23, 1871, Goldschmidt, pp. 94–95, no. 51.

90. Bismarck to Fabrice, April 24, 1871, *PEA,* I, 39–43, no. 19.

91. MAE, CP (Allemagne), 1: 18–19; *GW,* XI, 159–163.

92. Bismarck to Fabrice, Berlin, April 27, 1871, *PEA,* I, 45–47, no. 21; Busch, *Bismarck,* I, 69–72.

93. Lyons to Granville, Versailles, April 28, 1871, PRO, FO 27–1862.

94. Favre to Baude and Goulard, Versailles, April 25, 1871, MAE, CP (Belgique), 61: 414–415.

95. Favre to Delahaye, Versailles, April 26, 1871, Sorel, II, 288–289; Favre to Fabrice, Versailles, April 26, 1871, Favre, III, 325–326.

96. Fabrice to Bismarck, Soisy, April 28, 1871, Goldschmidt, pp. 108–109, no. 60. Favre set down his arguments in a memorandum (Favre to Fabrice, Versailles, May 1, 1871, GA, Frankreich, no. 70, 112–113: 64–69).

97. Fabrice to Bismarck, Soisy, April 30, 1871, Goldschmidt, p. 112, no. 64. Favre's desire to convert the preliminaries into a permanent treaty was not alone for reasons of speed. On May 1 he wrote that the preliminaries were more advantageous to France than the terms proposed by the Germans at Brussels (Favre to Baude and Goulard, Versailles, May 1, 1871, MAE, CP [Belgique], 62: 2).

98. Arnim to Bismarck, Brussels, April 28, 1871, Goldschmidt, pp. 109–110, no. 61.

99. Memorandum: Arnim to Bismarck, Brussels, May 1, 1871, *ibid.*, pp. 115–118, no. 67.

VIII

The Frankfort Negotiations

ON MAY 1 BISMARCK SENT A TELEGRAM to Fabrice proposing a personal meeting with Favre at Frankfort or Mainz "to dissipate the mistrust" arising from the Brussels negotiations and to consider a "reinforcement of the guarantees or . . . an exact fixing of the terms of paying the five billion."[1] The following day he made it very clear, however, that Favre's plan of recognizing the preliminaries as the final treaty had no appeal for him whatever. That would only be "to receive again at Brussels *solemn promises* which we have received at Versailles; it is not promises that we lack, but performance."[2]

Favre was, of course, eager for a personal meeting and he agreed to meet Bismarck on May 6 at Frankfort. He assured Bismarck that he was fully prepared to give "all the desirable guarantees" of France's adherence to the terms of the preliminaries.[3] Since Bismarck had ordered Arnim to Frankfort,[4] Favre instructed Goulard and de Clerq to join him there and he told Baude to be prepared to come to Frankfort should Balan be ordered there by Bismarck.[5]

Favre obviously was expecting great things from a personal meeting with Bismarck. He told Lyons that "the subordinate German authorities" had created so many difficulties and had shown so much distrust that he had despaired of reaching any understanding with them. He hoped that from his meeting with Bismarck would come a settlement of questions "respecting present arrangements and the acceleration" of a peace treaty.[6] If Favre included Fabrice in his indictment of the "subordinate German authorities" his suspicions were unfounded. Fabrice was well disposed toward the French and he repeatedly played the role of peacemaker. He did so on this occasion again, assuring Bismarck of his own conviction that the French honestly did want to settle differences and were prepared to make concessions to Germany.[7] In spite of such assurances Bismarck was in a less than optimistic mood when he left for Frankfort and his meeting with Favre.

Favre and Pouyer-Quertier arrived in Frankfort early in the evening of May 5 and proceeded to the Hotel de Russie where they made their headquarters. Bismarck and his suite arrived during the night and went to their quarters at the Hotel du Cygne.

The French were prepared to sign a definitive treaty at Frankfort. Favre had, of course, long expressed willingness to convert the preliminaries into a permanent treaty except for a few points which he wished changed, and Thiers had come around to this view.[8] Thiers's dispatches to Frankfort stressed above all else the need for speed[9] and this sense of urgency must have been communicated to Bismarck. He later said that he had gone to Frankfort not expecting to sign a final peace but rather in an attempt to end the interminable delays, secure additional guarantees for payment of the French indemnity, and get agreement on certain of the major problems which had arisen at Brussels but that when the opportunity of a final peace presented itself he had seized it. "What can one do? The snipe must be shot where it rises."[10]

At Frankfort Bismarck carried the brunt of the negotiations

for Germany, assisted by Arnim. Favre and Pouyer-Quertier headed the French delegation. Although Favre was the senior member of the team Pouyer-Quertier, who got along very well with Bismarck, often took the initiative in the bargaining. Colonel Laussedat was present as advisor to the French on territorial problems,[11] and at Bismarck's suggestion Goulard was brought into the conference since he was a member of the national assembly.[12] De Clerq, an able diplomat, was also present but he took no part in the discussions.

At noon on May 6 Favre and Pouyer-Quertier called on Bismarck at his hotel. The atmosphere at this first meeting was, in Favre's words, "completely unpleasant." Bismarck adopted a rather belligerent tone and announced that his government would be justified in considering the preliminary treaty as non-existent since its principal clauses had not been fulfilled. He referred specifically to that part of the treaty which called for withdrawal of the French army behind the Loire and said that its nonfulfilment had imposed additional expense on Germany. Faced with this situation and the delays at Brussels, Germany felt that she no longer had adequate guarantees of French compliance with the terms of the preliminary peace. As a result the emperor had ordered him to secure a separate convention stipulating clearly what guarantees of performance Germany had. Should France still refuse to adhere to her obligations Germany would then feel free to force a French withdrawal behind the Loire, to suppress the Commune as she saw fit, and to move peace negotiations from Brussels.

Favre in turn accused the Germans of causing the delays and offered to conclude a definitive peace treaty immediately. Bismarck did not refuse the offer but remarked that a peace treaty *per se* would not give Germany any real guarantees of French performance but that an immediate treaty might be acceptable if France would give *additional* guarantees. When Favre asked him to be more specific Bismarck said that the treaty of February 26 should be so modified as to stipulate "the successive restriction of our occupation proportional to the payment of each half-billion and, after the fourth, imposing it upon no more than six departments, with an effective force reduced to 50,000 men." He said that Germany would begin to evacuate French territory as quickly as order was restored in France. In addition, he asked that the German forces be given more security by allowing them to guard the gates of Paris and to patrol the neutral zone between their lines and the walls of Paris.

Favre agreed to consider these proposals and asked that discussion of details be put off to a later meeting. Bismarck said that he had been ordered to deliver an ultimatum to the French and would do so the next day. He felt it to be unnecessary now but he had no alternative and it would, he said, cover Favre when he had to account to the national assembly.[13]

Favre was pleased with the results of the negotiations so far. He felt that they had re-established mutual confidence which would soon lead to agreement on all principal points.[14] We don't know precisely what Bismarck's reactions were but he emerged from the conference room looking tired and worried and said that the French had been very obstinate.[15]

That night the two Frenchmen met with Bismarck again. The conversation ranged over a wide variety of subjects. Bismarck reiterated that the seeming inability of the French government to suppress the Commune jeopardized France's ability to carry out the terms of the preliminaries. He was in no hurry to hasten the evacuation of France until Germany had more effective guarantees of collecting the war indemnity and he suggested that such a guarantee might be found if

France would proceed to pay the first two billion of the sum. He also insisted on prolonging the occupation until Germany was convinced that order was restored in France, even though this might go beyond payment of the first half-billion francs and the conclusion of a peace treaty, as provided in the preliminaries. On the subject of Belfort, Bismarck refused to allow a radius greater than seven or eight kilometers unless he received in exchange the additional lands near Thionville, a demand which Favre refused.

Bismarck in turn refused to burden Alsace-Lorraine with any portion of the French debt. He did agree in principle to accept payment by France of the indemnification of the Eastern Railway. As for the war indemnity he wanted to specify fixed periods for its payment. This was an attempt to change the terms of the preliminaries, which had been couched only in very general terms as to when the payments of the indemnity were due, specifying only that one billion francs should be paid before the end of 1871 and the remaining four billion within three years of the ratification of the preliminaries. Favre and Pouyer-Quertier agreed to set fixed periods for the first two billion of the indemnity but refused to commit themselves for the remainder. Concerning the commercial treaties Bismarck insisted on receiving "most favored nation" status.

Favre was considerably less optimistic after this second meeting than he had been after the first although he did foresee agreement on all points except those of the Belfort radius and the Alsatian debt.[16]

On May 7, attired in full uniform and accompanied by his entire suite, Bismarck called on Favre to deliver in person the ultimatum of which he had spoken. The setting and circumstances were designed to give the greatest possible solemnity to his words. The ultimatum, which Bismarck read aloud, was essentially a repetition of his comments in the earlier conversations, stressing Germany's desire for additional guarantees and indicating that they might be found in a prolongation of the occupation until order was restored in France. Bismarck said that "we will try . . . to agree on the chief questions to be settled by the definitive peace treaty" but that if they did not reach agreement the German government would feel free to act as its interests dictated.

Favre announced that he accepted the ultimatum in light of the conversations which had preceded it, for within that context it referred to a situation which no longer existed, and he asked that discussions begin immediately.[17]

An hour after Bismarck's departure Favre called on him. The discussion which followed had, according to Favre, "a certain vivacity" and lead him to fear a renewal of the scenes which had often characterized his previous meetings with Bismarck. Bismarck's mood was made no better by the fact that he had that very morning received word from St. Petersburg of a recent French attempt to induce the czar to use his influence with Emperor William to bring about a peace treaty. Favre, of course, disclaimed any perfidy on France's part in so doing and said that he was merely trying to speed up the negotiations.[18]

After this incident the negotiations got back to the business at hand. In the matter of additional guarantees for Germany Favre and Pouyer argued long and hard against Bismarck's demands but they finally gave way and agreed to a prolongation of the occupation. Bismarck, in turn, conceded that the evacuation of northern France would begin after payment of the third half-billion francs regardless of the status of order in France. He also abandoned his demand that Prussian troops guard the gates of Paris but he did gain permission for them to patrol the neutral zone around the city. In the matter of the Belfort radius the French still refused Bismarck's demands for the lands near Thionville but indicated that they would prefer to find compensation for the wider radius either in a money payment or in some commercial matter.[19] Favre abandoned his insistence on a six-year period for the option of citizenship and they agreed that such option could be made until October 1, 1872. France undertook to indemnify the Eastern Railway although there was a difference as to the size of the payment. Bismarck still refused absolutely to accept any share of the French debt and he would not hear of the war indemnity being paid in any medium other than "cash or bills of the same value."[20]

On the evening of May 7 Laussedat arrived in Frankfort. He was horrified to find that Thiers had given Favre permission to cede the communes in the department of Moselle in return for the wider Belfort radius. Laussedat urged Favre to refuse the exchange only to be met with a "smile of resignation" and the remark: "Then you think, colonel, that it is so easy to refuse Prince Bismarck?" Laussedat carefully marshalled his arguments in a note which he presented to Favre on May 8. Favre admitted that the note would be very persuasive "if we were before an impartial judge . . . but you forget that we are doing business with an enemy who intends to profit by all his advantages and that we are vanquished."[21]

Negotiations on May 8 brought further agreement on a number of points. Bismarck hammered at the question of the territorial exchange. In return for the extended radius of Belfort, he wanted "a strip of land of about ten kilometers" on the Luxembourg border. This strip would include seven thousand people and about ten thousand hectares of land (one hectare equals, approximately, two and one-half acres); the land which the French wanted around Belfort contained about twenty-seven thousand people and six thousand hectares of land. Favre and Pouyer considered this an advantageous trade but they said that any question pertaining to national sovereignty must be left exclusively to the national assembly for final action. Consequently it was decided to phrase this portion of the treaty in terms of an alternative: France would gain the desired radius on condition that the assembly approve the revised border in the north.

Agreement was also reached on "navigation and copyrights, . . . temporary advantages for Alsatian industry, as well as right of requisition and imposition . . . in the event of payments being in abeyance." Bismarck agreed to allow twenty thousand French prisoners to return to France immediately for use against an insurrection which had broken out in Algeria. After Bismarck said that he would rather begin a shooting war again than to become involved in a tariff war and threatened to break off negotiations completely Favre agreed to grant "most favored nation" status to Germany in return for it being given to France.[22]

By May 8 Favre seemed resigned to accepting all of Bismarck's terms.[23] Ironically, Bismarck was so anxious lest peace elude him that he was willing to give up his demand for frontier changes in the north. In a communication to Berlin he said that, if the French should reject the exchange he "would prefer to abandon all extension of our frontier than to hinder the conclusion of peace for that reason."[24] It should be noted that he was not unaware of the mineral deposits located in that region. While, understandably, he had not stressed their existence in his negotiations with Favre, he did stress their value to Germany when he wanted to persuade the emperor to agree to the exchange.[25] But the fact that he was willing to give up the exchange altogether if necessary as well as the fact that the choice was ultimately left up to the decision of the French national assembly would indicate that his primary considerations were not economic, a fact which had been amply demonstrated already.

By May 9 agreement had been reached on all outstanding issues. However, Bismarck was so certain that the emperor would reject the three hundred and fifty million franc indemnity for the Eastern Railway which had been agreed to that he preferred not to submit it for consideration lest the signing of the treaty be delayed. In response to a wire to Berlin, Emperor William gave his approval to omitting this matter from the treaty and deferring it to subsequent negotiations.[26] In the interests of speed the French, too, agreed to this procedure.[27]

On May 10, in a salon of the Hotel du Cygne, the representatives of France and Germany gathered for the signing of the peace treaty. For France there were Favre, Pouyer-Quertier and Goulard. Bismarck and Arnim signed for Germany. Just before the signing a telegram arrived from Thiers giving his full approval of the Frankfort agreements and announcing a government victory at the fort of Issy. The news was well received and must have given a real boost to Favre's constantly sagging morale.

Immediately after the treaty was signed Bismarck agreed to consider the still unsettled question of the railways. Pouyer refused to lower the company's claim below three hundred and twenty-five million francs and that sum was agreed on. France was to pay that sum to the company as an indemnity against its holdings surrendered to Germany. France was also to surrender to Germany all of her rights in the railroad in the ceded territories and to assume all claims which might in the future be lodged by or on behalf of the company. In return for this the sum mentioned was to be deducted from the war indemnity. Thus in effect Germany did pay the indemnity and the clause was a compromise between the German and French positions in the matter.[28]

And so the treaty was signed. Its rapid conclusion came as a surprise to Bismarck.[29] The Brussels negotiations had dragged on for five weeks. The Frankfort negotiations had lasted but three days. Once in Bismarck's presence Favre's resistance had collapsed. Bismarck had improved Germany's position insofar as payment of the indemnity and the occupation were concerned, and Favre had dodged the issue of the frontier exchanges by referring it to the assembly. He now had to persuade the assembly to accept the treaty.

NOTES TO CHAPTER VIII

1. Bismarck to Fabrice, Berlin, May 1, 1871, *PEA,* I, 47–48, no. 23.
2. Bismarck to Fabrice, Berlin, May 2, 1871, *ibid.,* pp. 49–51, no. 25.
3. Favre to Bismarck, Soisy, May 2, 1871, GA, Frankreich, no. 72, 8–9: 21; Favre, III, 332–334.
4. Baude to Favre, Brussels, May 3, 1871, MAE, CP (Belgique), 62: 42.
5. Favre to Baude, Versailles, May 3, 1871, MAE, MD (Allemagne), 156: 334; Favre to Baude, Versailles, May 4, 1871, MAE, CP (Belgique), 62: 43.
6. Lyons to Granville, Versailles, May 3, 1871, PRO, FO 27–1863.
7. Fabrice to Bismarck, Soisy, May 4, 1871, GA, Frankreich, no. 70, 113–114: 25–30.
8. Lyons to Granville, Versailles, May 5, 1871, PRO, FO 27/1863.
9. Laussedat, p. 46.
10. *AD,* 1873, I, 144–149, no. 1180; *GW,* XI, 170–175; Busch, *Bismarck,* I, 478.
11. Baude to Favre, Brussels, May 7, 1871, MAE, MD (Allemagne), 156: 338.
12. Busch, *Bismarck,* I, 478.
13. Favre, III, 353–360.
14. Favre to Thiers, Frankfort, May 6, 1871, MAE, Papiers Thiers, Négociations de Francfort.
15. Busch, *Bismarck,* I, 478.
16. Favre to Thiers, Frankfort, May 7, 1871, MAE, Papiers Thier, Négociations de Francfort.
17. This account is taken from Favre, III, 360–364. The text of the ultimatum is in Goldschmidt, pp. 125–127, no. 74. The marginal notations

in Bismarck's hand indicate that he made it a sterner note than his advisers had planned.

18. Favre, III, 364–372.

19. Bismarck to Delbrück, Frankfort, May 7, 1871, *PEA,* I, 51, no. 26.

20. *Ibid.* On May 25 Bismarck told the Reichstag that "if there is one thing that I can attribute to myself as my personal part . . . it is the fact that Alsace is completely free of debts, and it was not easy to obtain" (May, p. 49, fn. 1).

21. Laussedat, pp. 40–43. Text of the note by Laussedat is in the Pièces justificatives, pp. 154–157, no. 3.

22. Favre, III, 372–374; Bismarck to Thile, Frankfort, May 8, 1871, *PEA,* I, 51–52, no. 26.

23. Favre to Thiers, Frankfort, May 8, 1871, MAE, Papiers Thiers, Négociations de Francfort.

24. Bismarck to Thile, Frankfort, May 8, 1871, *PEA,* I, 51–52, no. 26.

25. Bismarck to the emperor, Frankfort, May 9, 1871, *PEA,* I, 52–53, no. 28.

26. *Ibid.;* Favre to Thiers, Frankfort, May 9, 1871, MAE, Papiers Thiers, Négociations de Francfort.

27. Favre, III, 374.

28. *Ibid.,* pp. 375–376. The protocol of signature of the treaty specified that these "additional articles" should be considered an "integral part of the peace treaty" (*DDF* I, 13, no 4).

29. Lumley of the British legation to the foreign office, Brussels, May 11, 1871, PRO, FO 27/1863.

IX

Ratification

On May 12 Bismarck went before a cheering Reichstag to present the treaty and to give an account of the Frankfort negotiations. In a speech notable for its moderation of tone Bismarck said that he had gone to Frankfort hoping only to make some arrangement concerning "the terms fixed for payment of the war indemnity, and an improvement in the nature of the guarantees for that payment," but that he had seized the opportunity to conclude a definitive treaty. He admitted that not everyone would be pleased with the treaty but said that it represented "all that we could demand from France in reason. We have secured our frontiers by territorial annexation; we have, so far as it is humanly possible, ensured payment of our war indemnity." He expressed confidence in the intentions of the French government and hope "that this peace will be a lasting one, and that we shall not be called upon, for many years to come, to utilise the additional means of protection against a renewed attack with which we have now provided ourselves." The emperor would, he said, ratify the treaty, and ratifications would be exchanged by May 20.[1]

Bismarck's triumphant return to Berlin was not duplicated at Versailles. On May 13 Favre went before the assembly to ask for ratification of the treaty.[2] His policy in the negotiations with Bismarck had been a simple one. "It consisted in remaining sincere." He placed responsibility for France's woes squarely on "the criminals who have usurped power at Paris." The Commune had so shaken hopes that France could execute her agreements with Germany that it was impossible for him to refuse Bismarck's demand for a prolongation of the occupation until order was restored. He justified the advanced payment on the indemnity by saying that it would also advance the evacuation of France. He told the assembly that the exchange of frontier territories was a question for it to decide, since only the peoples' representatives could make such a decision. For the negotiators to have accepted this proposal would have been "usurpation" of powers belonging to the assembly. He then read the treaty and the assembly voted to consider it in committee on Monday, May 15.[3]

Favre was clearly on the defensive and determined to justify his actions at all costs. Thiers, too, was determined to secure approval of the treaty negotiated by his government. With a combination of ability, scorn, and determination he carried far more weight and influence than did his equally emotional but far less stable foreign minister. Opposition made Thiers even more obstinate.

In testifying before the parliamentary committee charged with examining the treaty, Thiers lost his temper badly when his actions were challenged by Count Chaudordy, former *"chef du cabinet"* of the foreign office. The two men had differed before and when Chaudordy said that Thiers could have got better terms if he had had recourse to the neutrals during the recent negotiations Thiers turned "violently" on the count, "accused him of having misrepresented diplomatic secrets . . . and challenged him to justify his statements." Chaudordy claimed that he could not do so without giving away professional secrets.[4]

Martial Delpit, a deputy, pungently testified to Thiers's powers of persuasion:

> He treats those who are not of his opinion as ignoramuses, men who do not know history and geography. With . . . that marvelous lucidity which he brings to the exposition of the most intricate questions, he opens a course of strategy for the benefit of the weak-minded of the Assembly. He does it so well that nobody has the courage to bring out a "perhaps."[5]

Thiers faced stiff opposition on the question of the exchange of frontier lands. A subcommittee was set up to consider this question and to report to the full parliamentary committee. Laussedat was named secretary to the subcommittee. He had opposed Favre at Frankfort and he now emerged as Thiers's chief opponent on this issue. On May 15 he told the subcommittee that in his opinion Favre could have got ten kilometers around Belfort without any concessions whatsoever had he only refused to discuss any exchange at all. He felt that the Germans had no real interest in the area around Belfort and had used it only to get something for themselves in the north. So persuasive was he that the committee agreed to recommend that the proposed exchange be rejected. When Thiers heard of this recommendation he refused to accept it and he asked the subcommittee to re-examine the issue.[6] A second meeting of the subcommittee was held on May 17. This time two of the members changed their votes but the chairman, General Chabaud-Latour, refused to use his prerogative to break the resulting tie, leaving it to the members of the subcommittee to explain their positions individually before the assembly. Thus, the official report went to the full committee in its original form. On May 18 Laussedat appeared before the entire committee. He repeated his arguments, said that General Doutrelaine fully agreed with him, and urged the committee to refuse the exchange of lands and to hold out for a radius of ten kilometers around Belfort. He was told that the committee had already drawn up its report in line with Favre's information and advice, thereby rejecting the subcommittee's report. Laussedat always felt that the territorial exchange would probably not have taken place had it not been for Thiers's "deplorable intervention."[7]

The assembly convened on May 18 to hear the recommendation of its committee. The Viscount of Meaux, secretary of the committee, read the report. He called the treaty "the saddest, but the most inevitable, that our history has known." Pouyer-Quertier had assured the committee that the government would do everything possible to hasten payment of the first one and one-half billion francs in order to end the occupation as quickly as possible. Concerning the border exchanges, he reported that the government "strongly" advised it. The committee had heard "representatives of the interested populations . . . industrialists, and the most competent military men." The witnesses who had opposed the exchange had done so because they alleged that it would render more difficult communications with Luxemburg, would surrender to Germany many French who had thought their fates fixed by the peace preliminaries, and would give up mining territory "of an incontestable riches and of a special quality." He then stated the arguments which had swayed the committee in favor of the exchange. The military value of Belfort was still considerable. The exchange would also have commercial value because the extended radius of Belfort would allow Alsatian industry to move there and thus remain French. In addition, France would save "mineral deposits necessary to our manufacturing." As to the populations concerned, the peace preliminaries were not final on population exchanges and, in any event, France would regain more Frenchmen than she would lose. Moreover, the committee had "reason to believe" that this exchange would "facilitate certain frontier rectifications." He named these as Raon-les-Leau, Raon-sur-Plaine, and Igney. "In complying with the change advised by the government, your committee expects that it will obtain these supplemental modifications." The committee, "not without debate," advised the assembly to adopt the treaty. By so doing it would serve notice that it "submits to the consequence of facts of which it is not the author."[8]

The assembly voted to debate the question of ratification immediately. Admiral Fourichon asked that debate be held only on the issue of the territorial exchange. For the rest of the treaty, he asked that the vote be taken without debate so that the Germans might be answered "by the dignity of silence."[9] General Chanzy attacked the treaty as an unwarranted aggravation of the terms of the preliminary peace. The mineral riches in the region demanded by Germany on the Luxemburg border made it essential for France to keep that region. He could detect only "new demands" without "discovering any compensations" for France. He pleaded with the assembly to reject a treaty which he termed "inexecutable."[10] Peltereau-Villeneuve then rose to speak. Since he was a minority member of the committee, his words give some insight into the committee debates. He felt that the only part of the treaty which was debatable was the territorial exchange. Those who were left to France by the peace preliminaries had acquired an "inalienable" right that "no one in the world, not even a sovereign assembly" could take away. Moreover, "very respectable authorities" had said that Belfort could be defended with a radius of seven or eight kilometers. The German demands would also interrupt communications with Luxemburg. Finally, he dwelt on the mineral deposits which France would surrender and which had been estimated, he said, at one billion, two hundred million francs. An "important and conscientious industrialist" had told the committee "vote this annexation and the days of the industry in the whole *arrondissement* of Longwy, the Ardennes, and the north are numbered."[11] Deputy Raudot rose to speak against the treaty. To him, anything proposed by Bismarck could not possibly be to France's advantage. Favre interrupted him: "We asked Mulhouse and the whole department of the Haut-Rhin, sir! That is what *we* asked." Raudot turned on Favre and began to make an observation about one who had declared that he would give up neither an inch of territory nor a stone of a fortress. He was not allowed to finish for he was interrupted by an uproar from the deputies. When he was again able to make himself heard he warned that to accept the treaty would be to become Bismarck's accomplice in gobbling up Luxemburg and the other small states on Germany's borders.[12]

General Chareton followed Raudot to speak against the treaty. He could see no great advantage to France in providing a haven for Alsatian industry. He called Alsace the "robe of Nessus clinging to Germany's flanks." It could one day be the "apple of discord" between north and south Germany. To welcome Alsatian industry into France would flood the French market with manufactured goods which, left in Germany, could give "ruinous competition" to the industry of Baden and Bavaria. Why, he asked, should Prussia be given this opportunity to rid herself of a serious embarrassment and, at the same time, acquire valuable mineral deposits in the north which France could use? He also maintained that Belfort no longer had either offensive or defensive value sufficient to justify the territorial exchange.[13]

The opponents of the treaty, concentrating their fire on the territorial exchange, had held the floor since the debate began. Following Chareton, Thiers defended the treaty. He had, he said, spent much of his life studying "the military geography of France and of Europe." He was "very surprised" at Chareton's conclusions. France had only political interests in the Luxemburg border. Invasions had never been launched by that route, as his studies of the Revolution and the First Empire had shown. And if Germany should ever raise the question of Luxemburg's future, France would have as much right to intervene if she had a common border of two leagues or seven leagues with Luxemburg. He professed to be "truly astonished" that Belfort's importance was questioned. He had "despaired" when Germany demanded Belfort and had thought it might be better to continue the war than to give it up. He had fought for it "with a despair so energetic and so sincere that I persuaded a very stubborn negotiator." Yet now he heard its importance denied. With Strasburg lost the importance of Belfort was enhanced and "those who say the contrary are blind." But to make Belfort fully effective it was necessary to have the wider radius. With it Belfort could be made "one of the most important" fortified places in Europe. He brushed aside the question of Belfort as an offensive site by saying that "the roads are always open" to a strong army and a good general. He repeated that Bismarck had offered this particular territorial exchange only after France had demanded Mulhouse. He felt that Bismarck had purely industrial reasons for his willingness to make the exchange, for it had become a "passion" with him to expand the prosperity of Germany's Rhenish provinces. Thiers did not feel that France was losing too much in this respect. "The industrial interest which we have there is of little worth" and would be more than compensated by "the riches of our other mining provinces."[14]

Thiers then played his trump card. He asked Meaux to read a letter from Colonel Denfert-Rochereau, wartime commander of the Belfort garrison and a popular war hero. His letter endorsed the territorial exchange and said that Belfort would be "stripped" of its importance without the larger radius.[15] Following the reading of this letter, two generals, Ducrot and Chabaud-Latour, defended the territorial exchange on military grounds.[16]

After their testimony the assembly voted cloture. The vote followed immediately and the treaty was adopted by a vote of 433 to 98. The 98 votes against the treaty were all cast against the territorial exchange only, which had been put to a separate vote.[17]

Favre felt that he and Bismarck could, through a personal meeting, settle certain details of frontier delimitation which were stated vaguely in the treaty, hence he proposed to go personally to Frankfort for the exchange of ratifications.[18] Bismarck demurred at first but changed his mind and announced that he would be present for the exchange.[19] On May 20 Favre and Pouyer-Quertier met Bismarck in Frankfort. The ratifications of the treaty were finally exchanged at about eleven o'clock in the evening although, because of the late hour, the final signatures were delayed until the following morning.[20]

The treaty of Frankfort is one of the really significant treaties of modern times, for it was a monument to the great fact of the day in European diplomacy: the emergence of a united Germany as the leading power of western and central Europe. At the same time the treaty had one fundamental weakness which threatened to undo it: the seizure of Alsace and Lorraine. Germany and Germans might claim that they were merely undoing wrongs perpetrated by earlier generations of Frenchmen, but the fact remained that modern nationalism had emerged since the seventeenth century and had created a French nation of which Alsace and Lorraine were part. Thus the treaty of Frankfort established a shaky foundation for Franco-German harmony.

Shaky or not, it existed and both sides now had to live with it. Thiers had successfully pushed the treaty through the national assembly and its complete fulfillment became a basic part of the foreign policy of his government.

NOTES TO CHAPTER IX

1. Busch, *Our chancellor,* II, 79–80. Germany, *Stenographische Berichte über die Verhandlungen des deutschen Reichstages* (Berlin: 1867–), 1871, I, 669–671, hereafter cited as *Reichstag debates.*
2. Favre, III, 381 and 391.
3. *Annales,* III, 2–7; Villefort, I, 89–92, no. 7.
4. Meaux, pp. 52–54.
5. Quoted in Hanotaux, I, 300–301.
6. Laussedat, Bk. III, 57–60.
7. *Ibid.,* 60–64 and 81.
8. *Annales,* III, 62–64.
9. *Ibid.,* pp. 64–65.
10. *Ibid.,* pp. 65–67.
11. *Ibid.,* pp. 68–70.
12. *Ibid.,* p. 73.
13. *Ibid.,* pp. 74–75.
14. *Ibid.,* pp. 76–81.
15. *Ibid.,* p. 81.
16. *Ibid.,* p. 81 and 82–84.
17. *Ibid.,* p. 84.
18. Favre, III, 420–421.
19. *Ibid.,* p. 421.
20. *Ibid.,* pp. 426–428. For text of the procès-verbal of the exchange of ratifications see *DDF,* I, 14–15, no. 5. On May 10 Bismarck instructed the Prussian ambassadors to the South German states that those countries could adhere to the peace treaties, but they must take the initiative (Goldschmidt, p. 128, no. 75). Those adherences were made at Berlin on May 15 and official notice of them was given to France at Frankfort on May 20. The text of the treaty of Frankfort can be found in *DDF,* I, 5–11, no. 2; *PEA,* I, 53–59, no. 29; *GP,* I, 38–43, no. 17; and Goldschmidt, pp. 129–137. The "additional articles" will be found in *DDF,* I, 11–13, no. 3.

X

The Convention of 1871

At Bismarck's request Favre and Pouyer-Quertier remained in Frankfort after the exchange of ratifications to discuss several matters privately. One concrete accomplishment resulted from these conversations: a convention providing for the payment of 125,000,000 of the first half-billion francs of the war indemnity in notes on the Bank of France. This was a real concession by Bismarck since it was directly contrary to the terms of the peace treaty. It was, moreover, a concession which he made against the advice of his financial experts.[1]

Most of the conversations, however, were of a more general nature and they were conducted in an atmosphere of mutual friendship. Favre asked Bismarck to ease the burden of the occupation armies. Bismarck said that this could be accomplished within the terms of the peace treaty and he urged that France take advantage of the provision whereby, after payment of two billion francs, she could propose substitution of a monetary guarantee for a territorial guarantee. Germany would try to accept any serious proposal, in which case the total evacuation of France could be accomplished shortly.[2]

It must have been with a relatively untroubled mind that Favre returned to Versailles. For the moment relations with

Germany were fairly good, and the bloody fight against the Commune was finally drawing to a close. Within a week of his return government troops subdued the rebellious capital.

The treaty of Frankfort had provided that the boundary commission should "proceed to the spot immediately after the ratifications of the present treaty . . . to trace the new frontier." After some delays the two delegations met at Metz in mid-June.[3]

The treaty also provided that the items which had been discussed but not settled at Brussels "will be the object of further negotiations which shall take place at Frankfort." France named to this commission de Clerq and Goulard, both veterans of Brussels. They proceeded to Frankfort the last week in May, 1871.[4] They were joined there on June 3 and 4 by Arnim and Uxkull, the German representatives. The two teams agreed to confine themselves to deciding general principles, leaving questions of application and detail to be worked out later by special commissions. In this way they could base their discussions on the draft articles which had been exchanged at Brussels and which had followed the same procedure.

At the first meeting on June 5 the conversations went so well that Goulard and de Clerq were optimistic about the prospects of a quick conclusion to the talks.[5] Their optimism was premature for these conversations were to last nearly six months and were often marked by bitter recriminations and charges of bad faith on both sides. But for the moment goodwill reigned. To give proof of his confidence in Thiers's government Bismarck ordered the withdrawal early in June of a sizeable body of troops.[6] Such manifestations on his part were prompted not by altruism but by the feeling that support of Thiers was most consistent with Germany's own self-interest since he was committed to fulfillment of the peace treaty. It was in the same vein of cautious optimism that Bismarck spoke to Count von Waldersee, the chargé d'affaires whom he was sending to Paris. Before Waldersee left Berlin Bismarck told him that while he did not believe Fabrice's gloomy warnings about a revival of hostilities with France he did have some doubts about France's ability to pay the war indemnity and he wanted a military man on the scene to appraise accurately French army preparations.[7]

Waldersee's appointment virtually completed the establishment of diplomatic relations between France and Germany, for on May 30 Favre had announced the appointment as French chargé d'affaires in Berlin of the Marquis of Gabriac.[8] It was, however, almost a month before Gabriac arrived at his post.

Waldersee's arrival in Paris on June 14 coincided with a deterioration of the brief period of good relations which had prevailed since the signing of the treaty of Frankfort. Waldersee had scarcely arrived in Paris when he received a note from Bismarck complaining that "certain experiences that we have in the course of the supplementary negotiations of Frankfort and of the frontier commission seem to prove that the French government is not disposed to respond in any way to our good nature."[9]

Bismarck had two specific complaints to make. Article VII of the treaty of Frankfort provided that one half-billion francs should be paid "within 30 days after the re-establishment of the authority of the French government in the city of Paris." Paris was recaptured on May 28. Bismarck notified the French government that he considered order to have been restored, within the meaning of Article VII, on June 1, which would have made the first payment due on July 1. Favre and Thiers considered June 20 to have been the effective date of restoration of authority in Paris, and they proposed to pay on July

20.[10] This was one of the situations to which Bismarck referred in his note, and it was the first item of business with which Waldersee had to deal upon his arrival in France. He presented his credentials to Thiers on June 17 and received a courteous welcome from both Thiers and Favre. Thiers justified the delay in payment on the grounds that he had to await the outcome of a great public loan which was scheduled for June 26 before France's financial situation could be clarified. He did, however, finally say that he would try to begin payment on July 1, but he also said that it would be impossible to pay the entire sum before July 10.[11]

Bismarck refused absolutely to accept this interpretation of the treaty without concessions in return, his usual gambit.[12] Waldersee was back at Versailles twice on June 19. Favre "made a great fuss and declared we wanted to cut his throat, and so on and so on."[13] He told Waldersee that the sack of the Bank of France and the destruction of the ministry of finance were obviously unforeseen and made payment difficult. Finally Thiers gave Waldersee a half-promise to pay during the early days of July,[14] a compromise which Bismarck agreed to accept if payment were completed by July 7.[15]

Since the great public loan on which Thiers relied so heavily was a stunning success for the government, Bismarck's first complaint was relatively easily met but the boundary question was not so easily solved. Early in June Favre told Fabrice that at Frankfort Bismarck had let it be understood that if the assembly would accept the territorial exchange specified in the treaty he would permit rectifications in France's favor at three border points, Donon, Avricourt, and Moyeuvre. He complained that although the assembly had acted on this assumption the German commissioners at Metz now refused to follow through on the commitment.[16] This was the second point about which Bismarck complained to Waldersee. In the first place, he objected to Favre's attempt to by-pass the Metz discussions and, secondly, he said that Favre had interpreted his "alleged" statements far too favorably for France. He did not deny having discussed such a border rectification but he said that it could only be in return for some equivalent concession on the part of France. He told Fabrice that before committing himself on this issue he would wait to see what equivalent might come out of the Frankfort negotiations.[17]

There were other incidents, too, which aggravated hard feelings between Germany and France. On June 15 General Trochu made a speech in the national assembly accusing the German government of complicity in the Commune. The speech had, of course, no official character, but Bismarck felt that the silence of the French government lent to it almost official approval.[18] And on June 29, in the presence of Thiers and Marshal MacMahon, the reconstituted French army held its first review at Longchamps, where less than four months before the victorious German armies had paraded before Emperor William I. The incident brought a sharp note from Waldersee protesting that France was violating Article X of the peace treaty, which forbade her to have more than eighty thousand men in the army around Paris and Versailles.[19]

It was at this juncture that Gabriac took up his post in Berlin, arriving there on July 4. His very first assignment was not a pleasant one. Favre had managed to soothe German feelings in the affair of the Trochu speech by a face-saving exchange of notes.[20] He was, however, smarting from Waldersee's note concerning the French army as well as another questioning France's good faith in the matter of payment of the first half-billion of the war indemnity,[21] and he instructed Gabriac to protest the tone of the notes. In Bismarck's absence Gabriac brought the matter to the attention of Balan and Thile, who assured him that Waldersee's suspicions and harsh tone did not reflect the attitude of the German government.[22]

Favre was out for bigger game than apologies for Waldersee's notes. He hoped to gain the complete evacuation of France and he had what he thought was the weapon with which he could accomplish it : an Alsatian customs agreement. It will be recalled that on April 9 France had signed a convention with a delegation from Alsace and Lorraine whereby manufactured items from the ceded territories would be permitted to enter France duty free until a definitive peace treaty was signed. French goods were to enjoy reciprocal privileges when destined for consumption in Alsace and Lorraine. Article IX of the treaty of Frankfort provided that the special favors granted to Alsatian products should continue for six months from March 1 but it said nothing about entry of French goods into Alsace-Lorraine for the same period of time. Early in the Frankfort negotiations the French called this to the attention of the German delegates, alleging that at Brussels the Germans themselves had agreed to the principle of reciprocity.[23] Berlin was quick to realize that the issue offered real possibilities and Arnim was told that Germany would recognize the principle of reciprocity only if France were prepared to allow special treatment for Alsatian products for a period of six years.[24] So important did Bismarck consider this issue that he sent Herzog of the Prussian ministry of commerce to take over the negotiations concerning commercial questions.[25]

The matter was important to Germany as well as to France, a fact which de Clerq and Goulard realized. They urged Favre not to give in to the German demands too easily. Tactfully but firmly they suggested that public opinion in Germany was bringing pressure on the government to bring home the occupation army and that this might be used to advantage to gain concessions from Germany in the matter of the Alsatian customs.[26]

Favre made no immediate reply to this suggestion but it did bear fruit for within two weeks he was working to connect the Alsatian customs question with that of an early evacuation of France and, typically, he pursued his goal simultaneously at Frankfort and Berlin.

At Frankfort de Clerq told Arnim that he thought France would accept Herzog's plan for a six year period of privilege for Alsatian goods and would, in addition, pay immediately the one and one-half billion francs due by May 1, 1872, if in return, Germany would withdraw the occupation army completely. Arnim felt that since France could automatically gain evacuation of all but six departments by paying two billion francs what she was really proposing was evacuation of the last departments in return for a favorable customs arrangement with Alsace and Lorraine.[27] Bismarck was quick to refuse to evacuate France except in accordance with the terms of the treaties of February 26 and May 10; if this was the price demanded by France, he would renounce any claim to special customs treatment for Alsace-Lorraine.[28]

Following Favre's instructions, Gabriac pursued the subject at Berlin, too. On July 11 a minister, whom he identified only as a member of the council, told him that Bismarck probably intended to withdraw the German troops after the payment of two billion francs. Gabriac inferred from this that the evacuation was eagerly desired in Berlin but he felt that France should wait until the Germans broached the subject.[29]

When de Clerq heard of this he guessed that the unnamed minister with whom Gabriac had talked was Delbrück but he interpreted the remark to be both an invitation for France to propose the exchange and an indication that it would not be refused.[30] Apparently encouraged by this, de Clerq pressed Arnim hard on the matter, rejecting any suggestion that something less than a complete evacuation might be possible.

Arnim said that he thought Germany would prefer to reduce the six-year period asked for Alsatian goods to four years rather than to evacuate France completely.[31] De Clerq countered by referring cryptically to negotiations going on elsewhere which indicated that Arnim was mistaken if he thought that Germany would under no circumstances evacuate all of France.[32] The pressure on Arnim built up as Thiers, too, entered into unofficial negotiations with him through one M. Spörry, a personal friend and an Alsatian industrialist. Spörry appeared in Frankfort to plead Thiers's case. Not too subtly, he told Arnim that sympathy for the ceded territories was waning in France and that the time was propitious for such an agreement, since later in the year the national assembly would be less likely to make concessions. There was nothing in this proposal that Arnim had not heard before and he refused to discuss evacuation, suggesting that Thiers turn his attention instead to a limited extension of the Alsatian customs agreement, leaving the question of evacuation for later discussion. Seeking a way out of the impasse, Arnim suggested to Bismarck that Germany might promise to consider the question of guarantees to replace the occupation if France would extend the customs agreement until January 1, 1872, thereby gaining time for further consideration of a permanent tariff arrangement while really promising nothing but discussion.[33]

By late July the Frankfort discussions had come to a virtual halt over these questions and de Clerq suggested that the conference adjourn for a while. Arnim favored such a move. He felt that most of the important issues had been discussed and that the assurances desired from France were set out in sufficiently binding form in the protocols of the conference.[34] Bismarck agreed to a temporary adjournment but he instructed Arnim to have the agreement in writing so that the French could not later blame Germany for the suspension of the conference.[35] Bismarck refused to take the initiative in reopening the negotiations so long as France insisted on identifying the Alsatian customs question with that of the evacuation or even with full reciprocity for French goods.[36]

Late in July, as the Frankfort negotiations were being adjourned, Favre asked permission to begin advance payment on the second and third half-billion francs due by the end of 1871. He did not make this a specific condition of early evacuation, for he feared a rebuff from the German government.[37] The fact was, however, that Favre had begun to shift his attack.

In response to a suggestion by de Clerq, Favre told Gabriac to sound the German government on the possibility of extending the existing arrangement about Alsace until the first of the year but he suggested that France would be willing to find her compensation in the frontier changes which he had mentioned to Fabrice early in June.[38] And on the issue of securing the evacuation of France, he now began to concentrate his attention on linking it not with a customs arrangement but with a rapid payment of the war indemnity. As early as July 18 he revealed that Pouyer-Quertier was preparing to "lift the veil" on such a scheme.[39] And just as Favre was changing his tactics he was also changing the locale of his major effort to German occupation headquarters, where a new commander-in-chief had been named in mid-June.

The personality and background of General Edwin von Manteuffel were such that he was almost destined to become a center of controversy during his stay in France. From the French point of view he was an excellent choice for the post. Conciliatory and sensitive to the nuances of French pride, he went out of his way to flatter Thiers, and the old man's vanity was one of his weak points. But if he was a good choice from the French point of view, the same cannot necessarily be said from Bismarck's viewpoint. Manteuffel had opposed Bismarck since 1866 and he deplored the ascendancy in Prussia of a "politician" over the military.[40] He was "burningly ambitious" and insisted on playing the politician.[41] His political activities succeeded in further confusing an already confused situation and he constantly tangled the lines of command as he clashed repeatedly with Waldersee and Arnim. Manteuffel's associates predicted an eventual showdown with Bismarck and when it did come Manteuffel, like Fabrice, learned to his discomfort the penalty of too great friendship with the French.

When Manteuffel assumed his post at the beginning of July there seemed no reason to anticipate the difficulties that would soon develop. His first meeting with Thiers and Favre was marked by mutual cordiality that boded well for the success of his mission. Another factor which promised good relations was Thiers's nomination of the Count of Saint Vallier to be France's representative at Manteuffel's headquarters. Although Saint Vallier was plagued with ill health he did a good job in a difficult assignment and he and Manteuffel worked well together.[42]

An incident which occurred shortly after Manteuffel arrived at his post served to cement these new friendships and to earn for him French gratitude. The peace treaty provided that upon payment of the first half-billion francs of the war indemnity the departments of Seine-Infèrieure, Somme, and Eure should be evacuated. France completed the payment on July 15 and expected the evacuation to proceed at once. The Germans insisted on postponing the evacuation until the money had been counted and the validity of the commercial paper was established. Manteuffel took it upon himself to break the deadlock. On July 20, in response to a personal plea from Manteuffel the emperor ordered the evacuation of the three departments without waiting for a certification of payment, in order "not to aggravate the position of M. Thiers."[43]

In view of the excellent relations between the French government and Manteuffel's headquarters it is not surprising that Favre shifted his main attempt to gain the evacuation of France from Frankfort and Berlin to Compiègne. Manteuffel showed himself more than willing to discuss the larger issues of Franco-German relations and in particular the possibility of advanced payment by France of the second billion francs of the indemnity in return for evacuation of the Paris forts on the right bank of the Seine and the departments of Seine, Oise, Seine-et-Oise, and Seine-et-Marne.[44] Favre was not to complete the negotiations, for late in July he resigned as foreign minister. His resignation did not stop the conversations, however, for they were continued with Pouyer-Quertier and Saint Vallier carrying the burden for France. So quietly were the negotiations carried on that Favre's successor, Charles de Rémusat, was unaware of them until they were virtually completed.

On August 3 and again on August 6 Pouyer-Quertier went to Compiègne where he and Saint Vallier discussed with Manteuffel and Stosch the problems involved in speeding up payments in order to hasten the evacuation of France.[45] By August 7 Pouyer-Quertier and Manteuffel had arrived at specific terms of a convention by which France would pay the third half-billion francs during the month of August (the second half-billion, from which was deducted the indemnity to the Eastern Railway, had been paid at the end of July and the beginning of August), in return for which Germany would evacuate the departments in question.[46] That same day Manteuffel notified Bismarck of the convention and urged him to approve it.[47] He also wrote to the emperor about the convention, said that Thiers had approved it, and spoke optimistically of receiving Bismarck's approval as well.[48]

Manteuffel's optimism was premature, as he was shortly to discover. From the beginning Stosch had had qualms about the propriety of Manteuffel's undertaking the negotiations and he had warned that Waldersee should be consulted.[49] It was good advice to have followed. Waldersee had heard rumors that Pouyer-Quertier was trying to arrange a speeded-up payment of the war indemnity but he seems to have received no concrete information.[50] One can imagine, then, his surprise upon receiving a copy of the convention on the morning of August 8. He was furious and his anger was only increased when news reports in the Paris press of August 9 announced the convention as an accomplished fact.[51] Rémusat, who disclaimed any knowledge of the negotiations, apologized to Waldersee, as did Pouyer-Quertier, who went to see him in person.[52] Waldersee felt that the negotiations represented an attempt to undermine his position with Bismarck and there was a stormy scene at Compiègne with Manteuffel during which Waldersee absolutely refused to write to the emperor in support of the convention.[53]

Despite this furor Manteuffel still professed to feel that Bismarck would approve the convention. Bismarck, however, was far from pleased with it. The emperor was inclined to accept the evacuation from a purely military point of view, but he asked Bismarck's advice about the political aspects of the matter. He asked if the question might not be tied in with that of an Alsatian customs agreement.[54] This must have come as a nasty shock to Bismarck, for he probably thought that particular issue a dead letter. In reply, Bismarck said that Germany would be the loser if this procedure were adopted and that Manteuffel's negotiations introduced an "extremely dangerous" leniency into relations with France.[55] He instructed

Waldersee to make it completely clear to the French that the German government disassociated itself entirely from Manteuffel's negotiations.[56] Bismarck cut short his vacation at Varzin to return to Berlin and he told Manteuffel to cease all negotiations since they were inconsistent with Bismarck's remaining in office.[57] He also instructed Arnim to prepare to go to Compiègne to investigate the situation there.[58]

When Bismarck arrived back in Berlin he had a long and at times heated conversation with Gabriac during which he vented his anger over the turn which relations with France had taken. He asked if France considered it good business to "deal with a general . . . who has no political powers" while Arnim, "the only plenipotentiary designated by us," had been put off by excuses of lack of instructions from Versailles. Since, he said, things could not go on in this fashion he was sending Arnim to Paris to regulate "all pending questions." Although he conceded that it might be in everybody's best interests to hasten the evacuation of France, he said that until Germany was convinced of the peaceful intentions of the French government "we prefer to keep as long as possible the pledge that we have in hand."[59]

Manteuffel, who had felt for some time that he was being persecuted by his government, answered Bismarck with a bitter letter.[60] He defended his policy as being in the best interests of Germany and he made it quite clear that he did not care whether Bismarck remained in office.[61] It surely must have been one of the more astonishing letters received by Bismarck, yet Manteuffel remained relatively unscathed by it. But for all his defiance of Bismarck, Manteuffel still recognized storm signals when he saw them and he realised that it was imperative for him to step aside if the convention were to be salvaged. He told the French henceforth to handle the question through Waldersee.[62] He also suggested that Pouyer-Quertier get in touch directly with Bismarck in an attempt to carry the negotiations to a successful conclusion.[63]

After Bismarck's first outburst against Manteuffel his anger seems to have cooled somewhat. In a personal letter of August 14 he went into some detail to describe to Manteuffel what he called the "obstinacy," even the "contempt," which the French had shown at Frankfort, and he sought to explain this behavior by their attempt to by-pass the usual diplomatic channels. He said that the delay which had been caused by the Compiègne negotiations made it unlikely that the temporary extension of the Alsatian agreement could now be secured by September 1. Calmly but firmly Bismarck stressed that there must be unity of negotiation if success were to be achieved.[64] Manteuffel was angry enough, however, that such efforts did not mollify him, and he prepared to go personally to Gastein to see the emperor.[65] He also continued to urge Pouyer to seek a direct interview with Bismarck. This would, he said, probably flatter Bismarck and would at least hasten the arrival in Paris of Arnim, whom Manteuffel considered moderate and far more conciliatory than Waldersee.[66]

On August 15 Pouyer proposed to Bismarck a meeting at a German city of the latter's choice. He said that he was "convinced that the conditions and payments that I can offer to Germany for the second billion" would be found acceptable. He carefully said not a word about the evacuation of France.[67] Waldersee arranged for Pouyer to meet Bismarck at Gastein, where the chancellor had joined the emperor.[68] Bismarck made it clear that he expected Pouyer to come armed with more than pious wishes, for "without concessions with regard to imports from Alsace, I am in no way ready to show leniency of any kind."[69] Perhaps coincidentally, the day after this telegram Pouyer pleaded the press of domestic affairs to postpone his visit to Gastein. But, he said, he would be happy to see Arnim arrive in Paris.[70]

Harry von Arnim arrived in Paris on August 26. Arnim was and is a highly controversial character, and his stay in France was a turbulent one. A sensitive man, forever complaining of being snubbed by Parisian society, he was not happy at his French post. Somewhat earlier Bismarck had complained that Arnim's "opinion about people . . . changed twice every other week, according as he had been well or ill treated." Since Bismarck also said that he expected his diplomats to "wheel like soldiers at the word of command," the erratic Arnim was bound to encounter difficulties sooner or later.[71]

Bismarck explained his attitudes about Arnim's mission in a dispatch of August 28. He realized fully that he would have to surrender the Paris forts when France had paid the third half billion francs of the war indemnity. Arnim was to learn whether France "can make us offers which would lead us to evacuate in advance and to be satisfied with other guarantees of payment." He refused even to consider immediate evacuation of the forts without some compensation in return. Any uncompensated favor done for France, he said, would only be interpreted as a sign of German weakness and would probably deprive Germany of all hope of getting the last three billion francs of the war indemnity without resorting to war. The only possible attitude for Germany was to maintain her rights strictly and Manteuffel's negotiations had already weakened the German position. If there had to be war, he said, let it not come from signs of weakness but from "a flagrant violation" of the treaty.[72]

Arnim called on Thiers and Rémusat on August 29. He made it clear that Bismarck had no intention of moving the main negotiations from Frankfort and said that his only reason for being in Paris was to give the French a chance to state their intentions to one who was familiar with the negotiations from the beginning. Arnim also made it clear that he was not authorized to discuss payment of the last three billion francs or evacuation of the last six departments. He and Rémusat did discuss at some length the means by which the Manteuffel negotiations might be followed through to a successful conclusion. Arnim said that he would have to have a financial agreement concerning payment of the remainder of the third half-billion as well as the fourth half-billion and interest due on March 1, 1872, and extension of the Alsace-Lorraine customs agreement until the end of 1871. In return for these he was willing to discuss the evacuation of all France except the last six departments.[73]

Rémusat was relieved at the tone of the conversation with Arnim and felt that it indicated a better disposition toward France on the part of Bismarck. Privately he let it be known that he did not intend to use the evacuation of the departments concerned in the Manteuffel negotiations as a bargaining point in his talks with Arnim for rapid payment of the third half-billion francs which was then being carried out, would soon bring that about anyway. Nor did he show any disposition to extend the Alsatian customs agreement in return for evacuation of all save the last six departments.[74]

Arnim's reaction to the initial negotiations was mixed. He was pleased with the financial side of the talks, but he was far from optimistic about the Alsatian affair. To Bismarck he lamented that the German position had been weakened since the beginning of August for France was paying the third half billion so rapidly that Germany's imminent evacuation of the Parisian forts and the four departments was a foregone conclusion and they had lost all value as diplomatic pawns. Therefore, the only real talking point which he had revolved around advanced payment of the fourth half-billion and the six departments which served as a guarantee for its payment. He urged that since France would soon be able to advance that payment as well and thus liberate six additional departments Germany's best interests lay in keeping the demands concerning Alsace within such limits that the French would accept them and, at the same time, advance payment on the fourth half-billion in order to gain evacuation of the six departments.[75] There was a further point for possible bargaining which Arnim might have mentioned: the French request, as yet unanswered, for changes in the Franco-German frontier.

Bismarck agreed with Arnim that Germany's demands in the matter of the customs agreement must be curtailed somewhat, and the two sides settled down to serious discussions. Arnim and Thiers finally agreed, on September 14, on the main points of two conventions. The first concerned the Alsatian customs. It would admit the products of Alsace and Lorraine into France duty free until December 31, 1871, a four month extension of the existing arrangement. For six months thereafter the tariff would be twenty-five per cent of that charged on German goods entering France. From June 1872 to June 1873 the charge would be fifty per cent of that on German goods. After June 1873 full rate would be charged.[76] The second convention provided that Germany would evacuate immediately the six departments (Aisne, Aube, Côte-d'Or, Haute-Saônc, Doubs, and Jura) which must be evacuated after payment of the first two billion francs. In return, France would anticipate payment of the fourth half-billion, as well as the interest due on May 1, 1872. The evacuated departments would remain neutral and Germany retained the right to re-occupy them should France fail to fulfill her obligations.[77]

Thiers had hurried along the discussions because he wished the assembly's approval of the agreements before it adjourned on September 17. The day that Arnim and Thiers reached their agreement Rémusat went before the assembly to ask for the unusual procedure of approval in advance of a convention to be negotiated with Germany on the basis of the points agreed to thus far.[78] He did not place before the assembly the financial side of the evacuation convention, partly because Thiers felt that, constitutionally, it was unnecessary, and partly because he thought that the assembly would feel that the favorable customs convention was sufficient compensation for the evacuation of the departments. Arnim had objected to the entire procedure of going to the assembly while negotiations were still in progress for he feared that word would appear in the press and reach his government in garbled form. In view of the urgency of the situation, however, he dropped his objections.[79]

The assembly debated the proposal on September 16. The committee which had examined the convention, by the narrow margin of one vote, recommended that the assembly suspend its usual procedure and give advance approval to the convention. The committee also recalled the border rectifications which had been mentioned at the time of the ratification of the treaty of Frankfort and suggested that the current negotiations furnished the occasion for requesting that those border changes be made. In addition, the committee made two recommendations concerning the terms of the convention. It wished the Alsatian goods allowed into France to be based on the production figures for 1869 and it also called for the admission into Alsace-Lorraine on a fully reciprocal basis of all French goods destined for general consumption in the two provinces.

When the debate was thrown open Thiers was present to defend the government's course of action against the charges of irregularity and to answer the objections that French industry would be injured by this convention. He managed to avoid an amendment which would have demanded the border rectifications by assuring the assembly that he shared the committee's sentiments in this regard. He was, however, unable to avoid the other two amendments recommended by the committee, and the assembly adopted them. Thiers "guaranteed" the assembly that the convention would "conform to the sentiment of these articles," but he insisted that he must have freedom of action concerning the actual text of the convention for, he said, it would be impossible to negotiate if he were bound by the exact terms set forth by the assembly. The assembly, by a vote of 512 to 32, gave Thiers the authorization which he asked.[80]

Understandably, Arnim was shocked when he read of the vote in the *Journal officiel* on the morning of September 17. His worst fears were realized and he was now caught in a crossfire from both Versailles and Berlin.

No sooner had Arnim learned of the assembly's action than he wrote to Thiers refusing to accept the stipulation of reciprocity.[81] And to make his position perfectly clear he sent Holstein to Versailles to see Thiers. The president discounted the importance of the assembly's action, saying that its wording need not be retained *in toto* but that any agreement which might be reached should, "without being that of article 3 [the reciprocity clause], give a little more satisfaction to the sentiment of the country." He sent word to Arnim not to take the affair too much to heart, for "we will arrange all that."[82] In short, Thiers thought that, for a change, he had an effective weapon which he could use to force concessions from Germany.

Even worse for Arnim than his embarrassment vis-à-vis the French was the reaction which he got from Germany. On the day of the announcement of the assembly's action he had hastily assured the foreign office that he had not exceeded his instructions.[83] In spite of such assurances, Bismarck was highly displeased by the turn which events had taken. In a series of acrimonious notes he belittled Arnim's diplomatic abilities, accused him of not having kept Berlin adequately informed of the progress of negotiations, and tartly reminded him that he could in no way bind Germany to any course of action without the approval of the imperial government.[84] Bismarck's methods are well illustrated by an incident which occurred at this time. On September 20 Abeken wrote to Bismarck from Baden-Baden on behalf of the emperor to ask for clarification of the Paris negotiations. The last paragraph of the dispatch contained the statement that the emperor was surprised but not worried by the action of the French government. Bismarck directed that this be forwarded to Arnim *without* the last paragraph, an action which would, of course, be much more calculated to alarm Arnim.[85]

The method in which the French government had presented the convention to the assembly made it seem as though the evacuation of the six departments was the exchange for granting the Alsatian customs arrangement desired by Germany. Bismarck insisted that the question of the evacuation could only be tied in with advanced payment of the war indemnity. As for the tariff arrangement, he said that France must find her compensation for that in "the complaisance by which *we consent* to allow financial guarantees . . . in place of territorial guarantees."[86] He felt that the assembly's reciprocity demands were a good excuse to invalidate the entire agreement and "to bring the conference into the path I have wished from the beginning."[87]

When Bismarck finally saw a complete copy of the agreement which Arnim had reached with Thiers, he was somewhat mollified for, with the exception of the reciprocity clause, it was not too different from what he had wished. He did insist on a clause allowing German reoccupation in the event of French noncompliance with the terms of the convention.[88] This last demand was not well received by Rémusat, who complained that "to take into consideration such an eventuality in a treaty would be as monstrous as including the conditions of divorce in a marriage contract."[89]

It was Germany which finally suggested a way out of the impasse by offering to shorten the period during which Alsatian goods should have a privileged position in the French tariff system if France would abandon the demand for full reciprocity for French goods.[90] The French belatedly suggested that if Germany would evacuate the department of the Marne in addition to those already agreed upon she would drop the troublesome reciprocity provision.[91] Germany refused to permit the evacuation of "a single department more" and France accepted the German proposal instead.[92]

By the beginning of October agreement had been reached on all basic points. However, certain technical details concerning payment of the fourth half-billion francs remained to be worked out. To expedite these matters Rémusat proposed a personal meeting between Bismarck and Pouyer-Quertier. Before doing so, however, he and Pouyer were careful to ask Arnim's advice in the matter, a tactful gesture undoubtedly designed to avoid the unpleasantness connected with the Compiègne negotiations in August.[93] Bismarck, then at Friedrichsruh, agreed to a meeting at Berlin, where he was going for the opening of the Reichstag.[94] Pouyer-Quertier was quick to accept the invitation to go to Berlin, and he may have seen a good omen in the fact that the first week in October brought the evacuation, by virtue of the payment of the third half-billion of the war indemnity, of the departments of Oise, Seine-et-Oise, Seine-et-Marne, and Seine, together with the

Parisian forts. He arrived in Berlin on October 8 and immediately began a series of conversations with Bismarck which lasted for four days. The two men had always worked well together and now they easily settled all outstanding issues. Two separate conventions were the result. This procedure was adopted because the first convention, that dealing with the Alsatian customs, had to be submitted for ratification by the legislative bodies of both France and Germany, while the second, dealing with the evacuation of the six French departments, did not. Also, since Bismarck had succeeded in divorcing the Alsatian question from that of evacuation, this convention had legally no relation to the treaty of May 10, hence it was called the "Convention of October 12." The second of the two conventions did, however, alter the terms of the Frankfort treaty and was styled "Additional convention to the peace treaty between France and Germany."

By the latter, Germany agreed to evacuate within two weeks after ratification of the convention the six departments of Aisne, Aube, Côte-d'Or, Haute-Saône, Doubs, and Jura, and to reduce the occupation forces in the remaining departments to fifty thousand men. In return, the French government agreed to pay in eight bi-weekly installments from January 15, 1872 to May 1, 1872 the fourth half-billion of the war indemnity plus one hundred and fifty million francs as one year's interest on the last three billion falling due on March 2, 1872. Bismarck made one concession in this regard and agreed to accept as part of the payment not the negotiable securities which he had asked but bills of exchange, and he agreed not to cash these unless the Thiers government should be overthrown and replaced by one which would not recognize the treaties or the debt.[95] Germany retained the right to reoccupy the evacuated departments should France not fulfill the obligations of the treaty, and France agreed that these departments would be neutralized and that she would maintain there only enough troops to keep order until the full payment should be made.

In the commercial treaty Bismarck agreed to cut short by six months the period of favorable treatment accorded to Alsatian products. Thus they would enter duty free until December 31, 1871. From then until June 30, 1872 they would enter at a rate one quarter of that charged on German goods (Germany's "most favored nation" status was restated), while the rate would be fifty per cent from July 1, 1872 to December 31, 1872. A few exceptions to these terms were stipulated. Certain French goods destined for use by the industry of Alsace-Lorraine, received similar treatment upon importation into the ceded territories and for the same periods of time. One further provision of the customs agreement dealt with the border rectifications which France had been demanding ever since the ratification of the treaty of Frankfort. Germany had already conceded the border changes in principle. France did not get all she wanted but Germany did agree to "retrocede" to France the communes of Raon-les-Leau, Raon-sur-Plaine, Igney and part of the commune of Avricourt. Bismarck stipulated that these were not included in this convention as compensation for the Alsatian agreement but rather because this retrocession needed the action of the Reichstag, too. France agreed to build one small railway station for Germany because of a disruption in service caused by this change of sovereignty.[96]

A protocol was appended stating that the two conventions formed "one treaty only" and the form of two conventions was adopted only to hasten the ratification of the financial and evacuation convention since the Alsatian agreement must be approved by the Reichstag. Thus "the stipulations of the financial agreement cannot be put into effect if, contrary to all expectation, the ratification of the other by France should be absent."[97] Thus, although Bismarck had refused to link the Alsatian and evacuation questions during the negotiations, he was clearly doing so in the ratifications and was refusing to evacuate the six departments unless he got the Alsatian settlement which he wanted. Nor did Bismarck intend to be frustrated in his goal by the Reichstag. He assured Pouyer-Quertier that, if the Reichstag did not accept the territorial and tariff convention, the six departments would be evacuated anyway.[98]

On October 25 Bismarck presented the conventions to the Reichstag. He said that he was satisfied with both conventions and on October 27, without debate, the Reichstag ratified the conventions.[99] On October 28 the Bundesrat was informed that the Reichstag had completed favorable action on the conventions. Since the emperor had already given his approval, the Bundesrat voted that the exchange of ratifications should take place.[100]

Since the French national assembly had already given prior approval to the government's course of action, it took no further action on the conventions. The assembly reconvened on December 4. When Thiers addressed it a few days later he recapitulated the course of the negotiations. He put the best possible face on the fact that full reciprocity for French goods had not been obtained by saying that French goods destined for use by Alsatian industry had constituted the greatest part of France's former trade with the ceded territories. He considered that sufficient compensation had been received when Germany reduced her claims for favored treatment for Alsatian goods from eighteen to twelve months. Besides, Bismarck had agreed to take his and Pouyer's signatures for full payment of the two billion francs without having recourse to the guarantees of bankers. And, of course, six departments had been evacuated.[101]

In the weeks between the signing of the October conventions and Thiers's address in December relations between France and Germany had again gone through a dizzying series of ups and downs. Immediately after the signing of the conventions relations had been unusually good, but that happy state did not last long.

Point four of the protocol of signature of the Berlin conventions stated that both parties recognized that it was important to end, as soon as it could be accomplished, the work of the Frankfort negotiations, and to that end both agreed to give their delegates "instructions which will permit them to proceed in a short time to the signature of the additional acts prepared at Frankfort." To expedite matters, "questions of detail, if their nature permits, will be regulated by "a commission of liquidation."[102]

This brought back onto center stage the Frankfort negotiations, which had virtually ceased altogether during August and September. With the Alsatian question settled, the German government felt that the Frankfort conversations could now be brought to a quick conclusion on the basis of the agreements which had been reached in July.[103] Consequently, the negotiations reopened on a full scale late in October, but Bismarck's hopes for a quick settlement were disappointed almost from the beginning. On October 26 Uxkull, who had replaced Arnim as chief German negotiator, reported that de Clerq by no means considered all important matters to have been settled in July. De Clerq had certain decided opinions on many subjects which he was not prepared to change except on specific instructions from the French government.[104] To Bismarck it must have seemed that the haggling would go on forever. He instructed Arnim to urge the French government to tell its delegates to confine the negotiations to matters already considered or they might prove to be endless.[105]

The discussion covered a wide variety of complex and highly technical subjects: pensions, the status of doctors and chemists, the property of joint-stock companies, mortgages, patents, religious corporations, insurance company properties, postal questions, diocesan boundaries, and the like. There was even a lengthy discussion of the preamble to the convention. Most of the questions had been under discussion at various times since the Brussels negotiations. One by one they were settled outright or were agreed to in principle, leaving the details to be worked out later by committees of liquidation. Two issues were particularly troublesome: the citizenship of the people in the ceded territories, and amnesty for French citizens in Germany.

Article II of the treaty of Frankfort stated that "French subjects native to [*originaire*] the ceded territories" could preserve their French citizenship by means of a declaration of intention to that effect made to the competent authorities before October 1, 1872. They would then be free to move their residence to France unhindered by the German officials. At Frankfort the French tried to gain an interpretation of the word *originaire* which would have excluded from the stated time limit those not yet of age. The Germans insisted that a declaration would have to be made on their behalf by their legal representatives before October 1, 1872. The Germans also insisted that the word applied to those born in the ceded territories but no longer resident there. Nothing the French did could make the Germans change their interpretation.[106] The best the French could obtain was an extension of the time limit until October 1, 1873 for natives of Alsace-Lorraine residing outside of Europe.

The second point of special conflict was that of amnesty.

France wanted very much to gain an amnesty for her citizens convicted of offenses other than those of a criminal nature in occupied territory or in the ceded provinces. In mid-November France submitted a draft article by the terms of which Germany would grant amnesty to all convicted "other than for crimes of common law" [*droit commun*] as well as to all prisoners of war interned in Germany and not yet freed. France would agree to grant reciprocal amnesty to Germans in similar situations, a concession which she had refused to grant in July.[107] This particular matter became the subject of an intensive diplomatic effort on France's part. Rémusat used every conceivable appeal to support his position, including the usual argument that the government would find it difficult to go before the assembly with a convention not containing such a clause.[108] De Clerq insisted that the amnesty was "a point of honor" for France,[109] and threatened to break up the conference over it.[110]

By this time Bismarck probably agreed with Gabriac's statement that the negotiations threatened to "last longer than those at Westphalia,"[111] and his attitude had hardened. He refused to grant any definite commitment of amnesty, insisting that this would have to be a matter for imperial clemency voluntarily extended.[112]

In this latest deadlock Bismarck was presented with a ready-made weapon to use against the French. A French jury at Melun acquitted a Frenchman accused of murdering a German soldier. On December 7 Bismarck wrote Arnim a note declaring that such actions had dispelled any confidence which the October negotiations might have engendered toward the French government.[113] This incident, obviously strengthening Bismarck's hand in his refusal to grant the requested amnesty, may have played a part in the French decision to abandon the condition with a request for the favor of the emperor.[114] With this last obstacle out of the way, agreement was quickly reached, and on December 11 France and Germany signed an "additional convention to the treaty of peace of May 10, 1871," consisting of nineteen articles and a nine point "protocol of closure" clarifying certain obscure points which had arisen in the course of the negotiations.[115]

The national assembly ratified the convention for France without debate, on January 9, 1872.[116] Emperor William I ratified the treaty for Germany and ratifications were exchanged at Paris on January 11 between Arnim and Rémusat.[117]

The convention of December 11 had stated certain agreements in principle and their details were left to be worked out by a series of mixed commissions of specialists. Not until 1878 was the work of these various commissions finished and not until then, seven years after the end of the war, could the ramifications of the treaty of Frankfort, properly speaking, be said to have come to an end.[118]

This convention of December 11, 1871 paved the way for a stabilization of relations between France and Germany. The return to normality was further symbolized by the exchange of ambassadors between the two countries in the early days of December. Arnim was named to the position at Paris and France nominated as her ambassador to Germany the Viscount of Gontaut-Biron. Considering the turbulence of Franco-German relations during the second half of 1871, the year closed on a note of comparative serenity which boded well for future relations.

NOTES TO CHAPTER X

1. Bismarck-Delbrück correspondence, Goldschmidt, pp. 151–152, no. 79.
2. Favre, III, 432.

3. Laussedat, Bk. II, 81–84.

4. Favre to de Clerq, Versailles, May 25, 1871, MAE, MD (Allemagne), 160 : 3.

5. Goulard and de Clerq to Favre, Frankfort, June 4, 1871, *ibid.*, 161 *bis;* Goulard and de Clerq to Favre, Frankfort, June 5, 1871, *ibid.*, fols. 4–10. In a long note to Fabrice, Favre set out some twenty points that he felt should be considered at Frankfort (Favre to Fabrice, Versailles, May 25, 1871, Goldschmidt, pp. 153–154, no. 81).

6. Bismarck to Fabrice, June 10, 1871, Favre, III, 472.

7. Waldersee, pp. 96–99.

8. Favre to Bismarck, Versailles, May 30, 1871, MAE, CP (Allemagne), 1 : 26; *DDF,* I, 30 fn. 1.

9. Bismarck to Waldersee, Berlin, June 14, 1871, *PEA,* I, 61–62, no. 33.

10. Favre to Nostilz [temporary commander of the occupation forces], June 15, 1871, Favre, III, 468–469; Nostilz to Favre, June 16, 1871, MAE, Papiers Favre.

11. Waldersee to Bismarck, Paris, June 17, 1871, *PEA,* I, 62–63, no. 34; Waldersee, pp. 100–101; GA, Schriftwechsel d. Ges. Paris über Züstände USW in Frankreich, 2 : 2–3.

12. Bismarck to Waldersee, Berlin, June 18, 1871, *PEA,* I, 63, no. 35; Busch, *Bismarck,* I, 494.

13. Waldersee, p. 101.

14. Waldersee to Bismarck, Paris, June 20, 1871, *PEA,* I, 63–65.

15. Waldersee (Germ.), I, 144.

16. Fabrice to Bismarck, Soisy, June 11, 1871, Goldschmidt, pp. 160–161, no. 87.

17. Bismarck to Fabrice, Berlin, June 12, 1871, Goldschmidt, pp. 161–162, no. 88; Nostilz to Favre, Soisy, June 13, 1871, MAE, MD (Allemagne), 160 : 67.

18. Bismarck to Waldersee, Berlin, June 28, 1871, *PEA,* I, 65–67, no. 37.

19. Waldersee to Favre, Paris, June 30, 1871, *DDF,* I, 34.

20. Waldersee to Bismarck, Paris, July 4, 1871, *PEA*, I, 68–69, no. 38.

21. Waldersee to Favre, Paris, June 30, 1871, *DDF,* I, 34–35; Waldersee (Germ.), I, 146. As a result of these charges Pouyer-Quertier paid one hundred million francs on July 1 and promised to pay the remainder at Strasbourg between July 5 and 10. The other 125,000,000 of the first payment had previously been made in Bank of France notes as stipulated by the treaty of Frankfort. In connection with this incident Waldersee noted in his journal that the French were "unreliable" and not to be trusted (Waldersee [Germ.], 144–146).

22. Favre to Gabriac, Versailles, July 3, 1871, *DDF,* I, 33, no. 17; Gabriac to Favre, Berlin, July 5, 1871, *ibid.,* pp. 36–37, no. 19; Gabriac to Favre, Berlin, July 7, 1871, MAE, CP (Allemagne), I : 45–51.

23. Goulard and de Clerq to Favre, Frankfort, June 5, 1871, MAE, MD (Allemagne), 161 *bis* : 4–10.

24. De Clerq to Favre, Frankfort, June 13, 1871, MAE, Papiers Favre.

25. Goldschmidt, p. 160.

26. De Clerq and Goulard to Favre, Frankfort, June 14, 1871, *DDF,* I, 26–27, no. 10.

27. Arnim to Bismarck, Frankfort, July 4, 1871, Goldschmidt, pp. 169–171, no. 96.

28. Bismarck to Arnim, Berlin, July 10, 1871, *ibid.,* pp. 177–178, no. 101.

29. Gabriac to Favre, Berlin, July 11, 1871, MAE, CP (Allemagne), 1 : 63.

30. De Clerq to foreign office, Frankfort, July 12, 1871, MAE, MD (Allemagne), 161 *bis* : 205.

31. De Clerq to Favre, Frankfort, July 13, 1871, *DDF,* I, 45–46, no. 25.

32. Arnim to Delbrück, Frankfort, July 13, 1871, Goldschmidt, pp. 180–183, no. 103.

33. Arnim to Bismarck, Frankfort, July 21, 1871, *ibid.,* pp. 186–191, no. 106.

34. Arnim to Thile, Frankfort, July 24, 1871, *ibid.,* pp. 193–196, no. 106.

35. Bucher to the chancellery, Varzin, July 31, 1871, *ibid.,* p. 196, no. 109.

36. Bismarck to Arnim, Berlin, Aug. 4, 1871, *ibid.,* pp. 202–203, no. 112.

37. Gabriac to Favre, Berlin, July 29, 1871, MAE, CP (Allemagne), 1 : 123 and 124–128.

38. Favre to Gabriac, Versailles, July 27, 1871, *ibid.,* fol. 119; Gabriac to Favre, Berlin, July 31, 1871, *ibid.,* fol. 131.

39. Favre to Goulard, Versailles, July 18, 1871, MAE, MD (Allemagne), 160 : 207–208.

40. Herzfeld, Hans, *Deutschland und das geschlagene Frankreich, 1871–1873: Friedensschluss, Kriegsentschädigung, Besatzungszeit* (Berlin: 1924), pp. 68–69.

41. Stosch, pp. 247–249.

42. Henri Doniol, *M. Thiers, le comte de Saint Vallier, le général de Manteuffel. La libération du térritoire, 1871–1873* (Paris: 1897), pp. 15–16.

43. Saint Vallier to Favre, Compiègne, July 19, 1871, Louis Adolphe Thiers, *Occupation et libération du territoire* (Paris: 1903), I, 18, no. 14 and 19–24, no. 15, cited hereafter as *Occ. et lib;* Abeken to Waldersee, Ems, July 20, 1871, *PEA,* I, 72, no. 41.

44. Rémusat to de Clerq and Goulard, Versailles, Aug. 16, 1871, Marquis de Gabriac, *Souvenirs diplomatiques de Russie et d' Allemagne (1870–1872)* (Paris: 1896), pp. 315–318. On July 22 Manteuffel wrote to Thiers: "I have written that the payment of the first four half-billion should be speeded up in such a way that in a few months the number of German troops in France would be reduced to the number of 50,000 men stipulated in the peace" (Manteuffel to Thiers, Compiègne, July 22, 1871, *Occ. et lib.,* I, 28–30, no. 17). On July 18 Favre wrote to Goulard that such negotiations had been mentioned at Com-

piègne (Favre to Goulard, Versailles, July 18, 1871, MAE, MD [Allemagne], 160: 207–208).

45. Stosch, pp. 257–258.

46. Pouyer-Quertier to Rémusat, Compiègne, Aug. 7, 1871, *DDF,* I, 56, no. 38.

47. Manteuffel to Bismarck, Compiègne, Aug. 7, 1871, GA, Frankreich, no. 72, 123: 58.

48. Manteuffel to the emperor, Compiègne, Aug. 7, 1871, Goldschmidt, pp. 206–207, no. 155.

49. Waldersee (Germ.), I, 148–149.

50. *Ibid.,* p. 148.

51. Waldersee to the foreign office, Paris, Aug. 9, 1871, GA, Frankreich, no. 70, 123: 137.

52. Keudell to the foreign office, forwarding telegram from Waldersee, Aug. 11, 1871, *ibid.,* fol. 80.

53. Waldersee (Germ.), I, 150–152.

54. Abeken to the foreign office, Homburg, Aug. 9, 1871, GA, Frankreich, no. 70, 123: 41–42.

55. Bismarck to Abeken, Aug. 10, 1871, *ibid.,* fol. 55.

56. Bismarck to Waldersee, Berlin, Aug. 12, 1871, Goldschmidt, pp. 211–212, no. 119.

57. Thile to Manteuffel, Berlin, Aug. 12, 1871, *ibid.,* pp. 210–211, no. 118.

58. Bismarck to Thile, Varzin, Aug. 12, 1871, GA, Frankreich, no. 70, 124–125.

59. Gabriac to Rémusat, Berlin, Aug. 14, 1871, *DDF,* I, 61–65, no. 42.

60. Herzfeld speaks of attacks in the *Frankfurter Zeitung* against Manteuffel during July which the general felt resulted from Bismarck's illwill. He answered through the intermediary of Stosch and Freytag with articles in the *Neuen Reich* (Herzfeld, p. 80). Stosch records that Manteuffel received anonymous articles through the mails attacking him and says that the newspaper articles galled Manteuffel (Stosch, pp. 256–257).

61. Manteuffel to Bismarck, Compiègne, Aug. 13, 1871, *PEA,* I, 72–74, no. 42.

62. Saint Vallier to Rémusat, Compiègne, Aug. 13, 1871, *DDF,* I, 60–61, no. 41.

63. Saint Vallier to Rémusat, Compiègne, Aug. 13, 1871, *Occ. et lib.*, I, 44–48, no. 23.

64. Bismarck to Manteuffel, Berlin, Aug. 14, 1871, *PEA,* I, 75–76, no. 44.

65. Stosch, p. 258.

66. Saint Vallier to Thiers, Compiègne, Aug. 15, 1871, *Occ. et lib.,* I, 50–54, no. 25; Saint Vallier to Rémusat, Compiègne, Aug. 15, 1871, *DDF,* I, 66, no. 43.

67. Pouyer-Quertier to Bismarck, Paris, Aug. 15, 1871, *DDF,* I, 66–67, no. 44.

68. Bismarck to Waldersee, Munich, Aug. 15, 1871, GA, Frankreich, no. 70, 124–125: 37–38; Waldersee to Bismarck, Paris, *ibid.,* fols. 42–43.

69. Bismarck to Waldersee, Munich, Aug. 16, 1871, Goldschmidt, pp. 212–213, no. 120 (2).

70. Pouyer-Quertier to Bismarck, Versailles, Aug. 17, 1871, MAE, CP (Allemagne), 1 : 223.

71. Charles Lowe, ed., *Bismarck's Table-talk* (London: 1895), p. 214.

72. Bismarck to Waldersee, Gastein, Aug. 28, 1871, *PEA,* I, 81–85, no. 50.

73. Arnim to Bismarck, Paris, Aug. 30, 1871, *ibid.,* pp. 85–86, no. 51.

74. Instructions of Rémusat to Direction politique, Aug. 31, 1871, *DDF,* I, 71–72, no. 52; Rémusat to Gabriac, Versailles, Aug. 31, 1871, MAE, CP (Allemagne), 1 : 274–279.

75. Arnim to Bismarck, Paris, Sept. 2, 1871, *PEA,* I, 86–87, no. 52.

76. Arnim to Bismarck, Paris, Sept. 14, 1871, *ibid.,* p. 88, no. 54; *DDF,* I, 78, fn. 2.

77. Arnim to Bismarck, Paris, Sept. 18, 1871, GA, Frankreich, no. 72, 16–17 : 17a.

78. Arnim to Bismarck, Paris, Sept. 14, 1871, *PEA,* I, 88, no. 54; *Annales,* V, 622–623.

79. Arnim to Bismarck, Paris, Sept. 18, 1871, GA, Frankreich, no. 72, 16–17 : 17a.

80. *Annales,* V, 684–703.

81. Arnim to Thiers, Paris, Sept. 17, 1871, *Occ. et lib.,* I, 67, no. 32.

82. Holstein to Arnim, Paris, Sept. 18, 1871, GA, Frankreich, no. 72, 16–17 : 22–26.

83. Arnim to foreign ministry, Paris, Sept. 17, 1871, *PEA,* I, 89–90, no. 56; Arnim to Thile, *ibid.,* pp. 90–91, no. 58.

84. Bismarck to Arnim, Berlin, Sept. 19, 1871, *ibid.,* p. 91, no. 59; Bismarck to Arnim, Berlin, Sept. 21, 1871, GA, Frankreich, no. 72, 16–17 : 1–3.

85. Abeken to Bismarck, Baden-Baden, Sept. 20, 1871, GA, Frankreich, no. 72, 16–17 : 4–5.

86. Bismarck to Arnim, Berlin, Sept. 19, 1871, *PEA,* I, 91, no. 59.

87. Bismarck to Arnim, Berlin, Sept. 22, 1871, Goldschmidt, pp. 229–231, no. 133.

88. Bismarck to Arnim, Berlin, Sept. 21, 1871, *PEA,* I, 94, no. 61.

89. Arnim to Bismarck, Paris, Sept. 22, 1871, Goldschmidt, pp. 227–228, no. 131.

90. Gabriac to Rémusat, Berlin, Sept. 28, 1871, MAE, CP (Allemagne), 1 : 392.

91. Rémusat to Gabriac, Versailles, Sept. 29, 1871, *DDF,* I, 78, no. 58.

92. Gabriac to Rémusat, Berlin, Sept. 30, 1871, *ibid.,* pp. 78–79, no. 59.

93. Arnim to Bismarck, Paris, Oct. 2, 1871, *PEA,* I, 97, no. 64; Rémusat to Gabriac, Oct. 2, 1871, Gabriac, Pièces justificatives, pp. 326–327, no. 2.

94. Gabriac to foreign ministry, Berlin, Oct. 4, 1871, BN, Papiers Thiers, XXXIII, NAF 20633; *DDF,* I, 79, fn. 1.

95. Pouyer-Quertier to Thiers, Berlin, Oct. 9, 1871, *DDF,* I, 80–81, no. 63.

96. Pouyer-Quertier to Thiers, Berlin, Oct. 11, 1871, *ibid.,* pp. 85–86, no. 67.

97. For text of the conventions see *DDF,* I, 89–95, nos. 70 and 71; *GP,* I, 91–96, nos. 55 and 56.

98. Pouyer-Quertier to Thiers, Berlin, Oct. 13, 1871, *DDF,* I, 88–89, no. 69.

99. *Reichstag Debates,* 2d session, 1871, I, 57–59.

100. *Protokolle über die Verhandlungen des Bundesraths des deutschen Reichs* (Berlin: 1871–), 1871, u. 285, no. 488, hereafter cited as *Bundesrat minutes.*

101. *Annales,* VI, 7–9.

102. Additional convention of October 12, 1871, *DDF,* I, 91–95, no. 7; *GP,* I, 91–95, no. 55.

103. Bismarck to Uxkull, Berlin, Oct. 20, 1871, Goldschmidt, pp. 246–247, no. 140.

104. Uxkull to Bismarck, Frankfort, Oct. 26, 1871, *ibid.,* pp. 247–248, no. 141.

105. Bismarck to Arnim, Berlin, Nov. 4, 1871, *ibid.,* pp. 248–250, no. 142.

106. Sorel, II, 328–329.

107. *DDF,* I, 36, fn. 2; Rémusat to Gabriac, Versailles, Nov. 26, 1871, MAE, CP (Allemagne), 3: 217–218; Goldschmidt, pp. 261–262.

108. Rémusat to Gabriac, Versailles, Nov. 15, 1871, MAE, CP (Allemagne), 3: 95–108.

109. Weber and Uxkull to Bismarck, Frankfort, Nov. 12, 1871, Goldschmidt, pp. 251–254, no. 143.

110. Weber to Delbrück, Frankfort, Nov. 13, 1871, *ibid.,* pp. 254–256, no. 144.

111. Gabriac to de Clerq, Berlin, Nov. 15, 1871, MAE, CP (Allemagne), 3: 124–128.

112. Bismarck to Arnim, Berlin, Nov. 21, 1871, Goldschmidt, pp. 265–267, no. 148; Gabriac to Rémusat, Berlin, Nov. 21, 1871, *DDF,* I, 101–102, no. 79.

113. Bismarck to Arnim, Berlin, Dec. 7, 1871, *PEA,* I, 107–109, no. 72.

114. Rémusat to de Clerq and Goulard, Versailles, Dec. 9, 1871, *DDF,* I, 113, no. 95; Arnim to Bismarck, Paris, Dec. 11, 1871, Goldschmidt, pp. 268–269, no. 150.

115. Villefort, I, 89–98 and II, 201–202, no. 15. See also Goldschmidt, pp. 269–285, no. 152.

116. *Annales,* VI, 486.

117. Villefort, I, 102–104. The Reichstag was not in session at this time. The convention had called for its ratification, on behalf of Germany, by the emperor. However, on January 8 the Bundesrat resolved to concur in the convention and the closing protocol (*Bundesrat minutes,* 1872, pp. 2–3, no. 4).

118. The commission charged with fixing the new diocesan boundaries, following two papal decrees of July 1874, issued its final protocol on October 7, 1874 (Villefort, IV, 140–141, no. 28). The ratification of the

final convention of the frontier delimitation commission was exchanged at Metz on May 31, 1877 (*ibid.*, p. 100, no. 19). The so-called "mixed commission of liquidation of Strassburg," which dealt primarily with financial affairs, met from May 28, 1872 until July 1, 1878 (*ibid.*, V, 293–301).

XI

The Convention of June 29, 1872

IN SPITE OF THE RE-ESTABLISHMENT of full diplomatic relations between France and Germany, Thiers left Saint Vallier at Manteuffel's headquarters, ostensibly to deal with matters concerning the occupation.[1] One suspects, however, that there were less prosaic reasons for maintaining the mission at Nancy, for the Manteuffel connection was a potentially valuable channel of communication with Berlin. Saint Vallier warned Thiers that Manteuffel's "sane" views were too often cancelled at Berlin by what he called Arnim's "preconceived hostility" toward France.[2] That the Manteuffel connection did still have value was indicated late in January when the general returned from a visit to Berlin with the news that a reconciliation had been effected between Bismarck and himself.[3]

On his return from Berlin Manteuffel also told Saint Vallier that the German government would welcome a total evacuation of France if an adequate guarantee could be found as a substitute for the territories then held as a guarantee of payment. He said that if Germany could feel secure about French internal affairs she would be ready to open negotiations on this subject in May or June.[4]

This idea was not entirely new for somewhat earlier Bleichröder, who often served as Bismarck's intermediary in financial affairs, had hinted as much to Gontaut-Biron.[5] This coincided exactly with Thiers's own thinking and, apparently encouraged by such broad hints, he instructed Gontaut to stress that France was willing to give concrete demonstration of her desire for peace by paying her debts promptly and even by anticipating them. He warned Gontaut not to raise the issue prematurely but said that if he were asked what France meant by "anticipating" he was to say that after May, 1872, when France would have paid the 650,000,000 francs due under her treaty obligations, she would then be willing to negotiate for payment of the last three billion francs before 1874 when that sum would be due.[6] He wrote in the same vein to Saint Vallier, who reported that Manteuffel had passed these ideas along to Berlin.[7]

Bismarck refused to be drawn into a conversation when Gontaut brought the matter up at a social affair. In a subsequent visit, however, Bleichröder assured Gontaut that Bismarck did wish to see negotiations open and awaited only an opening on the part of France.[8] Thiers instructed Gontaut to be agreeable to any financial plan acceptable to the Germans. France would be ready to negotiate in May, he said.[9]

All of this talk of anticipated payments was a clear indication of France's remarkable economic recovery and Thiers was prepared to back his words with cash for he had on hand funds sufficient to pay immediately the 650,000,000 francs due on May 1. He was anxious to arrange for this payment, the prelude to the larger negotiations, for Arnim was about to leave for Berlin on February 28. The night before Arnim's departure he, Thiers, and Pouyer-Quertier agreed to a convention by which France would pay in the first week of March the sum due on May 1.[10] Thiers took advantage of the meeting to broach the subject of anticipating payment of the last three billion francs of the indemnity. In reality he proposed only a partial anticipation, for his scheme called for France to borrow the sum from leading European bankers to pay to Germany at the rate of 100,000,000 francs per month for thirty months or, if possible, for thirty-six months. This would have extended the terminal date for payment of the war indemnity from 1874 until 1875. In return, he wished a promise of complete evacuation of France. Arnim promised to present the plan to Bismarck.[11] Thiers made it clear to Arnim that he did not intend to enter into formal negotiations until he had on hand the means to carry them through to a successful conclusion.[12] He now felt that April would be the earliest that he could expect to launch the scheme.

Arnim's stay in Berlin was to be a brief one for he was to leave almost immediately for Rome and a special mission to the Vatican. Within hours of his arrival in Berlin the shadowy Bleichröder called on Gontaut to say that Bismarck was anxious to receive the French proposals and to negotiate the matter with the ambassador. He also pointed out that there was little to hope for so long as France insisted on total evacuation, for the German government was disposed to accept only progressive evacuation in proportion to actual payments. Gontaut, who had received no instructions on the subject, merely pointed out that the preliminary peace treaty did not say that France would be evacuated *only* when the three billions had been paid but that Germany would consider *replacing* the territorial guarantee of partial occupation by a financial guarantee.[13]

Manteuffel, too, urged Thiers to open negotiations. He felt that Pouyer-Quertier would be the proper person to undertake the task. When Pouyer's resignation as finance minister ruled that out, Manteuffel sent word to Thiers that anyone, even Gontaut, of whom the general had a very low opinion, would be well received at Berlin if he came armed with specific proposals. He claimed to have it on good authority that Bismarck wished to be able to present the French proposals to the Reichstag when it met during the second week in April.[14]

Thiers was not to be rushed in his plans, however, and a part of his plan consisted of a diplomatic offensive designed to bring pressure on Germany to hasten the evacuation of France. He told Le Flô, the ambassador at St. Petersburg, to make a special effort to persuade the czar "that he should influence his uncle in the direction of evacuation."[15] Le Flô was persistent in his efforts until finally Gorchakov drove him away by telling him an anecdote about a losing gambler whose lamentations slowed the game, whereupon another player told him: "Payez d'abord et lamentez-vous après."[16]

By the middle of April it was becoming apparent that Thiers's plans had gone awry. He was now ready to negotiate but the Germans seemed to be dragging their feet. Arnim had returned to Berlin but was showing no disposition to return to Paris. On April 11 Thiers complained that the state of the international money market was such that France must soon make her plans if she wished to obtain a large loan and he must know if Bismarck intended to follow up the discussions recently begun and, if so, when. He instructed Gontaut to see either Arnim or Bismarck but he also told Gontaut to take care not to act as though he had been chosen to conduct the negotiations for, he said, Bismarck "has always let me know that this business should pass between him and me by an intermediary to be designated by him."[17] Three days later, acting under the influence of a warning from Manteuffel to avoid dealing with Arnim,[18] Thiers again wrote to Gontaut, instructing him to go directly to Bismarck and saying that he would deal where and with whom Bismarck wished.[19] Apparently before receiving this second letter, Gontaut saw Arnim on April 15. Arnim said that Thiers's proposals would be seriously discussed upon his return to his post but he was vague about his plans to leave for Paris. He said that Germany was anxious to open the negotiations and wished to conclude them before the end of June.[20] Rather pointedly Arnim said that France and Germany should negotiate "without the aid of foreign powers."[21]

When they heard of this conversation Thiers and Rémusat reversed themselves yet again and gave Gontaut freedom "to proceed *when* and as you would wish" in opening the negotiations.[22] This was precisely what Manteuffel had warned against. He thought that Arnim was the last person Gontaut should have seen because he was convinced that Arnim was trying to keep the negotiations in his own hands. To lend credence to his arguments he showed Saint Vallier a letter dated April 17—two days *after* the conversation between Arnim and Gontaut—in which Bismarck expressed concern over France's silence and wondered if France had changed her mind about opening negotiations. Again Manteuffel urged strongly that Gontaut deal only with Bismarck. He also sent Bismarck a telegram reassuring him as to Thiers's desire to negotiate.[23]

Thiers immediately instructed Gontaut to get in touch directly with Bismarck to try to set the matter in motion.[24] Gontaut, who must by this time have been thoroughly confused, dutifully followed instructions and requested an interview with Bismarck.[25] When after several days he had heard absolutely nothing from Bismarck, he was sufficiently irritated to consider declining an interview should one now be offered.[26] Gontaut was none too convinced of the wisdom of the negotiations in any case and, after the bewildering reversals in his instructions and the assurances that Bismarck was eagerly waiting to hear from him, one can understand his annoyance at the silence which greeted his request for an interview. Nevertheless, a rupture at the very outset of negotiations was precisely what Thiers did not want, and Rémusat instructed Gontaut to forget his personal feelings and to accept quickly any proferred interview.[27]

The fact was that by late April Bismarck had apparently decided to handle the negotiations at Paris. Arnim arrived in Paris on April 30 and saw Thiers at Versailles on May 2. In the ensuing conversations Thiers spelled out for Arnim his plan to borrow three billion francs from European bankers, the sum to be payable directly to the German government at the rate of one hundred million francs per month for thirty months beginning during the summer of 1872. In return he asked an end to the occupation of France. If, he said, Germany wished to divide the evacuation into two parts, then it would be necessary to divide the financial arrangement into two parts as well.[28]

Bismarck considered the scheme unacceptable. He indicated what he considered an adequate compensation for a rapid evacuation: payment of one billion francs by France over a period of eight to ten months plus the deposit of non-French bills of exchange for the remaining two billion francs. In addition, he said that Belfort at least should remain occupied until final payment of the debt and the regions to be evacuated should be constituted militarily neutral areas. He told Arnim to continue to explore the subject but to accept any new suggestions by Thiers only *ad referendum* since the emperor, who preferred territorial guarantees, had so far refused to give authorization for Arnim to negotiate on any basis at all.[29]

One source of trouble in this matter lay in differing interpretations of the peace treaty. Article VII of the treaty of Frankfort said that the last three billion francs should be payable on March 2, 1874. It became apparent during these conversations in 1872 that Germany considered that the sum should be paid *by* that date and that the occupation could continue until it was paid regardless of how long the payment might take. The French view was that France owed nothing *until* March 2, 1874 and Thiers contended that any attempt by Germany to prolong the occupation beyond that date "would be contested by Europe. . . . If France were to begin payment of her debt on March 1, 1874 and proceeded to this payment with all the speed permitted by circumstances, nothing more could be asked."[30] Given these two interpretations, the French contended that their willingness to pay in advance a debt not due for two years was a real concession to Germany in return for which they expected some equivalent compensation in the form of the evacuation of the occupied territory. The Germans contended that when France paid in advance on the sum due two years hence they were only doing what their treaty obligations and prudence dictated if France were to be fully evacuated by March 2, 1874 and, while they were willing to discuss at least a partial evacuation of France before that date they insisted on some guarantee or compensation which, according to their lights, they did not already have.

As the negotiations dragged on into May without making any real progress tempers grew short. The French were annoyed with Arnim, and Bismarck was no less irritated with them, not least because of Thiers's efforts "at St. Petersburg and Vienna to have 'Europe' engage in a diplomatic action against us."[31]

On May 17 Thiers offered Arnim a plan which he felt to be more in keeping with German thinking: to raise one billion francs by loan, a second billion to be raised by lottery in Germany, the third being covered by "foreign securities of recognized stability." In return, he expected evacuation to be "carried out as soon as payment is effected."[32]

On May 25 Bismarck instructed Arnim to have Thiers send an official proposal through Gontaut. He was tired of dealing with both Thiers and Rémusat, and the confidential nature of the negotiations thus far allowed the French to disavow them whenever they wished.[33] The same day Arnim had an interview with Thiers at the Elysée Palace. Thiers agreed that the negotiations must now be placed on an official footing and wrote out a resumé of his proposals. The financial aspects were essentially the same as his plan of May 17. However, he had now abandoned his demand for complete evacuation of France. Instead he now asked evacuation of two of the last six departments after payment of the first, third, and sixth half-billion francs.[34] In spite of Bismarck's instructions Arnim did not insist that Thiers send this offer to Gontaut but sent it to Bismarck himself.[35]

Although the emperor was reluctant to give up the occupation, by June 1 he had approved the idea of gradual evacuation in return for gradual payment of the war indemnity. Bismarck said that Thiers's idea of evacuating two departments for each billion paid was acceptable, but he said that the evacuated departments must be neutralized and Germany must retain the right of reoccupation in the event of nonpayment of the remainder. He insisted, too, that Germany must retain Belfort and the departments of Meurthe-et-Moselle and Meuse until final payment. He was less happy about Thiers's financial schemes. He refused to allow a lottery loan to be issued in Germany, and he emphasized that he wished to remain aloof from France's negotiations with European bankers because involvement in such negotiations would furnish a means of bringing pressure on Germany to favor France so as to facilitate payment of the war indemnity.[36] In spite of the fact that Thiers's latest proposals had served to narrow considerably the gap which divided the two sides it was not until June 11 that Gontaut was told that France could assume as accepted at least the principles of progressive payment in advance and proportionate evacuation.[37]

The following day Arnim was instructed to proceed with the negotiations. His instructions were specific and he presented Germany's terms to Thiers on June 14. Essentially they were a return to Thiers's original plan but with the important difference of partial rather than full evacuation. One billion francs would be paid by February 1, 1873, in return for which the departments of Haute-Marne and Marne would be evacuated. The second billion would be paid by January 1, 1874, and the Ardennes and Vosges departments would be evacuated. The third billion would be paid by March 2, 1875. In return for allowing France this one year deferment in paying the last billion Germany demanded as a guarantee of its payment the deposit into her treasury of an equivalent sum in non-French negotiable securities. With their redemption would come evacuation of Belfort and the departments of Meuse and Meurthe-et-Moselle. The evacuated departments were to be neutralized and Germany was given the right of reoccupation in the event of nonfulfillment. It was also provided that, although the number of departments occupied would be reduced, the size of the army of occupation would remain the same.[38]

On June 15 Thiers journeyed to Paris to see Arnim and expressed a desire to have a personal interview with Bismarck in order to facilitate conclusion of an agreement. He said that in general he subscribed to the German proposals but then he raised a number of objections. He had hoped, he said, for a more rapid evacuation and he felt that Germany could without risk evacuate all of France upon payment of one and one-half billion francs. He said that he could now give assurances that the first billion would be paid in December 1872 and the second before the end of 1873 but he would find it difficult to arrange for the deposit of non-French securities. Thiers was especially anxious to have the two Marne departments evacuated after the payment of one-half billion rather than one billion as proposed by Bismarck, and Arnim gave him reason for hope on this score. Bismarck had insisted on holding two departments and Belfort until the last of the indemnity had been paid and Arnim now suggested that if Thiers would accept this view they could reconsider the substitution of a financial guarantee for those areas after two billion francs had been paid. Thiers agreed in principle.[39]

On June 18, from Varzin, Bismarck replied to Arnim's letter about this interview. He felt that an interview with Thiers would be fruitless. He said that it had been difficult enough to persuade the emperor to agree to the principle of gradual evacuation in return for gradual payment of the indemnity without trying to gain his approval of yet further German concessions. Because Thiers had been particularly concerned about the payment of the last billion Bismarck suggested that it would facilitate negotiations if they could defer discussion about that for the moment and concentrate instead on payment of the first two billion since he was not prepared to commit himself without the advice of his financial experts.[40]

Meanwhile the French had followed up Thiers's visit to Arnim by producing a draft treaty embodying their ideas.[41] The first article said that the three billion francs' indemnity would be "discharged by means of a loan contracted by France" but said nothing about it being paid directly to Germany. In response to Arnim's questions about this Rémusat said that to word the article in such fashion would exclude the possibility of raising the sum by public subscription, for the public obviously could not pay directly to the German treasury. Since France had found public subscription to be the "most powerful and surest method" of raising the necessary sums, the question of calling in Europe's bankers would become necessary only with payment of the third billion or its guarantees.[42] France proposed that the first half-billion francs should be paid "within two months of the ratification of the present convention," fifteen days after which the Haute-Marne and Marne departments should be evacuated. She further proposed to pay the second and third half-billion during 1873, the fourth on March 1, 1874, and the fifth and sixth by March 1, 1875. According to her scheme Germany would evacuate the departments of Vosges and Ardennes after payment of the third half-billion. This would leave occupied only the departments of Meurthe and Meuse and Belfort until the last billion francs should have been paid, but France reserved the right to furnish "after the discharge of the fourth half-billion securities or bankers' guarantees which . . . shall be substituted for the territorial guarantee, if they are accepted and recognized by Germany as sufficient." The proposed Article VII said that as the departments were evacuated the size of the occupation forces in the remaining departments should be reduced proportionately. Arnim made it clear that this was unacceptable but Rémusat told him that Thiers had inserted it mainly for the record and would not insist on it if Germany objected too strenuously.[43] France agreed to neutralize the evacuated departments and recognized Germany's right of reoccupation "if the financial engagements entered into were not completely fulfilled." Arnim questioned this limitation to violations of financial engagements only but he was assured that this could easily be remedied according to his wishes.

Arnim forwarded the French proposals to Berlin and received from the foreign office on June 25 a draft convention which had already received the emperor's approval. Arnim was authorized to sign a convention in conformity with it if France would agree to its terms. On June 27 Arnim presented the convention to Thiers. There were actually few major differences between the two drafts and on June 29 an agreement was signed. Except for the preamble, which Arnim changed because of Thiers's wish to be named specifically, the German proposals were the ones followed.[44]

Article I provided that France should pay one half-billion francs two months after the exchange of ratifications. The French had proposed to pay at any time *during* the two month period, which was too imprecise for the Germans. The second half-billion francs were to be paid on February 1, 1873. The second billion was to be paid on March 1, 1874 and the third was payable on March 1, 1875. It was provided that any or all of the last three payments might be anticipated in whole or in part.

Article III stated that the Marne and Haute-Marne departments should be evacuated two weeks after payment of one half-billion francs, the Ardennes and Vosges two weeks after payment of the second billion, and the Meuse and Meurthe, as well as the canton of Belfort, two weeks after payment of the third billion. Article IV gave France the right to substitute, "after the payment of two billions . . . financial guarantees which . . . shall be substituted for the territorial guarantees, if they are accepted and recognized as sufficient by Germany." Article VI provided that "in case" the size of the occupation forces should be reduced, the amount of their maintenance should be reduced proportionately. Articles VII and VIII neutralized the evacuated departments and gave Germany the right to reoccupy "in case of the nonfulfillment of the engagement entered into." The French stipulation of "financial" engagements was, therefore, dropped.

France attached great importance to the treaty and when Rémusat presented it to the assembly on July 1 he assured them that its adoption would "consolidate peace and secure our independence."[45] The assembly voted to send the treaty to committee for consideration the following day.[46] On July 6 the committee's brief report was read by the Duke of Broglie. He said that the government had assured the committee that it would build barracks in the departments whose evacuation would be delayed to prevent billeting of German troops on the people of the last occupied places. Thus "the good of one part of our compatriots" would not become "the misfortune of another." The committee "unanimously" recommended ratification of the treaty, and the assembly proceeded to vote immediately. There were only four dissenting votes.[47] The Reichstag was not in session at this time, but was not called upon to take any action on the treaty. The Bundesrat, on July 5, simply took notice of the deposit of the special convention with France under the printed papers of that body.[48] Ratifications of the treaty were exchanged at Paris on July 7, 1872.

Just four days after the exchange of ratifications, Thiers's government asked the assembly for permission to borrow a sum "necessary to produce a capital of three billion" francs. The assembly gave its approval on July 15. On July 20 the government announced the terms of the loan: a public sale of bonds at $84\frac{1}{2}$. The day before the loan Thiers signed a contract with a group of European banking houses by the terms of which the bankers guaranteed the subscription of the loan and put at the disposal of France some 700,000,000 in coin to be used to pay Germany. When the subscription opened it was an even more spectacular success than the loan of 1871 had been.

The subscription amounted to 43,900,000,000 francs in capital, of which France refused forty billion.[49]

Scarcely was the convention of June 29 signed than the French government began to receive complaints from departmental officials about the unpleasant prospect of having larger numbers of occupation troops crowded into the last four departments and being billeted on the inhabitants. Since the new barracks which the government had promised the assembly it would build could not be ready in time for the mid-September evacuation date, it was agreed that the evacuation of the departments of Marne and Haute-Marne should be delayed until the barracks were finished, so as to work no hardship on the inhabitants of the four last departments.[50]

All in all 1872 had been a good year for France in her relations with Germany. In spite of the last minute hitch in plans, the occupation had been reduced when in November the two departments of the Marne were finally evacuated. One minor point of unfinished business was cleared away in August when the boundary commission signed two conventions fixing the Franco-German border in the communes of Raon-les-Leau, Raon-sur-Plaine and Avricourt.[51] Financially the picture was extremely bright. The public loan of the summer had been a spectacular success. Before the end of December France finished paying the third billion francs of the war indemnity and Thiers told Arnim that the fourth billion would probably be paid by March 1, 1873 and, in any case, by July 1.[52]

Thiers was well aware that Arnim was pessimistic about both the longevity and the goodwill of both him and his government. To offset this he had the satisfaction in September, when the emperors of Germany, Austria-Hungary, and Russia had gathered in Berlin, of having William I, Bismarck, and Moltke all go out of their way to assure Gontaut-Biron of their goodwill toward France in general and Thiers in particular.[52] As 1873 came in Thiers had reason to be satisfied with his achievements and his prospects.

NOTES TO CHAPTER XI

1. Thiers to Saint Vallier, Versailles, Jan. 11, 1872, *DDF,* I, 124–125, no. 107.
2. Saint Vallier to Thiers, Nancy, Jan. 12, 1872, *Occ. et lib.,* I, 115–121, no. 61.
3. Saint Vallier to Thiers, Nancy, Jan. 25, 1872, *ibid.,* pp. 129–137, no. 65.
4. *Ibid.*
5. Vicomte de Gontaut-Biron, *Ma mission en Allemagne, 1872–1873* (Paris: 1906), pp. 63–66.
6. Thiers to Gontaut-Biron, Jan. 28, 1872, *Occ. et lib.,* I, 138–144, no. 67; Gontaut-Biron, pp. 67–68.
7. Thiers to Saint Vallier, Jan. 29, 1872, *Occ. et lib.,* I 144–150, no. 68; Saint Vallier to Thiers, Nancy, Jan. 30, 1872, *ibid.,* pp.150–156, no. 69.
8. Gontaut-Biron to Rémusat, Berlin, Feb. 8, 1872, *ibid.,* pp. 156–162, no. 70; Gontaut-Biron, pp. 86–87.
9. Thiers to Gontaut-Biron, Versailles, Feb. 12, 1872, *Occ. et lib.,* I, 168–171, no. 75; Gontaut-Biron, pp. 87–88.
10. Villefort, I, 125–126.
11. Arnim to Bismarck, Berlin, Mar. 3, 1872, GA, Frankreich, no. 70, 131–132: 71–76.
12. Thiers to Gontaut-Biron, Versailles, Mar. 7, 1872, *Occ. et lib.,* I, 207–211, no. 88.
13. Gontaut-Biron to Thiers, Berlin, Mar. 2, 1872, *DDF,* I, 132–133, no. 113; Gontaut-Biron, p. 88.
14. Saint Vallier to Thiers, Nancy, Mar. 7, 1872, *Occ. et lib.,* I, 204–207, no. 87; Saint Vallier to Thiers, Nancy, Mar. 18, 1872, *ibid.,* pp. 217–223, no. 92.
15. Thiers to Le Flô, Versailles, Mar. 8, 1872, Bouniols, pp. 166–169.
16. Reuss to Bismarck, St. Petersburg, April 10, 1872, GA, Frankreich, no. 70, 132–133: 8; Busch, *Bismarck,* II, 59–60.
17. Thiers to Gontaut-Biron, April 11, 1872, *Occ. et lib.,* I, 241–244, no. 100.
18. Saint Vallier to Thiers, Nancy, April 12, 1872, *ibid.,* pp. 245–248, no. 101.
19. Thiers to Gontaut-Biron, Versailles, April 14, 1872, *ibid.,* pp.249–253, no. 102.
20. Gontaut-Biron to Rémusat, Berlin, April 16, 1872, *ibid.,* pp. 254–262, no. 104.
21. Gontaut-Biron to Rémusat, Berlin, April 19, 1872, MAE, CP

(Allemagne), 5: 432–435; Gontaut-Biron to Thiers, Berlin, April 20, 1872, *Occ. et lib.,* I, 277–281, no. 122.

22. Thiers to Gontaut-Biron, Versailles, April 18, 1872, *DDF,* I, 141–143, no. 122; Rémusat to Gontaut-Biron, Versailles, April 19, 1872, MAE, CP (Allemagne), 5: 428–431.

23. Saint Vallier to Thiers, Nancy, April 22, 1872, *Occ. et lib.,* I, 283–289, no. 114.

24. Thiers to Gontaut-Biron, Versailles, April 24, 1872, *ibid.,* pp. 303–304, no. 120. Gontaut was by no means convinced of the wisdom of speeding the indemnity payment because he felt that Bismarck, free of treaty obligations, might consider beginning the war again to distract attention from internal difficulties. Too, he felt that France might become so preoccupied with internal matters that she would isolate herself (Gontaut-Biron, p. 90, fn. 1).

25. Gontaut-Biron to Rémusat, Berlin, April 24, 1872, MAE, CP (Allemagne), 5: 453–357.

26. Gontaut-Biron to Rémusat, Berlin, April 28, 1872, *ibid.,* fol. 502.

27. Rémusat to Gontaut-Biron, Versailles, April 29, 1872, *ibid.,* fol. 503.

28. This account of the exchange at the beginning of May has been drawn from several sources: Arnim to Bismarck, Paris, May 6, 1872, *PEA,* I, 115–119, nos. 81 and 82; Thiers, *Memoirs,* pp. 341–345, appendices, nos. 8 and 9; *DDF,* I, 152–155, nos. 128–129.

29. Bismarck to Arnim, Berlin, May 12, 1872, *PEA,* I, 120–121, no. 84.

30. Arnim to Bismarck, Paris, May 11, 1872, *ibid.,* pp. 119–120, no. 83.

31. Bismarck to Arnim, Berlin, May 17, 1872, *ibid.,* pp. 125–126, no. 88.

32. Thiers to Arnim, Versailles, May 17, 1872, Thiers, *Memoirs,* pp. 346–348, appendix no. 12; *DDF,* I, 156–158, no. 132; *PEA,* I, 123–125, no. 87.

33. Thile to Arnim, Berlin, May 25, 1872, *PEA,* I, 126, no. 89.

34. Thiers to Arnim, Paris, May 25, 1872, Thiers, *Memoirs,* pp. 349–350, appendix no. 14; *Occ. et lib.,* I, 347–348, no. 136.

35. Arnim to Bismarck, Paris, May 26, 1872, *PEA,* I, 127–130, nos. 90–91.

36. Bismarck to Thile, Varzin, June 1, 1872, *ibid.,* pp. 130–131, no. 92.

37. Gontaut-Biron to Thiers, Berlin, June 11, 1872, MAE, CP (Allemagne), 6: 183–184.

38. Arnim to Thiers, Paris, June 14, 1872, Thiers, *Memoirs,* pp. 355–356, Appendix no. 17; *DDF,* I, 162–163, no. 136.

39. Arnim to Bismarck, Paris, June 15, 1872, *PEA,* I, 133–135, no. 94.

40. Bismarck to Arnim, Varzin, June 18, 1872, *ibid.,* pp. 135–138, no. 95.

41. Draft convention of June 16, 1872, MAE, CP (Allemagne), 6: 246–248. For text of draft convention of June 18 see *PEA,* I, 140–142, no. 97; *GP,* I, 140–141, no. 85; *DDF,* I, 164–166, no. 139; Thiers, *Memoirs,* pp. 362–364, Appendix no. 21. Thiers's *Memoirs* contain, in

addition, a note of June 17 from Henckel von Donnersmarck to Thiers suggesting a proposed convention (pp. 359–360, Appendix no. 19), as well as a draft convention submitted to the French on June 18 (pp. 361–362, Appendix no. 20).

42. Rémusat to Arnim, Versailles, June 20, 1872, MAE, CP (Allemagne), 6: 253–258.

43. Arnim to Delbrück, Paris, June 19, 1872, *PEA,* I, 138–140, no. 96.

44. Arnim to Delbrück, Paris, June 29, 1872, *ibid.,* pp. 143–144, no. 100.

45. *Annales,* XII, 633–634; *Annual Register,* 1872, I, 187; Charles de Rémusat, "Les débuts de M. de Rémusat au Ministère des Affaires Etrangères (Extrait de ses Mémoires inédits)," in *Revue d'histoire diplomatique,* 1931, XLV, 185–186.

46. *Annales,* XII, 634.

47. *Ibid.,* pp. 723–725.

48. *Bundesrat minutes,* 1872, p. 296, no. 445.

49. Hanotaux, I, 478–482.

50. Rémusat to Montgascon, chargé at Berlin, Versailles, Aug. 21, 1872, *DDF,* I, 176, no. 150.

51. Villefort, IV, 79–82, nos. 10 and 11.

52. Arnim to Delbrück, Paris, Dec. 10, 1872, *PEA,* I, 158, no. 122.

53. Gontaut-Biron to Rémusat, Berlin, Sept. 14, 1872, *DDF,* I, 184–188, no. 156.

XII

The Convention of March 15, 1873

By mid-January 1873 Thiers was sufficiently optimistic about France's financial situation that he was ready to open negotiations with a view to substituting financial guarantees for payment of the last billion francs, thereby ending the occupation before 1875.

Thiers raised the question in conversation with Arnim and was pleased to find that Arnim seemed eager to pursue the subject.[1] However, when Gontaut-Biron broached the same subject at Berlin, Bleichröder, who professed to speak for Bismarck, discouraged him from pursuing the matter.[2] Thiers was confused by this puzzling reception of his offer and told Gontaut to try discreetly to discover the reason for Berlin's apparent hesitancy about opening negotiations.[3]

Gontaut was unable to shed any light on the matter other than the information, which he said he had on good authority, that the objections to such negotiations came from a source other than Bismarck and that Bismarck wanted to defer the negotiations until he had overcome "dispositions which must be modified."[4]

In view of the fact that the Emperor William had always been reluctant to substitute financial guarantees for territory already occupied it requires no great stretch of the imagination to see that Gontaut's anonymous informer probably was referring to the emperor as the source of the delay. A conversation with His Majesty in late January did serve to convince Gontaut that this was so.[5]

Thiers had come to the conclusion that Berlin was displeased that he had tried to negotiate with Arnim.[6] He was apparently reassured by Gontaut's opinion that the emperor was the real source of trouble and early in February he arranged a meeting with Arnim in order to pursue the matter further. Thiers said that France expected to complete payment of the second billion (the fourth of the entire indemnity) before the middle of May. Under the terms of the convention of June 29 she would then be entitled to demand the evacuation of the departments of Vosges and Ardennes. He hoped that Germany would see fit to reduce the occupation army instead of crowding its full complement of fifty thousand men into the two departments of Meuse and Meurthe. He was prepared to forego insistence on evacuation of the Vosges and Ardennes in May in order to spare the inhabitants of the last two departments from having to support fifty thousand men. In return for this he asked that Germany evacuate all four departments in July since, in any event, France's financial situation would permit payment of the last billion during September and Germany would then be forced to evacuate the departments.[7]

Arnim reported the conversation to Bismarck but he omitted an element in the proposals: Thiers's willingness to negotiate on the basis of leaving the departments of Vosges and Ardennes occupied for a specified period beyond payment of the fourth billion if, in return, Germany would evacuate all four departments before complete payment of the fifth billion.[8] Arnim also proposed to Bismarck a complicated plan whereby Belfort alone would be held until the very last moment, while the four evacuated departments would be neutralized until March

1874 with Germany retaining the right of reoccupation. Characteristically, his reason was that pressure on France could thus be maintained for a longer time and would give Germany a weapon in the event of a change of governments in France. He felt that any such change would probably lead to irregularity in payment of the war indemnity and that would in turn furnish the pretext for reoccupation. The alternative as he saw it was that Thiers would pay off the fifth billion by August and Germany would then have to evacuate France while retaining no influence at all in that country.[9]

Bismarck was in no way disposed to accept Thiers's proposals as forwarded by Arnim. He said that unless Thiers would allow the Vosges and Ardennes to remain occupied after payment of the fourth billion, the occupation army would simply have to be concentrated in the Meuse and Meurthe departments until the fifth billion should be paid.[10]

Meanwhile Bismarck had received from Manteuffel the gist of Thiers's proposals as he had sent them to Saint Vallier. Bismarck proceeded to apprise Manteuffel of an "important point of divergence" between the information received from Arnim and that which reached him from Nancy, and he told Manteuffel to clarify the matter.[11] Manteuffel immediately suggested that Thiers use his headquarters as the proper channel for making it very clear to Bismarck that Arnim had not reproduced his ideas correctly. He further suggested that after each interview with Arnim Thiers send a resumé of the conversation to Gontaut to enable him to combat any further erroneous reports from Arnim.[12]

Thiers was quick to take advantage of Manteuffel's offer. In a letter of February 23 he said that France could promise to pay all of the last billion francs of the indemnity by September 1, 1873. He was prepared to prolong the German occupation of Vosges and Ardennes for two months if in return

Germany would speed up by two months the evacuation of Meuse, Meurthe-et-Moselle and Belfort.[13]

This second offer received a different reception from the first, erroneous one. On March 1 Gontaut dined at Bismarck's home. Bismarck said that he had submitted Thiers's proposals to the emperor and that he hoped shortly to obtain permission to evacuate all of France, excepting only the canton of Belfort, on July 1. Belfort he proposed to hold until payment of the entire five billion francs.[14]

Bismarck was as good as his word and on March 3 he sent to Arnim a draft convention which reflected the emperor's thoughts on the question of the evacuation. It proposed that the fifth billion would be paid in four equal installments on June 1, July 1, August 1, and September 1, 1873. Upon payment of the July 1 installment the emperor would give the order to evacuate the four remaining departments within four weeks. Belfort alone would remain occupied, and it would be evacuated upon payment of the remaining principal and interest due on September 1, 1873. The evacuated departments must be neutralized, and France must agree to erect no new fortifications there. Bismarck instructed Arnim that he could ask for neutralization until March 1, 1874, as Arnim himself had earlier suggested, since that would certainly be in Germany's interests if it could be obtained. In addition, Germany wished to retain the right to reoccupy the evacuated departments should France not keep her engagements taken in the convention.[15]

Arnim received these instructions on March 4. The following day he went to Versailles to see Thiers. Thiers was ill at the time and he asked only for the general outline of Bismarck's terms. Thiers complained of the reservation concerning Belfort and of the delay in evacuation of the four departments after July 1. He said that while he did not attach too much importance to these reservations they did furnish a weapon which his enemies could use against him.[16] Thiers's arguments apparently made an impression on Arnim for he stressed to Bismarck that the French placed an almost "legendary importance" on Belfort and he asked if it might not be possible, since that fortress could not be given up until complete payment, to evacuate the four departments between May 15 and June 15, for this would be of great help to Thiers.[17] In reply, Bismarck angrily told Arnim to hew more closely to his instructions. His proposals were a matter of "take it or leave it," and any variation of them he considered unacceptable. He instructed Arnim to present the German demands in their entirety.[18]

Before receiving Bismarck's reply Arnim went to Versailles to see Thiers. Thiers presented him with a proposed convention. It proposed that the sums remaining due to Germany should be paid in six installments falling due on the 5th of each month, beginning in April and ending in September. The evacuation of the four departments was to be completed between July 1 and July 5. Thiers wished inserted in the convention a special clause to the effect that Belfort would be evacuated simultaneously with the payment of the final sums due in September. The convention accepted the principle of neutralization of the evacuated departments and the German right of reoccupation.[19] Thiers rejected, however, Arnim's request for neutralization of the evacuated departments for six months after Belfort's evacuation, comparing it to the restrictions which Napoleon had placed on Prussia.[20]

Bismarck was thoroughly annoyed and worried over what he considered the lack of response to his proposals. He asked Gontaut to call on him in an effort to get to the bottom of the affair. Gontaut found the chancellor "preoccupied and very annoyed" at having received no reply to his proposals. His annoyance was directed at Arnim rather than at the French, however. He said that it had not been easy to gain the emperor's acceptance of the idea of the negotiations and he felt that Arnim's delays threatened the entire affair. Gontaut was unable to shed any light on the delays other than to suggest that Thiers's illness and the press of duty had probably prevented Arnim from seeing the president. Bismarck was unimpressed with this argument and said that Arnim could always have dealt with Rémusat if Thiers were unable to handle the matter. Gontaut took advantage of the opportunity to protest the retention of Belfort after July 1 to guarantee the payment of only a portion of one billion francs. Bismarck, "smiling," put him off with a remark that one could always see about that later. To Gontaut this raised the possibility of a softening of Bismarck's attitude. Gontaut urged Thiers to send immediately his response to Bismarck's offers.[21]

Thiers did send Gontaut his propositions as stated earlier to Arnim. He also said that he was prepared to lengthen the occupation of the four departments until August 1 and advance the payment of the indemnity from September 1 to August 1 if he could thereby secure the evacuation of Belfort and the departments simultaneously.[22]

Bismarck's concern over the slow pace of the negotiations and his alarm over the state of Thiers's health were reflected in a letter which he sent to Manteuffel. He also sent a copy of his proposals and told Manteuffel to take the matter up directly with Saint Vallier.[23] Saint Vallier forwarded the German proposals to Versailles. Thiers replied that this was the first knowledge he had that Germany had formulated a definite set of proposals. He immediately told Saint Vallier that he would withdraw his own draft convention and would accept Bismarck's proposals with three reservations only: there must be a statement of the size of the garrison to be left at Belfort, the evacuation of Belfort must be ten days after final payment of the indemnity, and the evacuation of the four last departments must take place within two weeks after payment of one-half billion francs on July 1 rather than the four weeks specified by Bismarck.[24]

Before word of this had reached either Gontaut or Bismarck the two men had met once again. Gontaut mentioned Thiers's plan to extend the occupation until August 1 if all of France would be evacuated at that time. Bismarck was noncommital on this point since it would involve France paying part of the last billion in Bank of France notes. Bismarck told Gontaut to see Delbrück on such financial matters and said that if they met with his approval then would be time enough to try to gain the emperor's consent. Gontaut then presented Thiers's counterproposals. Again Bismarck was noncommittal. He did say that four weeks was the minimum time necessary to permit the evacuation of France and that it would be impossible to promise payment and evacuation at the same time. He promised to take the plan under consideration and to let Gontaut know his answer within a week. Then, rather to Gontaut's surprise, Bismarck asked if Thiers would prefer to have Toul or Verdun substituted for Belfort as the last occupied point in France. Gontaut said that he would have to have new instructions on this point.[25]

Shortly after returning from this meeting with Bismarck Gontaut received word from Paris telling him not to insist on Thiers's counterproposals but instead to accept Bismarck's offer with the reservations which Thiers had already indicated in his reply to Saint Vallier.[26] When they met again the following afternoon Gontaut was able to tell Bismarck that it now seemed possible to reach agreement with little difficulty. He did tell Bismarck that he had been ordered to accept the substitution of Verdun for Belfort. Bismarck, who had raised the question, said that he would have to get the permission of the emperor to this substitution.[27]

Thiers and Rémusat were now quite prepared to have Gontaut sign an agreement with Bismarck. Thiers sent Gontaut credentials authorizing him to sign a convention, together with instructions to be accommodating about the size of the German garrison of Verdun as well as the territory to be attached to that fortress for purposes of the occupation.[28] Rémusat hoped that the signing would take place at Berlin rather than at Paris because he did not want to have to deal with Arnim any more.[29]

Rémusat was mistaken if he thought that he had seen the last of Arnim. On March 12 Bismarck had *ordered* Arnim to present the full text of the German proposals to Thiers. Bismarck insisted that four weeks were necessary to accomplish the complete evacuation of France. He also consented that payment of the installments of the indemnity could take place within the period of the first to the fifth of each month, but he insisted on the evacuation having the same elastic clause. He agreed to evacuate Belfort within two weeks after the final payment of the indemnity, and he agreed to leave there a garrison no larger than that then existing. If, however, Thiers should insist on having Verdun, Bismarck was agreeable provided that he have the right to raise the size of the garrison at that fortress and that France give two way stations between Metz and Verdun to facilitate communications between Germany and Verdun.[30]

Upon receipt of Bismarck's order Arnim sent a telegram to Berlin insisting that Thiers *had* been told of the German terms on March 5.[21] He then went off to Versailles to see Thiers. Arnim told Thiers that he had orders to sign a convention and, after some discussion and an apparent meeting of the minds, Thiers instructed Rémusat to prepare for signing of the convention the next day. He also informed Gontaut that it would not be necessary for him to sign any convention in Berlin.[32] When Arnim returned from Versailles he sent a telegram to Bismarck requesting permission to sign a convention with the French government on the following day, March 14.[33] Instead, he received a telegram from Bismarck informing him that he had already reached agreement with Gontaut and that the signing of the convention would take place at Berlin.[34] Arnim was clearly being rebuked and he stiffly informed Thiers that, since there was no further business to transact, he would not return to Versailles to take up the president's time.[35]

By the night of March 13 virtually everything had been settled which could lead to a quick conclusion to the negotiations at Berlin. Gontaut must have been perplexed, then, when Bismarck returned to the idea of Belfort as the last occupied place. He said that if Thiers would return to the Belfort scheme a convention could be signed immediately but that if he held out for Verdun as a substitute this could delay the signing for several days since the military were opposed to the substitution unless the road between Verdun and Metz were protected by way stations maintained by German troops.[36]

Thiers reminded Gontaut that it was Bismarck who had first suggested the substitution of Verdun for Belfort and he insisted on it now. He did, however, consent to the military way stations between Verdun and Metz.[37]

Finally, on the evening of March 14 Gontaut wired that he and Bismarck had agreed on a convention which combined "your text and that of Prince Bismarck." They had agreed on Verdun with a radius of three kilometers as the substitute for Belfort. There would also be two way stations on the Verdun-Metz road with half a battalion of men at each. The garrison of Verdun would be raised no more than one thousand men above the number then stationed there. Belfort and the four departments would be evacuated within four weeks after July 5, while Verdun would be evacuated within two weeks after September 5.[38] Thiers immediately authorized him to sign on the basis of those terms.[39]

On March 15 Bismarck and Gontaut met to sign the convention. Bismarck had just come from a meeting with the emperor and the military. Unexpectedly, the military had demanded the right to exercise along the Verdun–Metz road the same rights that they exercised in the occupied departments. Gontaut was unprepared for this demand but he accepted it on his own initiative. With that clause disposed of, the convention was signed early in the evening of the same day.[40] As Gontaut had said, the final convention was essentially Bismarck's proposals of March 3 as modified by Thiers's reservations of March 11.

On March 17 Rémusat officially announced to the assembly the signing of the convention. The members of the assembly already knew of it but the news was greeted with bravos and applause. When Rémusat finished his announcement there were cries from the Left of "Vive la République" and from the Right of "Vive la France."[41] Deputy Christophle moved that Thiers "has deserved well of the country," and his motion met with applause from the Left and center Left. There were some objections from the Right. Deputy Gaslonde summed it up when he said that the country, "which has paid the ransom," had made possible the evacuation quite as much as Thiers's efforts. After a few such objections the assembly did vote its thanks to Thiers and appointed a committee to transmit the resolution to the president. A "member on the right" said: "Three quarters of an hour of deification is quite enough."[42]

The following day Rémusat presented a bill of ratification and asked for the assembly's approval. The assembly sent the bill to committee and voted to consider ratification the next day.[43] On March 19 Victor Lanfranc presented the brief committee report which "unanimously" recommended that the treaty be ratified. The assembly voted approval immediately. No one had stood or raised his hand against the treaty.[44] The Reichstag was in session between March 12 and June 25 but it was not called upon to ratify the treaty. On March 18 the convention was presented to the Bundesrat and entered among its printed papers.[45] Ratifications of the convention were exchanged at Berlin on March 22.[46]

In mid-May Manteuffel suggested that his government would not be averse to evacuating Verdun before September 1 if adequate financial guarantees could be arranged.[47] Thiers was receptive to any scheme which would end the occupation, of course, but any plans which he had for following up the suggestion came to an abrupt halt when he resigned as President of France on May 24.

His resignation had no direct relation to foreign policy matters but it could have had a significant effect had a violently anti-German attitude been adopted by the new government. News of the resignation had a profound effect in Berlin and popular rumor had it that a revolution had taken place in Paris.[48] Berlin's anxiety was allayed, however, by the election of Marshal MacMahon as Thiers's successor. Both the new president and his foreign minister, the Duke of Broglie, were careful to reassure the German government of their intention of following a peaceful foreign policy and of paying off the indemnity exactly in keeping with France's treaty obligations.[49]

About a month after the installation of the new government Broglie tried to reopen the subject of an evacuation of Verdun in return for some financial concession by France.[50] When on June 25 Gontaut tried to discuss this matter Bismarck said that he could not open negotiations. The emperor was the final arbiter in such matters but he was in poor health and could not be disturbed. Gontaut thought that this excuse was given in good faith and he was not inclined to look behind it for any ulterior motive.[51] He was also unable to open negotiations at any subsequent time.

The entire affair was quickly becoming academic in any case as the date for the final payment of the indemnity drew nearer. The last four departments and Belfort were evacuated on schedule by August 1. At the end of August there appeared one possible obstacle to the complete evacuation of France. There had been in session at Strasbourg since May 1872 a special mixed commission established by the convention of December 11, 1871, whose function was to regulate the execution of Article IV of the treaty of Frankfort as well as other financial details arising from the transfer of the ceded provinces to Germany.[52] A dispute over the sums threatened to delay the evacuation of Verdun for Germany considered this matter as simply a complement to the treaty of Frankfort and did not propose to leave France entirely until the affair was settled. Finally, on September 6, Gontaut and Delbrück reached agreement and instructed the members of the commission to conclude their work.[53]

France having paid the last installment of the war indemnity, the evacuation of Verdun began on September 13. On September 16, Conflans and Jarny, the last occupied portions of French territory were evacuated.[54]

Although the end of the occupation was a day of national rejoicing for France it must have brought particular satisfaction to the men who for so long had been working to bring it about. Thiers had retired to private life. Manteuffel returned to Berlin to receive a field-marshal's baton. Saint Vallier had the grace to write to Thiers to thank him for his help and assistance during the days of the occupation. He said no more than the truth when he said that Manteuffel remained a good friend of France and deserved her thanks.[55]

The correspondent of the *Annual Register* gave his readers a word picture of the final moments of the occupation at Verdun. His description is quite moving and still conveys the excitement and the emotions of an historic occasion:

At seven o'clock in the morning, the handful of men who remained under General von Manteuffel's command assembled on the esplanade of the fortress, where they underwent their last inspection upon French territory. The staff, having ridden round the ranks, drew up in front of the men; and then, the word of command 'Present arms!' having been given, General von Manteuffel rose in his saddle, swiftly drew his sword and waved it aloft, shouting 'Hoch lebe der Kaiser! Hurrah!' The cheer was caught up by the men, and the bands bursting forth with the 'Heil dir im Siegerkranz,' the troops marched down the esplanade and through the Porte de France, out of the little frontier town which had gallantly braved the German cannonade less than three years before. Scarcely had they departed than the tricolor flag was everywhere hoisted, and tricolor rosettes decorated the breasts of the women and the coats of the men. At twelve o'clock the French troops arrived, and were received at the railway station by a crowd of departmental and municipal functionaries. Their march through the town to the citadel resembled a triumphal procession, the streets being lined by an enthusiastic crowd, shouting 'Vive la République!' 'Vive l'Armée' and 'Vive Thiers!' and ladies and children presenting them with bouquets of flowers. . . .[56]

The great drama was over and France was once again free. But the implications and ramifications of the treaty of Frankfort remained to poison relations between France and Germany. France could not and did not rest until she had her revenge. Baude had predicted that one day France would have a Bismarck and that Germany would be surprised to be treated as she had treated France. Clemenceau may not have been a Bismarck, but in 1919 he undid the work of Bismarck as represented by the treaty of Frankfort.

NOTES TO CHAPTER XII

1. Arnim to Bismarck, Paris, Feb. 2, 1873, *PEA,* I, 163–164, no. 114; *DDF,* I, 194, fn. 2; Thiers to Gontaut-Biron, Versailles, Jan. 20, 1873, *DDF,* I, 193–195, no. 162.

2. Gontaut-Biron to Thiers, Berlin, Jan. 15, 1873, *DDF,* I, 193, fn. 1; *Occ. et lib.,* II, 154–157, no. 244.

3. Thiers to Gontaut-Biron, Versailles, Jan. 20, 1873, *DDF,* I, 193–195, no. 162.

4. Gontaut-Biron to Rémusat, Berlin, Jan. 28, 1873, *ibid.,* p. 200, no. 162.

5. Gontaut-Biron to Thiers, Berlin, Feb. 1, 1873, *Occ. et lib.,* II, 182–193, no. 250.

6. Thiers to Gontaut-Biron, Versailles, Jan. 31, 1873, *ibid.,* pp. 177–182, no. 249.

7. Thiers to Gontaut-Biron, Versailles, Feb. 9, 1873, *ibid.,* pp. 206–211, no. 256; *DDF,* I, 204–206, no. 170; Thiers to Saint Vallier, Versailles, Feb. 10, 1873, *Occ. et lib.,* II, 213–214, no. 258.

8. Arnim to Bismarck, Paris, Feb. 5, 1873, *PEA,* I, 167–168, no. 116.

9. Arnim to Bismarck, Paris, Feb. 7, 1873, *ibid.,* pp. 168–172, no. 117.

10. Bismarck to Arnim, Berlin, Feb. 17, 1873, *PEA,* I, 174–176, no. 119.

11. Bismarck to Manteuffel, Berlin, Feb. 18, 1873, *DDF,* I, 208–209, no. 174.

12. Saint Vallier to Thiers, Nancy, Feb. 20, 1873, *Occ. et lib.,* II, 229–231.

13. Thiers to Saint Vallier, Versailles, Feb., 23, 1873, *DDF,* I, 209–210, no. 175; *Occ. et lib.,* II, 238–241, no. 266.

14. Gontaut-Biron to Thiers, Berlin, Mar. 1, 1873, *DDF,* I, 211, no. 176.

15. Bismarck to Arnim, Berlin, Mar. 3, 1873 (with annexed draft convention), *PEA,* I, 176–179, no. 120 plus annex.

16. Arnim to Bismarck, Paris, Mar. 8, 1873, *ibid.,* pp. 179–181, no. 122.

17. Arnim to Bismarck, Paris, Mar. 8, 1873, *ibid.,* p. 179, no. 121.

18. Bismarck to Arnim, Berlin, Mar. 8, 1873, *ibid.,* p. 182, no. 123.

19. Arnim to Bismarck, Paris, Mar. 8, 1873, *ibid.,* pp. 179–181, no. 122; "Projet de rédaction proposé par M. Thiers," Mar. 9, 1873, MAE, CP (Allemagne), 9: 226–227.

20. Thiers to Gontaut-Biron, Versailles, Mar. 9, 1873, *Occ. et lib.,* II, 274–279, no. 280.

21. Gontaut-Biron to Thiers, Berlin, Mar. 9, 1873, *DDF,* I, 213–216, no. 179.

22. Thiers to Gontaut-Biron, Versailles, Mar. 9, 1873, *ibid.,* p. 216, no. 180; *Occ. et lib.,* II, 273, no. 279, *Ibid.,* pp. 274–279, no. 280.

23. Saint Vallier to Thiers, Nancy, Mar. 10, 1873, *Occ. et lib.,* II, 281–287, no. 283.

24. Manteuffel to Bismarck, Nancy, Mar. II, 1873, *PEA,* I, 183, no. 125.

25. Gontaut-Biron to Thiers, Berlin, Mar. 11, 1873, *Occ. et lib.,* II, 294–295, no. 289; Gontaut-Biron to Thiers, Berlin, Mar. 11, 1873, *ibid.,* pp. 296–305, no. 290.

26. Rémusat to Gontaut-Biron, Mar. 11, 1873, *DDF,* I, 217, fn. 3; MAE, CP (Allemagne), 9: 55; Rémusat to Gontaut-Biron, Versailles,

Mar. 11, 1873, MAE, CP (Allemagne), 9: 56–58; Thiers to Gontaut-Biron, Versailles, Mar. 12, 1873, *DDF,* I, 217–218, no. 182.

27. Gontaut-Biron to Thiers, Berlin, Mar. 12, 1873, *Occ. et lib.,* II, 315–321, no. 297; Gontaut-Biron to Thiers, Berlin, Mar. 12, 1873, *ibid.*, pp. 308–309, no. 293, and *DDF,* I, 218, no. 183. The text of these proposals, together with Gontaut's written observations, are in MAE, CP (Allemagne), 9: 68–72.

28. Thiers to Gontaut-Biron, Versailles, Mar. 13, 1873, *Occ. et lib.*, II, 321, no. 298.

29. Rémusat to Gontaut-Biron, Paris, Mar. 12, 1873, MAE, CP (Allemagne), 9: 63; Rémusat to Gontaut-Biron, Paris, Mar. 12, 1873, Gontaut-Biron, pp. 286–288.

30. Bismarck to Arnim, Berlin, Mar. 12, 1873, *PEA,* I, 184–185, no. 128.

31. Arnim to Bismarck, Paris, Mar. 13, 1873, GA, Frankreich, no. 70, 139–140: 8–9.

32. Thiers to Gontaut-Biron, Versailles, Mar. 13, 1873, *Occ. et lib.,* II, 322–323, no. 300.

33. Arnim to the foreign office, Paris, Mar. 13, 1873, *PEA,* I, 185–186, no. 129.

34. Bismarck to Arnim, Berlin, Mar. 13, 1873, *ibid.,* pp. 186–187, no. 130.

35. Arnim to Thiers, Paris, Mar. 14, 1873, *Occ. et lib.,* II, 330–331, no. 304.

36. Gontaut-Biron to Thiers, Berlin, Mar. 14, 1873, *ibid.,* pp. 327–329, no. 302; *DDF,* I, 222, fn. 1.

37. Thiers to Gontaut-Biron, Versailles, Mar. 14, 1873, *Occ. et lib.*, II, 329–330 and 336, nos. 303 and 309; Thiers to Gontaut-Biron, Paris, Mar. 14, 1873, *DDF,* I, 220–221, no. 186.

38. Gontaut-Biron to Thiers, Berlin, Mar. 14, 1873, *Occ. et lib.,* II, 339–340, no. 313.

39. Thiers to Gontaut-Biron, Versailles, Mar. 15, 1873, *ibid.,* p. 348, no. 318.

40. Gontaut-Biron to Thiers, Berlin, Mar. 15, 1873, *ibid.,* pp. 349–350, no. 319; *DDF,* I, 223, no. 188; Gontaut-Biron to Rémusat, Berlin, Mar. 17, 1873, MAE, CP (Allemagne), 9: 152–155.

41. *Annales,* XVI, 513–514; *Annual Register,* 1873, Pt. I, 125.

42. *Annales,* XVI, 514–516.

43. *Ibid.,* pp. 532–533.

44. *Ibid.,* p. 568; Villefort, IV, 16–17; *Annual Register,* 1873, pt. 1, 125.

45. *Bundesrat minutes,* 1873, p. 84, no. 123.

46. Gontaut-Biron to Rémusat, Berlin, Mar. 22, 1873, *Occ. et lib.,* II, 364, no. 331.

47. Saint Vallier to Thiers, Nancy, May 15, 1873, *ibid.,* pp. 412–414, no. 356.

48. Gontaut-Biron to Broglie, Berlin, May 30, 1873, MAE, CP (Allemagne), 10: 229–235.

49. Broglie to Gontaut-Biron, Paris, May 26, 1873, *DDF,* I, 237, no. 204; MacMahon to Saint Vallier, Versailles, May 28, 1873, GA, Frankreich, no. 70, 141–142: 7; Arnim to William I and Arnim to Bismarck, Paris, June 8, 1873, GA, Schriftwechsel mitd. Kaiserl. Botschaft, Paris, 1873, 2: 52 and 54.

50. Broglie to Gontaut-Biron, ca. June 19–20, 1873, *DDF,* I, 249, fn. 1; Broglie to Gontaut-Biron, Versailles, June 22, 1873, *ibid.,* p. 250, no. 220.

51. Gontaut-Biron to Broglie, Berlin, June 26, 1873, *ibid.,* p. 252, no. 222.

52. Gontaut-Biron to Broglie, Berlin, Aug. 31, 1873, *ibid.,* p. 258, no. 229. For the pertinent papers and reports of this commission see France, *Documents diplomatiques* ("Livres jaunes") (Paris: 1861–), 1872–1873, "Commission Franco-Allemande de liquidation réunie à Strasbourg," December, 1873, pp. 125–176.

53. Gontaut-Biron to Broglie, Berlin, Sept. 6, 1873, *DDF,* I, 259, no. 231; Gontaut-Biron to Broglie, Berlin, Sept. 6, 1873, MAE, CP (Allemagne), 11: 99 *bis* and 111–117.

54. Saint Vallier to MacMahon, Verdun, Sept. 16, 1873, *DDF,* I, 261, no. 235.

55. Saint Vallier to Thiers, Paris, Sept. 27, 1873, *Occ. et lib.,* II, 421–423, no. 362.

56. *Annual Register,* 1873, Part I, 148–149.

Appendix A

Brussels Negotiations German and French Proposals

GERMAN PROPOSALS

What follows is, apparently, the original and a composite of several different sets of propositions given by the German plenipotentiaries at Brussels to their French counterparts. Found in MAE, MD (Allemagne), 156 : 74–95, it is inserted under date of March 31, 1871, and is written in French. I give it here verbatim.

Projet de Traité
communiqué
par les Plénipotentiaires Allemands

A.

Cession de territoire – option pour la nationalité – Pensions – Libération des militaires – Cautionnements – Archives – Rapports entre frontaliers – Batellerie (Canaux & Rivières).

Les Hautes Parties Contractantes sont convenues des dispositions suivantes concernantes les territoires cédés.

1

Le Gouvernement Allemand succède aux droits et aux obligations du Gouvernement français résultant de contrats ou d'autres titres qui concernent les territoires cédés. Les arrières des recettes et des dépenses seront mis au compte du Gouvernement Allemand.

2

Les sujets français domiciliés sur les territoires cédés jouiront pendant l'espace d'un an, à partir du jour de l'échange des Ratifications de la faculté pleine & entière d'émigrer en France, résultant de la législation Allemande. Dans le cas que, pendant cette époque, la nouvelle législation militaire serait introduite dans le territoire cédé, ce droit n'en serait pas atteint. Tous ceux qui ne voudront pas profiter du droit d'émigration resteront sujets Allemands et auront à remplir les devoirs qui leur incombent en qualité de sujets Allemands.

Le délai d'un an est étendu à deux ans pour les sujets originaires des territoires cédés qui, à l'époque de l'échange des Ratifications du présent traité se trouvent hors du territoire français. Aucun habitant des territoires cédés ne pourra être poursuivi, inquiété ou recherché, dans sa personne ou dans ses lieux, pour cause de sa conduite politique pendant les événements de la dernière guerre.

2ème Projet allemand Nouvelle rédaction de l'alinéa 1, l'ancien devenant alinéa 2.

Le nouveau Gouvernement des territoires cédés déclarera, dans les trois mois après l'échange des ratifications, lesquels des fonctionnaires ou officiers publics, en activité de service à l'époque de la signature du présent traité, il entend confirmer dans leur emploi. Il est garanti à ces employés confirmés le montant de leurs appointements actuels pendant la durée de leur service. Quant aux fonctionnaires & officiers publics le nouveau Gouvernement n'a aucun objection de leur payer les appointements arriérés ou une indemnité quelconque.

3

Les pensions, tant civiles que militaires, régulièrement acquises, avant le 19 juillet 1870, à des personnes neés dans les territoires cédés et y domiciliées à l'époque de la signature du présent traité, restent à leurs titulaires si ces derniers ne profitent pas de la faculté que leur accorde de 2.

Ces pensions seront acquittées à l'avenir par le Gouvernement Allemand.

2ème Projet Allemand Nouvelle rédaction.

Les militaires et marins français originaires des territoires cédés seront, sur leur demande, immédiatement libérés du service & renvoyés dans leurs foyers.

Il est entendu que ceux d'entre

4

Les sujets français originaires des territoires cédés, qui font partie de l'armée ou de la flotte française, seront, lorsqu'ils le désirent, immédiatement libérés du service et renvoyés dans leurs foyers.

eux qui déclarent vouloir rester au service français ne seront point inquiétés, pour ce fait, soit dans leurs personnes, soit dans leurs propriétés.

Il est entendu que ceux d'entre eux qui déclarent vouloir rester au service français ne seront point inquiétés, pour ce fait, soit dans leurs personnes, soit dans leurs propriétés.

5

Le Gouvernement français remettra au Gouvernement allemand toutes les sommes versées au profit d'habitants des territoires cédés, y compris les communes, corporations y établissements publics, dans le trésor, dans la caisse des dépôts & des Consignations ou dans toute autre caisse française, à titre de cautionnements, dépôts ou consignations.

Le Gouvernement français prend le même engagement à l'égard des sommes qui ont été prélevées dans les territoires cédés, telles que centimes additionnels ou d'autres pour faire face aux dépenses départementales, communales ou locales et qui ont été versées dans les caisses de l'État, tant que ces sommes n'auront pas déjà été employées, dans le but indiqué, à des dépenses conformes à la loi et au budget.

Seront également compris dans ces sommes les masses et primes d'engagements des soldats originaires des territoires cédés et qui voudront faire cesser leur engagement, soit dans l'armée, soit dans la marine française.

Seront exclus des dispositions sur mentionnées les cautionnements des fonctionnaires et officiers publics qui ne seront point confirmés dans leur emploi par le Gouvernement Allemand.

Cependant le Gouvernement français garantira ces cautionnements aux propriétaires.

6

2ème Jrojet allemand Nouvelle rédaction.

Les archives, pièces originales, registres et autres documents écrits, cartes et plans, qui se rapportent à l'histoire ou à l'administration civile et judiciarie des territoires cédés, seront délivrés au Gouvernement allemand, soit qu'ils s'y trouvent conservés, soit qu'ils aient été transportés hors de leurs limites; sont notamment compris dans cette rétrocession; l'original des relevés topographiques ainsi que les planches y relatives et les documents écrits, plans et modèles qui se rapportent aux forter-

Les archives, actes, documents, registres et autres écrits, cartes et plans, qui se rapportent à l'histoire des territoires cédés, ainsi qu' à leur administration civile et judiciaire, seront remis au Gouvernement Allemand, soit qu'ils se trouvent conservés ou déposés dans les limites des territoires cédés ou hors de ces Pays nommément les originaux des cartes du Pays cédé, les plaques, clichés, qui s'y rapportent, ainsi que les plans des fortresses.

Les collections d'objets d'art et d'antiquité appartenant aux territoires cédés seront remises au Gouvernement allemand; même dans le cas où elles

esses et places de garnison des territoires cédés.

Les collections d'objets d'art et d'antiquité appartenant à ces mêmes territoires seront également rétrocedées, dans le cas où, pour les mettre, à l'abri des accidents de guerre, elles auraient été déplacées, en totalité ou en partie.

seraient retirées de ces Pays, entièrement ou en partie.

7

Pour assurer l'exécution des dispositions contenues aux 5 et 6, les Parties Contractantes nommeront, immédiatement après l'échange des Ratifications, des Commissaires qui designeront les objets à remettre.

L'extradition des objets aura lieu immédiatement après la décision de la commission.

8

Dans le but de ménager et de faciliter, autant que possible, les rapports de bon voisinage et de commerce existant entre les habitants des districts limitrophes, les Parties Contractantes exemptéront réciproquement certaines espèces de ce commerce de tout droit d'entrée et de sortie, nomément : le commerce des marchandises déstinées à être perfectionnées ainsi que de celles qui sont expédiées sans que la vente en soit assurée, enfin, le petit commerce de frontière.

Les Commissaires, qui auront à se réunir, en vertu du 7 de l'Article préciseront les objets et les espèces de ce commerce, de même que les conditions concernant les facilités à accorder. A cet effet, ils prendront pour base les stipulations arrêtées dans l'Article 4 et 5 du traité de commerce et de douanes entre le Zollverein et la Suisse, en date du 13 mai 1869.

9

Sur la Moselle, sur le Canal de la Marne au Rhin et sur le Canal des houillières de la Sarre, ainsi que sur toutes les voies navigables étant en communication avec ces eaux, dans les deux

Pays, les bateliers, navires ou bateaux appartenant à l'une ou à l'autre Partie Contractante, ainsi que leurs chargements, ne pourront être frappés de droits de douane, de navigation, de patente et, en général de droits ou charges de quelque nature que ce soit, autres ou plus élevés que ceux qui seront imposés aux bateliers, navires ou bateaux nationaux et à leurs chargements; ils ne pourront non plus être soumis à des formalités autres ou plus onéreuses que celles auxquelles sont assujétis les bateliers, navires ou bateaux nationaux et leurs chargements.

10

Une Commission spéciale sera chargée de résoudre les difficultés resultant du démembrement des districts judiciaires, notamment en ce qui concerne les procès en cours d'instance, tant au civil qu'au criminel et l'exécution des peines encourues.

B et C

Chemins de fer

Le Gouvernement Allemand ne reconnaît pas les concessions accordées à la Compagnie des Chemins de fer de l'Est pour l'exploitation des Chemins de fer situés dans le territoire cédé. Le Gouvernement Allemand garde ces chemins de fer qu'il exploite à l'heure qu'il est. Mais il fera établir par des experts la valeur du réseau des chemins de fer en question, ainsi que celle de ses accessoires, et cherchera à s'entendre avec les propriétaires sur le montant du prix de rachat.

En cas que le Gouvernement allemand ne réussirait pas à s'arranger à l'aimable avec la Compagnie des Chemins de fer de l'Est, il se réserve de se prévaloir du droit d'expropriation, en procédant par voie legislative pour fixer ainsi le montant des indemnités à payer. Il est bien entendu que les accessoires du chemin de fer ne comprendront pas le matériel roulant (waggons, locomotives). Celui-ci sera restitué aux propriétaires français par le Gouvernement allemand, en tout qu'il est en sa possession.

Le Gouvernement allemand ouvrira des négociations avec le Gouvernement français pour sauvegarder les droits des propriétaires des obligations dont le tronçon cédé à l'Allemagne est chargé.

L'Allemagne reconnaît et confirme les concessions accordées par la France pour les chemins de fer de Munster à Colmar, de Steinbourg à Bouxviller, de Colmar au Rhin et de Nancy à Château-Salins avec unbranchement sur Vic. L'Allemagne est subrogée à tous les droits qui résultaient pour la France des concessions précitées.

L'Allemagne se concertera avec les concessionnaires sur le maintien des concessions accordées par la France pour un chemin de fer partant de Saarbourg et passant par Fenestrange, Saar-Union et Saaralbe à Saarguemines.

Exécution des contrats et jugements

La solution des difficultés résultant du démembrement des circonscriptions judiciaires et plus particulièrement de celles qui se rattachent à des procès en cours d'instances où à l'application des peines encourues sera déférée à des commissions mixtes.

D

Canal de la Sarre

Le Canal des houillières de la Sarre construit en vertu de la convention entre la Prusse et la France du 4 avril 1861, étant situé entièrement sur le territoire cédé, les hautes Parties Contractantes sont d'accord que la Convention susdite est et demeure abolie. De même les hautes Parties Contractantes sont d'accord que les Conventions conclues entre la Prusse et la France, le 18 juillet 1867 et le 26 avril 1870 pour l'établissement d'un chemin de fer entre Sarreguemines et Sarrebruck et pour des facilités à accorder à la circulation des voyageurs et des marchandises sur le chemin de fer, sont et demeurent abolies.

E

Armateurs

La France s'oblige à indemniser les propriétaires et équipages de ceux des navires Allemands, ainsi que les Propriétaires de celles des cargaisons qui ont été capturées, détruites ou endommagées par ses croiseurs ou dans ses parts. Cette indemnité sera réglée d'après les bases suivantes;

1. Immédiatement après l'échange des Ratifications du présent traité, tous les navires marchands allemands ainsi que leurs cargaisons et les chargements appartenant à des sujets allemands, qui ont été capturés sous pavillon neutre ou sur des navires munis de saufs-conduits, seront restitués dans l'état où ils se trouvaient, *bona fide,* au moment de leur remise.

2. Dans le cas où les navires ou les cargaisons spécifiés dans le 1 n'existeraient plus, il sera tenu compte de leur valeur. Si celle-ci avait subi une dépréciation depuis le moment de la capture, les propriétaires recevront une indemnité proportionnelle.

F

Allemands expulsés

En ce qui concerne les Allemands expulsés du territoire français par suite de l'état de guerre, les Parties Contractantes sont convenues des stipulations suivantes :

1. Tous les Allemands expulsés conserveront la jouissance pleine et entière de tous les biens qu'ils ont acquis en France.

2. Ceux des Allemands qui avaient obtenu l'autorisation exigée par les lois françaises pour fixer leur domicile en France, sont réintégrés dans tous leurs droits y peuvent, en conséquence, établir de nouveau leur domicile sur le territoire français.

Le délai stipulé par les lois françaises pour obtenir la naturalisation sera considérée comme n'ayant pas été interrompu par l'état de guerre pour les personnes qui profiteront de la faculté ci-dessus mentionnée de revenir en France dans un délai de six mois après l'échange des Ratifications de ce traité, et il sera tenu compte du temps écoulé entre leur expulsion et leur retour sur le territoire français comme si elles n'avaient jamais cessé de résider en France.

3. Ceux des Allemands qui se seraient établis en France sans avoir obtenu l'autorisation mentionée dans les paragraphes précédents ou qui n'auraient pas voulu se prévaloir du droit d'être admis au domicile, n'en aurent pas moins la faculté de rentrer en France pour liquider leurs affaires et d'y demeurer, dans ce but jusqu' à l'échéance des six mois qui suivront l'échange des Ratifications.

4. Le droit d'expulser du territoire français et de faire conduire au délà de la frontière les étrangers se trouvant en France, est formellement suspendu en ce qui concerne les Allemands rentrés en France, conformément aux deux articles précédents, jusqu' au terme et pour le délai indiqué au 3.

5. La dénomination d'allemands pour l'application des stipulations précédentes comprend toutes les personnes appartenant aux divers États Allemands ayant pris part à la guerre ou qui appartenaient à ces États lors de leurs résidence en France, si elles ne sont pas encore naturalisées. La dénomination de *territoire français* s'applique à toutes les parties du territoire dépendant de la France y compris les colonies.

G

Indemnités au profit des sujets allemands

Le Gouvernement français s'engage à payer aux Gouvernements alliés d'Allemagne, dans un délai de quatre semaines, à partir de l'échange des Ratifications du présent traité, une somme qui sera employée par ces Gouvernements à secourir, dans une mesure équitable, les sujets allemands expulsés et à compenser les pertes que les mesures edictees par le gouvernement français, ses autorités ou agents, pour la saisie, sur terre, de propriétés privées Allemandes, auraient pu faire éprouver aux propriétaires.

H

Réintégration dans des droits périmés

Les Hautes Parties Contractantes s'engagent mutuellement à étendre aux sujets et citoyens respectif les mesures qu'elles pourront juger utile d'adopter en faveur de ceux de leurs nationaux qui, par suite des evénements de la guerre, auraient été mis dans l'impossibilité d'arriver en temps utile à sauvegarde ou à la conservation de leurs droits.

I

Respect de la propriété privée sur mer

La déclaration arrêtée à Paris, le 16 avril 1856 par les Gouvernement signataires du traité de Paris, ayant crée une base importante pour le droit maritime en temps de guerre, et les Parties Contractantes désirant en développer les principes dans le même sens, déclarent vouloir à l'avenir, regarder comme une règle obligatoire, à perpétuité, ce qui suit :

Les navires de commerce, sous pavillon ennemi et la Marchandise ennemie, à l'exception de la contrebande de guerre, ne pourront être ni saisis ni endommagés. La saisie ne pourra avoir lieu que dans le cas où seraient saissables, d'après les principes du droit des gens, les navires sous pavillons neutre ou la marchandise neutre. Les Parties Contractantes inviteront les Gouvernements de tous les États maritimes à accéder à la présente déclaration.

L

Circonscriptions diocésaines

1. Les Parties Contractantes étant d'avis que les circonscriptions diocésaines des évêchés Catholiques devront coincider avec la délimitation territoriale des deux Pays, prendront les mesures nécessaires à cet effet.
2. Les Communautés réformées des territoires cédés cesseront

de faire partie de l'association réprésentée par le Conseil Central des Églises réformées siégeant à Paris.

De même, les adhérents de la Confession d'Augsburg ne seront plus répresentées au Consistoire de Paris.

Par contre, les communautés Augsbourgeoises qui resteront à la France cesseront d'être en relation avec le Consistoire supérieure et le Directoire de Strasbourg.

M et N

Restitution de dessins et documents

Un article concernant la restitution des dessins, documents et autres manuscrits, cartes et plans, dont l'extradition a été stipulée par les traités du 30 mai 1814 et 20 novembre 1815, ainsi que des objets d'art, etc., ayant été enlevés à l'Allemagne par la France.

O

Traités de commerce, de navigation, littéraire, chemins de fer

1. Les traités conclus en date du 2 avril 1862 entre les États faisant partie de l'Association de douanes et de commerce Allemande, d'un côté et la France de l'autre côté, savoir; le traité de commerce, le traité de navigation, la convention relative au service international des chemins de fer dans ses rapports avec la douane, la Convention pour la garantie réciproque des oeuvres d'esprit et d'art, ainsi que les stipulations y relatives contenues dans les Protocoles du 2 août 1862 et du 14 décembre 1864, y compris les amplifications et changements qu'ils avaient subis jusqu'au commencement de la guerre—seront rétablis en vigueur. Ils seront, en outre, étendus aux territoires cédés par la France, en vertu du traité de paix.

Seront également confirmés, le traité entre la France et les villes libres hanséatiques de Brême, Hambourg et Lubeck du 4 mars 1865 et le traité entre la France et le Grand Duché de

Mecklenbourg-Schwerin du 9 juin 1865, y compris la déclaration y relative du 19 fevrier 1868.

P et Q

Remise en vigueur des conventions antérieures

Tous les traités et conventions conclus entre les États de l'Empire Allemand et la France qui étaient en vigueur avant le 19 juillet 1870 sont confirmés, en tant qu'il n'y est pas dérogé par le présent traité. Toutefois, les hautes Parties Contractantes s'engagent à soumettre, dans le terme d'une année ces traités et conventions, à une révision générale, afin d'y apporter, d'un commun accord, les modifications qu'ils seront jugées conformes à l'intérêt des deux Parties. En attendant, les traités et conventions conclus entre la Prusse et la France, en tant qu'ils restent en vigueur, ainsi que la convention conclue, le 16 avril 1846 entre le Grand Duché de Bade et la France, concernant l'exécution des jugements ou arrêts rendus en matière civile et commerciale, sont étendus au territoire nouvellement acquis par l'Empire allemand.

R

Prisonniers

Un article concernant la restitution des prisonniers et des ôtages, en tant qu'elle ne serait pas déjà effectuée.

S

Cessions territoriales

La France renonce en faveur de l'Empire Allemand, à tous ses droits et titres sur les territoires ci-après mentionnés, savoir :

____

____

____

L'Empire allemand possédera ces territoires, à perpétuité, en toute souveraineté et propriété.

Une commission internationale, formée des délégués des hautes Parties Contractantes, sera chargée, aussitôt après l'échange des Ratifications du présent traité, de se rendre sur les lieux et de procéder à l'abonement de la nouvelle frontière. Cette commission sera, en outre, chargée d'opérer le partage, tant des terres, capitaux et autres propriétés appartenant, en commun, aux départements, arrondissements, cantons et communes que la nouvelle délimitation viendrait à séparer, que des dettes collectives qui leur incombent. En cas de désaccord entre les commissaires au sujet de la démarcation ou des mesures d'application qui en découlent, il en sera référé à la décision des Gouvernements respectifs.

T

Relations postales

Les Hautes Parties Contractantes conviennent, aussitôt après la Ratification du présent traité, d'ouvrir des négociations pour la conclusion, entre l'Allemagne et la France, d'une convention postale, ayant pour but d'assurer le développement des correspondances réciproques et de tout ce qui s'y rattache.

En attendant la signature de cette Convention, il est convenu :

1. Que les Conventions de poste conclues, le 14 octobre 1856 entre Bade et la France, le 19 mars 1858 entre la Bavière et la France, le 21 mars 1858 entre la Prusse et la France, le 25 novembre 1861 entre l'ancien office de la Tour et Taxis et la France, ainsi que les conventions additionnelles y relatives, seront remises en vigueur, sauf en ce qui concerne les taxes réduites au profit des zones frontières prévues par ces mêmes conventions et qui devront être considérées comme nulles et non avenues.

2. Que les relations postales entre les territoires cédés et la France seront provisoirement réglées par un accord spécial entre les offices de poste respectifs, reposant sur la base du partage par moitié des taxes perçues et ne dépassant par un maximum de 2

silber-gros ou 25 centimes par lettre simple affranchie.

La convention postale projetée entre les hautes Parties Contractantes consacrera la liberté et la gratuité du transit postal, de telle sorte que les parquets clos échangés entre l'une des hautes Parties Contractantes et un État tiers puissent passer librement et sans frais d'aucune sorte sur le territoire de l'autre partie, à moins que l'office chargé du traduit n'ait lui-même à supporter de ce chef des dépenses particulières qui lui seraient alors remboursées par l'office qui aura emprunté son entremise.

Les Hautes Parties Contractantes s'engagent à faire leurs efforts pour que le principe de la franchise complète du transit postal devienne autant que possible, la base générale des relations internationales de poste.

U

Canal de la Moselle

Les Hautes Parties Contractantes sont convenues de ce qui suit, relativement à la canalisation de la Moselle entre Frouard et Thionville.

1. La France libere la portion du Département de la Moselle cédée à l'Allemagne des obligations relatives à la canalisation de cette rivière, soit que ces obligations découlent, pour ce Département, des décisions prises le 31 août 1864 et 25 avril —— par le Conseil Général de la Moselle, soit qu'elles résultent pour l'État, d'après le texte de la loi du 31 juillet 1867 (Bulletin 1867 —no. 15,310, p. 203), de l'acceptation des subventions offerts ou reposant sur tout autre titre légal. La France cède à l'Allemagne les droits qu'en vertu de l'Article précité elle aurait pu faire valoir contre les industriels habitant les portions de territoire cédées. Elle se substitue à toutes les obligations contractées en vertu de la même loi, soit par la portion du Département de la Moselle cédée, soit par les industriels susmentionnés, sous forme d'emprunts ou de contrats particuliers.

2. Les hautes Parties Contractantes feront exécuter la canalisation de la Moselle entre Frouard et Thionville, chacune sur

son propre territoire, dans les mêmes conditions de navigabilité que le Canal de la Marne au Rhin. Une Commission composée d'hommes de l'art, choisis par les deux Parties, sera chargée de résoudre les questions techniques relative à l'exécution de ces travaux. — Dès que les avis de cette commission auront reçu l'approbation des Gouvernements respectifs, les travaux seront repris sur les deux territoires et exécutés de manière à ce que l'achèvement de la Canalisation puisse être obtenu dans le plus bref délai possible.

3. Les taxes de navigation, sur toute l'étendue du Canal de la Moselle seront fixées, en France comme en Allemagne, d'après un tarif uniforme, et proportionellement aux distances parcourues. Le taux de ces taxes sera ultérieurement déterminé de commun accord entre les hautes Parties Contractantes.

V

Produits du sol et de l'industrie de l'Alsace et de la Lorraine

1. Il est convenu entre les hautes Parties Contractantes que tous les produits du sol ou de l'industrie des territoires cédés qui, à la date de l'échange des Ratifications du présent traité existeront sur ces mêmes territoires ou se trouveront placés dans un entrepôt de douanes en dehors des nouvelles limites, seront, pendant un délai de six mois, considérés comme produits français et pourront à ce titre moyennant justification de leur origine, être importés et vendus, tant en France que dans les colonies françaises, en exemption de tous droits de douane.

Il est également entendu :

1. que les produits manufacturés français importés dans les territoires cédés avant le 1*er* septembre 1871 en vertu de commandes faites ou de contrats particuliers, passés avant le 1*er* mars 1871 par des commerçants établis sur ces mêmes territoires, etc.

2. que les produits manufacturés des territoires cédés, importés en France jusqu'au 1*er* septembre 1871, en vertu de commandes faites ou de contrats particuliers passés, avant le 1*er* mars 1871, par des commerçants français.

Seront réciproquement admis en franchise.

La perte des brevets d'invention sanctionnée par le 3 de l'article 32 de la loi du 5 juillet 1844 sur les brevets d'invention, modifiée par la loi du 31 mai 1856, ne sera pas encourue par les habitants des territoires cédés qui, à la date de l'échange des ratifications du présent traité auront obtenu en France des brevets d'invention et voudront importer en France des objets fabriqués sur les territoires cédés, similaires de ceux pour lesquels ils sont brevetés.

W

Contribution de guerre

Payement

Le payement de la contribution de guerre de cinq milliards de francs et intérêts à payer pour une partie de cette somme sera effectué d'après les stipulations suivantes :

1. Les intérêts à cinq pour cent des trois milliards de francs dont le payement se fera plus tard, seront payés par trimestre post numerando. Le 1*er* terme sera le 2 juin 1871.

2. Le payement des trois milliards cités dans le 1 sera effectué au plus tard, aux dates suivantes :

le 2 mars le 2 juin le 2 septembre le 2 décembre	1872
le 2 mars le 2 juin le 2 septembre le 2 décembre	1873
le 2 mars	1874

à quotes parts égales. Le Gouvernement français a cependant le droit de faire les paiements plus tôt, en prévenant quatre semaines d'avance.

Simultanément avec de tels payements seront payés les intérêts échus pour les sommes anticipées.

3. Le Gouvernement français effectuera tous les payements à Berlin à la Caisse générale de l'Empire Germanique.

4. Les Paiements se feront en or. Outre les monnaies d'or, au pied de francs, dont la convention monétaire du 23 septembre 1865—entre la France, l'Italie, la Belgique et la Suisse—a fixé le poids et le titre, d'autres monnaies et lingots en or dont le poids et le titre seront constatés par le Gouvernement Allemand, peuvent être donnés en payement, le Kilo d'or fin à 3.444 4/9 francs.

On ne donnera cependant, pas de pièces et de lingots d'or dont le titre serait moins de 900/1000.

S'il convenait au Gouvernement français de faire des paiements, en partie en argent, on admettra :

a. des pièces de cinq francs du poids et du titre établis par la convention précitée;

b. des monnaies en argent monnayé au poids voulu (donc à l'exclusion de la petite monnaie) émises par les États de l'Empire Allemand, au taux de 8/10 gros, égal un franc;

c. d'autres monnaies en argent et lingots d'argents d'après leur poids et leur titre, à constater par les autorités allemandes, le kilo d'argent fin égal à 222 2/9 francs.

5. On acceptera également le payement en argent prussien, y compris le papier monnaie prussien, au taux de 3 f. 75 c. le thaler prussien ou de 8 gros égal 1 franc.

X

Sépultures

Le Gouvernement français s'engage à prendre les mesures nécessaires pour la conservation des sépultures des sujets allemands tués ou décédés pendant la guerre, et pour que ces tombeaux jouissent d'une protection égale à celle qui est acquise aux tombes des citoyens français.

Y

Privilège de la Banque de France

Le privilège de la Banque de France dans l'étendue des territoires cédés perdant toute valeur à dater du jour de l'échange des Ratifications du présent traité et les mesures adoptées par cette Banque pour la conduite de ses opérations dans les mêmes territoires, devant prendre fin, les hautes Parties Contractantes concerteront les dispositions nécessaires pour faciliter à la Banque de France la liquidation de ses affaires dans un délai raisonnable.

FRENCH PROPOSALS

The following is a composite of two items in the foreign ministry archives: "Conférence de Bruxelles, 1871, Projet de traité—contre propositions Françaises, avril 1871" (MAE, CP, [Belgique], 61: 186–211) and "Conférence de Bruxelles, Traité de paix, avant projet Française, mars–avril, 1871" (MAE, MD [Allemagne], 156: 162–174).

Préambule : à rédiger.

Paix et amitié : Il y aura paix, amitié et bonne intelligence entre la République française et l'Empire allemand.

Abornement : Une commission internationale, composée de représentants des Hautes Parties contractants, sera chargée immédiatement après l'échange des ratifications du présent traité d'opérer sur le terrain le tracé de la nouvelle frontière, conformément aux stipulations de l'article . . . . ci-dessus.

Amnistie : Pour contribuer de tous leurs efforts à la pacification des esprits, les Hautes Parties Contractantes déclarent et promettent que, dans leurs territoires respectifs et dans les pays cédés, aucun individu compromis à l'occasion de la dernière guerre, de quelle que classe et condition qu'il soit ne pourra être poursuivi, inquiété ou troublé dans sa personne ou dans ses propriétés à raison de sa conduite ou de ses opinions.

Il est également entendu que les poursuites entamées contre individus seront suspendus et que les condamnations prononcées à quelque titre que ce soit seront immédiatement levées.

Titres et archives : Les titres domaniaux et archives, les plans et les cartes des différents pays, villes et forteresses cédées par le présent traité, ainsi que les documents administratif et de justice civile y relatifs seront remis dans l'espace de six mois à dater de l'échange des ratifications aux commissaires de l'Empire Allemand nominés à cet effet.

Les Hautes Parties Contractantes s'engagent à se communiquer réciproquement sur la demande des autorités administratives supérieures, tous les documents et informations relatifs à des affaires concernant à la fois les territoires cédés et la France.

L'Empire allemand s'engage à remettre aux commissaires spéciaux nommés à cet effet, les pièces du comptabilité des places de guerre et les archives des divisions et subdivisions militaires, écoles, tribunaux, penitentières, prisons et autres établissements militaires situés dans les territoires cédés.

Ainsi que les bibliothèques et collections de modèles qui en dépendent.

Il en sera de même des archives, registres, contrôles, et autres papiers appartenant à des corps de troupes et d'armée saisis pendant le cours de la guerre.

Banque de France : Les Hautes Parties Contractantes s'engagent à prendre, d'un commun accord, les mesures nécessaires pour faciliter à la banque de France la suppression des succursales qu'elle possédait dans les territoires cédés et la liquidation à bref délai des opérations d'escompte, dépôt, avances et autres engagées par elle dans ces mêmes territoires.

Cautionnements et dépôts : Le Gt. Français remettra au Gt de l'Empire Allemand dans le terme de . . . mois à dater de l'échange des ratifications du présent traité :

1. Le montant des sommes déposées par les communes, départements et établissements publics des territoires cédés;

2. Le montant des primes d'enrôlement et de remplacement appartenant aux militaires et marins originaires des territoires cédés qui auront opté pour la nationalité Allemande et seront passés au service de l'Empire;

3. Le montant des cautionnements des comptables de l'État;

4. Le Montant des sommes versées pour consignations judiciaires, par suite de mesures prises par les autorités administratives ou judiciaires dans les territoires cédés.

Contrats : Tous marchés ou adjudications consentis par les autorités Allemandes et ayant pour objet soit la vente des propriétés domaniales, forêts ou autres situées à L'Ouest de la nouvelle frontière spécifiée dans L'Art. . . . ci-dessus, soit l'exploitation de ces propriétés, sont d'un commun accord entre les H.P.C. considérés commes nuls et non avenues et leur exécution si fait n'a été déjà sera immédiatement suspendue.

Les adjudications qui auraient de ce chef-des réclamations à élever ne pourront le pouvoir ni auprès du Gouvernet. Français ni contre lui.

Corporations : Les corporations religieuses légalement établiés dans les territoires cédés pourront librement disposer de leurs propriétés mobilières et immobilières dans le cas où la législation nouvelle sous laquelle elles passent n'autoriserait pas le maintien de leurs établissements.

Militaires et marins : Les individus originaires des pays cédés qui font partie de l'armée ou de la marine Française à un titre autre que celui de remplacements ou d'engagés volontaires seront immédiatement libérés du service militaire et renvoyés dans leurs foyers.

Il est entendu que ceux d'entre eux qui déclareront vouloir rester au service de la France ne seront point inquiétés pour ce fait, soit dans leur personnes, soit dans leurs biens. Les mêmes garanties sont assurés aux employés civiles de toutes classes originaires des territoires cédés qui manifesteront l'intention de conserver les fonctions qu'ils occupent.

Ceux des militaires et marins qui, sur leur demande, seront congédiés du service auront droit de réclamer la liquidation de leur quote part dans les masses régimentaires et primes d'engagement.

Droits acquis, concessions et contrats : Le Gouv*t*. de l'Empire Allemand respectera tout droit légalement acquis par les individus ou personnes civiles dans les territoires situés à l'Est de la nouvelle frontière. Il reconnait et confirme en tant que de besoin les concessions de chemins de fer, routes, canaux et mines accordées soit par le Gouv*t*. français soit par les départements ou les communes sur les territoires cédés dans toutes les dispositions et pour toute leur durée.

Il sera de même des contrats passés par le Gouv*t*. Français, les départements ou les communes pour le fermage ou l'exploitation des propriétés domaniales, départementales ou communales situées sur les territoires cédés.

L'Empire Allemand demeure subrogé à tous les droits et à toutes les charges qui résultaient de ces concessions et contrats pour le Gouvernement français. En conséquence les subventions en espèces ou en nature, les créances des entrepreneurs de construction, fermiers et fournisseurs, de même que les indemnités pour expropriation de terrain ou autres qui n'auraient pas encore été acquittées seront soldées par le Gouv*t*. Allemand.

Quant aux obligations pécuniaires ou autres que ces mêmes concessions des territoires cédés, le Gouv*t*. de l'Empereur s'engage à en assurer et faciliter l'exact accomplissement au profit des concessionaires fermiers ou contractants.

Nationalité : Les individus originaires des territoires cédés qui y sont actuellement domiciliés et qui entendront conserver la nationalité française jouiront pendant l'espace de 6 ans à partir de l'échange des ratifications du présent traité moyennant une déclaration préalable faite à l'autorité compétente de la faculté de transporter leur domicile en France et de s'y fixer : auquel cas la qualité de citoyens français leur sera maintenue.

Ils seront dans tous les cas libres de conserver leurs immeubles situés sur le territoire cédé.

La même faculté d'option est réservé aux enfants mineurs originaires des territoires cédés jusqu'à l'expiration de l'année dans laquelle les atteindront leur majorité.

Offices ministériels : L'Empire Allemand reconnait les changes et offices de notaires, avoués, huissiers et greffiers, courtiers et agents de change, établis sur les territoires cédés. Dans le cas où le nouveau régime administratif et judiciaire sous lequel ces territoires se trouveront placés ne permettrait pas le maintien de ces mêmes charges et offices, le Gouvernement de l'Empire Allemand s'engage à accorder aux titulaires actuels un juste indemnité pour la perte de leur position et un délai moralement suffisant pour apurer leur gestion et liquider les intérêts privés dont ils étaient légalement chargés.

Pensions : Les pensions tant civiles que militaires et ecclésiastiques et les dotations quelconques liquidées au profit d'individus originaires des territoires cédés qui opteront pour la nationalité allemande restent acquises à leurs titulaires ainsi qu'aux veuves et orphelins et seront désormais, à dater du 2 mars 1871, acquittées par le Gouv*t*. de l'Empire Allemand.

Le même gouvernement tiendra compte aux fonctionnaires civils de tous ordres, aux militaires et marins appartenant par leur naissance aux territoires cédés et qui deviendraient sujets allemands des droits qui leur sont acquis par les services rendu au Gouv*t*. français ils jouiront notamment du bénéfice résultant de l'immovibilité ——— pour la Magistrature et des garanties assurées à l'armée.

L'Empire Allemand s'engage à respecter et à laisser librement fonctionner, conformément aux statuts qui les régissent les caisses de retraite, de prévoyance, de secours, tontines ou autres associations du même genre établies dans les territoires cédés par des fonctionnaires publics ou employés et agents départementaux ou communaux de touts classes et alimentées par des retenues sur les traitements, des dons ou des subventions volontaires.

Prisonniers et ôtages : Prisonniers de guerre faits de part et d'autre tant par terre que par mer, et tous les ôtages enlevés ou donnés qui n'ont pas encore été restitués seront immédiatement mis en liberté et autorisés à rentrer dans leurs foyers.

Prises : Pour attenuer les maux de la guerre et pour une dérogation exceptionnelle à la jurisprudence généralement consacrée, les batimens allemands et français capturés pendant le cours de la dernière guerre qui n'ont point encore été l'objet d'une condamnation de la part des tribunaux de prises respectifs, seront restitués.

Les batiments et cargaisons seront réciproquement rendus dans l'État où ils se trouveront lors de la remise après paiement de toutes les dépenses et de tous les frais ausquels auront pu donner lieu la conduite, la garde et l'instruction des dites prises ainsi que du fret acquis aux capteurs, et enfin il ne pourra être réclamé de part ni d'autre aucune indemnité pour raison de prises coulées ou détruites pas plus que pour les préhensions exercées sur les marchandises qui étaient propriétés ennemis alors même qu'elle n'auraient pas encore été l'objet d'une décision des tribunaux de prises respectifs.

Il est bien entendu, d'autre part, que les jugemens prononcés par les mêmes tribunaux sont définitifs et acquis aux ——— ayant droit.

Rapports entre frontaliers : Pour faciliter la circulation des produits agricoles sur les frontières respectives, les céréales en gerbe ou en épis, les foins, les pailles et les fourrages verts seront réciproquement importés en franchise de droits.

Réclamations particulières : La décision de toutes réclamations entre les citoyens et sujets respectifs pour dettes, propriétés, effets ou droits quelconques qui, conformément aux usages reçus et au droit des gens, doivent être reproduites à l'époque de la paix sera renvoyée devant les tribunaux compétents et dans ce cas, il sera rendu une prompte et entière justice dans les pays où les réclamations seront faites respectivement.

Réglements de comptes — commission mixte : Une commission mixte composée de délégués en nombre égal par les Hautes parties contractantes immédiatement après l'échange des ratifications du présent traité, sera chargée de liquider toutes les sommes à rembourser à la France par l'Empire Allemand à quelque titre que ce soit notamment.

1. Les dettes contractées par la France pour l'administration intérieure et l'exécution du travaux d'utilité publique dans les territoires cédés;

2. Les sommes à rembourser soit par les départements, arrondissements, villes, communes et établissements publics, associations ou corporations compris dans ces mêmes territoires, soit par les habitans de ces pays devenus sujets allemands sur les prêts qui leur ont été consentis par la caisse des dépôts et consignations ou par toute autre caisse publique;

3. La part contributive des pay cédés dans la dette publique de France.

4. Le montant des réquisitions ou contributions qui auraient pu être prélevées par les armées allemandes dans des conditions de nature à en justifier le remboursement après son achèvement le travail de cette commission sera soumis à la ratification des hautes parties contractantes.

Partage de la dette publique afférente à l'Alsace : Art. . . . La quote part afférente aux territoires cédés par l'Art. . . . ci-dessus dans la dette publique de France est, de commun accord entre les hautes Parties Contractantes fixée à la somme ronde de 741 millions de francs. Cette somme sera déscomptée, au profit de la France sur le montant total de l'indemnité de guerre stipulée dans l'Art. . . . du présent traité.

Contributions et réquisitions de guerre—atteintes à la propriété privée : Art. . . . —La Commission mixte, mentionnée dans l'Art . . . sera également chargée;

a. de la liquidation du montant des contributions et réquisitions prélevées par les armées allemandes, depuis leur entrée sur le territoire française jusqu'au 2 Mars 1871, lorsque le prélévement de ces contributions et réquisitions sera reconnu avoir été fait en dehors des principes du droit des gens et ne pouvoir ni être considéré comme l'exercise temporaire du droit de lever les impôts d'État, ni justifié par les nécessités de l'entretien ou des mouvements des troupes allemandes.

Les répétitions à exercer de ce chef par le Gouvernement français comprendront notamment;

1. Les fournitures ou acquisitions soldées en bons;

2. Les contributions en argent qui ne rentrent pas dans la catégorie des contributions autorisées par le droit des gens;

3. La restitution des cautionnements exigés par l'autorité Allemande, en vue de garantir la sécurité des armées Allemandes.

b. De liquider les contributions ou réquisitions prélevées par les autorités Allemandes depuis le 2 Mars, en dehors des conditions stipulées dans les divers arrangements conclus, à Versailles, à Ferrières, et à Rouen, pour regler les conditions de l'occupation du territoire français;

c. Le montant des indemnités dues pour atteintes portées à la propriété privée, contrairement aux règles du droit des gens et en dehors des actes légitimes de guerre.

Exécution des contrats et jugements; — appels et pourvois en cassation : Tous actes et contrats ou jugements, intervenus, avant la Ratification du dit traité de paix, entre parties habitant, l'une le territoire resté français et l'autre le territoire devenu Allemand seront, pour leur exécution et, s'il y a lieu, pour leur recours en appel ou en cassation, régis par la législation sous l'empire de laquelle ils ont été souscrits ou rendus.

Chemins de fer de l'Est : A dater de l'échange des Ratifications du présent traité, le Gouvernement Allemand est, en ce qui concerne la portion du réseau située sur les territoires cédés, subrogé à tous les droits et à toutes les obligations résultant, pour le Gouvernement français, des lois, décrets, cahiers des charges et statuts qui constituent la Compagnie anonyme des Chemins de fer de l'Est. En conséquence, le droit de dévolution et de rachat qui appartenait au Gouvernement français à l'égard de ces chemins de fer, est transféré au Gouvernement allemand, dans les conditions ainsi que sous les réserves et obligations auxquelles il se trouve légalement subordonné par les actes de concession et leurs annexes.

Dans le cas, toutefois, où il conviendrait au Gouvernement allemand d'acquérir, dès à présent, la pleine et entière jouissance des droits éventuels auxquels il est subrogé par le ler alinéa de cet article, il est entendu, entre les hautes Parties Contractantes, qu'une Commission mixte composée de délégués choisis, en nombre égal, par elles et par la susdit Compagnie, sera instituée pour déterminer conformément aux clauses et conditions des actes de concession, l'indemnité due à la Compagnie pour la rétrocession immédiate de la partie du réseau des Chemins de fer de l'Est située à l'Orient de la nouvelle frontière.

La même commission sera chargée d'élaborer un réglement spécial pour le service international des Chemins de Fer entre les lignes dont la Compagnie de l'Est viendrait à faire la cession et celles dont elle conserverait l'exploitation sur le territoire français.

Les arrangements arrêtés par la Commission dont il s'agit, ne deviendront définitivement obligatoires qu'après avoir été approuvés par les hautes Parties Contractantes et sanctionnés par une note favorable émanant de l'Assemblée extraordinaire des actionnaires de la Compagnie anonyme des Chemins de fer de l'Est.

Échange des détenus : Les individus originaires, soit des territoires cédés, soit de France, et détenus, en qualité de condamnés ou d'inculpés, dans les établissements pénitentiaires situés sur les territoires devenus Allemands, pour crimes ou délits commis sur ces territoires, resteront les mains de l'autorité allemande jusqu' à l'expiration de leur peine ou leur acquittement. Les individus originaires, soit de France, soit des territoires cédés, et détenus, en qualité de condamnés ou d'inculpés, dans les établissements pénitentiaires de France ou des colonies, pour crimes ou délits commis sur les territoires devenue Allemands, seront remis à l'autorité Allemande.

Par contre : les individus originaires, soit des territoires cédés, soit de France et détenus, en qualité de condamnés ou d'inculpés, dans les établissements pénitentiaires situés sur les territoires devenus Allemands, pour crimes ou délits commis en France ou aux colonies, seront remis à l'autorité française,. Les individus originaires, soit des territoires cédés, soit de France, et détenus, en qualité de condamnés ou d'inculpés dans les établissements pénitentiaires situés en France ou aux colonies, pour crimes ou délits commis en France ou aux colonies, resteront entre les mains de l'autorité française jusqu' à l'expiration de leur peine ou à leur acquittement.

Ratifications.

Appendix B

Treaties and Conventions Between France and Germany, January 1871 to May 1873

I ARMISTICE CONVENTION OF JANUARY 28, 1871 (Hertslet, III, 1905–1906, no. 434)

No. 434—CONVENTION OF ARMISTICE between France and the Germanic Confederation. Signed at Versailles, 28th January, 1871.

Art. Table

Preamble

1. Armistice to last to the 19th February. Armies to preserve their positions. Armistice to apply to naval forces. Captures made after conclusion of armistice to be restored, as well as prisoners. Military operations in departments of the Doubs, Jura, and Côte d'Or, as well as the siege of Belfort, to continue until arrangements are made.
2. Armistice concluded to enable Government of National Defense to convoke an assembly to decide on peace or war. Assembly to meet at Bordeaux.
3. Fortresses around Paris to be occupied by German troops.
4. German army not to enter Paris during armistice. The enclosure shall be disarmed of its cannon, and the carriages sent into the forts. Armed garrisons to be prisoners of war, except 12,000 men for internal service in Paris. Arms to be delivered up. Soldiers to be interned and delivered up as

prisoners of war if peace is not concluded. Officers to preserve their arms.

7. National Guard, etc., charged with maintenance of order to preserve order. Rifle corps to be disbanded.
8. Facilities to French commissioners for the revictualling of Paris.
9. Revictualling of Paris after delivery of forts, etc.
10. Permits for leaving Paris.
11. City of Paris to pay war contribution of 200,000,000 francs.
12. Public securities not to be removed during armistice.
13. Import of arms, etc. into Paris during armistice interdicted.
14. Exchange of prisoners of war.
15. Postal service for unsealed letters.

ANNEX. Demarcation of armies before Paris. Surrender of forts and delivery of armament. 29th January, 1871.

1. Lines of demarcation before Paris.
2. Roads by which persons may pass the line of demarcation.
3. Surrender of forts and redoubts.
4. Delivery of the armament and material.

(Translation)

Between Count Bismarck, Chancellor of the Germanic Confederation, acting in the name of His Majesty the Emperor of Germany, King of Prussia, and M. Jules Favre, Minister of Foreign Affairs of the Government of National Defence, furnished with the necessary powers, have decided upon the following conventions :

Arts. I to XV (see table).

Done at Versailles, 28th January, 1871.

(L.S.) JULES FAVRE (L.S.) v. BISMARCK

Arts. I to IV (see table).

Versailles, 29th January, 1871.

(L.S.) JULES FAVRE (L.S.) v. BISMARCK

II. PRELIMINARY TREATY OF PEACE, FEBRUARY 26, 1871
(Hertslet, III, 1912–1916, no. 438)

No. 438—PRELIMINARY TREATY OF PEACE between France and Germany. Signed at Versailles, 26th February, 1871.

Art. Table

Accession of Bavaria and Württemberg

(Translation)

Between the Chancellor of the Germanic Empire, Count Otto de Bismarck Schönhausen, furnished with full powers from His

Majesty the Emperor of Germany, King of Prussia; the Minister of State and of Foreign Affairs of His Majesty the King of Bavaria, Count Otto de Bray-Steinburg; the Minister for Foreign Affairs of His Majesty the King of Württemberg, Baron Auguste deWächter; the Minister of State, President of the Council of Ministers of His Royal Highness the Grand Duke of Baden, Monsieur Jules Jolly, representing the Germanic Empire, on the one part; and on the other part, the Chief of the Executive Power of the French Republic, Monsieur Thiers, and the Minister for Foreign Affairs, Monsieur Jules Favre, representing France; the full powers of the two contracting parties having been found in good and due form, the following has been agreed upon, to serve as a preliminary basis to the definitive peace to be concluded hereafter.

Renunciations by France in favor of Germany

Art. I. France renounces in favor of the German Empire all her rights and titles over the territories situated on the east of the frontier hereafter described.

Line of new frontier between France and Germany

The line of demarcation begins at the north-west frontier of the Canton of Cattenom, towards the Grand Duchy of Luxemburg, follows on the south the western frontiers of the Cantons of Cattenom and Thionville, passes by the Canton of Briey, along the western frontiers of the Communes of Montjois-la-Montagne and Roncourt, as well as the eastern frontiers of the Communes of Marie-aux-Chênes, St. Ail, Habonville, reaches the frontier of the Canton de Gooze, which it crosses along the Communal frontiers of Vionville, Bouxières, and Onville, follows the south-west frontier, south of the district of Metz, the western frontier of the district of Château-Salins, as far as the Commune of Pettoncourt, taking in the western and southern frontiers thereof to follow the crest of the mountains between Seille and Moncel, as far as the frontier of the district of Sarreburg, to the south of Garde. The demarcation afterwards coincides with the frontier of that district as far as the commune of Tanconville, reaching the frontier to the north thereof, from thence it follows the crest of the mountains between the sources of the White Sarre and Vezouze, as far as the frontier of that Canton of Schirmeck, skirts the western frontier of that Canton, includes the Communes of Saales, Bourg-Bruche, Colroy-la-Roche, Plaine, Ranrupt, Saulxures, and St. Blaise-la-Roche of the Canton of Saales, and coincides with the western frontier of the Departments of the Lower Rhine and the Upper Rhine as far as the Cantons of Belfort, the southern frontier of which it leaves not far from Vourvenans, to cross the Canton of Delle at the southern limits of the Communes of Bourogne and Froide Fontaine, and to reach the Swiss frontier skirting the eastern frontiers of the Communes of Jonchery and Delle.

International boundary commission to be appointed

The German Empire shall possess these territories in perpetuity in all sovereignty and property. An international commission, composed of an equal number of representatives of the two High Contracting Parties, shall be appointed immediately after the exchange of the ratifications of the present treaty, to trace on the spot the new frontier, in conformity with the preceding stipulations.

Duties of commissioners

This commission shall preside over the division of the lands and funds, which have hitherto belonged to districts or communes divided by the new frontiers; in case of disagreement in the tracing and the measures of execution, the members of the commission shall refer to their respective governments.

Map of frontier

The frontier, such as it has just been described, is marked in green on two identic copies of the map of the territory forming the Government of Alsace, published at Berlin in September, 1870, by the Geographical and Statistical Division of the Staff, and a copy of which shall be annexed to both copies of the present treaty.

Alteration in boundary map. France to retain town and forts of Belfort

Nevertheless, the alteration of the above tracing has been agreed to by the two Contracting Parties. In the former Department of the Moselle, the villages of Marie-aux-Chênes, near St. Privat-la-Montagne, and Vionville to the west of Rezonville, shall be ceded to Germany. In exchange thereof, France shall retain the town and fortifications of Belfort, with a radius which shall be hereafter determined upon.

Indemnity to be paid by France

Art. II. France shall pay to His Majesty the Emperor of Germany the sum of 5,000,000,000 francs (5 milliards).

Time of payment of indemnity

The payment of at least 1,000,000,000 (one milliard) francs shall be effected within the year 1871, and the whole of the remainder of the debt in the space of 3 years, dating from the ratification of the present.

Evacuation of French territory by German troops

Art. III. The evacuation of the French territory occupied by German troops shall begin after the ratification of the present treaty by the National Assembly sitting at Bordeaux. Immediately after that ratification, the German troops shall quit the interior of Paris, as well as forts on the Left Bank of the Seine, and within the shortest possible delay agreed upon between the military authorities of the two countries, they shall entirely evacuate the Departments of Calvados, Orne, Sarthe, Eure et Loire, Loiret, Loire et Cher, Indre et Loire, Yonne, and also the Departments of the Seine Inférieure, Eure, Seine et Oise, Seine et Marne, Aube, and Côte d'Or, as far as the Left Bank of the Seine. The French troops shall fall back at the same time behind the Loire, which they shall not be allowed to pass before the signature of the definitive treaty of peace. The garrison of Paris is excepted from this disposition, the number of which shall not exceed 40,000 men, and the garrisons indispensably necessary for the safety of the strongholds.

Gradual evacuation according to payments made

The evacuation of the Departments between the Right Bank of the Seine and the eastern frontier by German troops shall take place gradually after the ratification of the definitive treaty of peace and the payment of the first 500,000,000 (half milliard) of the contribution stipulated by Article II, beginning with the Departments nearest to Paris, and shall continue gradually, according to the proportion of the payments made on account of the contribution; after the first payment of a 500,000,000 (half milliard) that evacuation shall take place in the following departments: Somme, Oise, and the parts of the Departments of the Seine Inférieure, Seine et Oise, Seine et Marne, situated on the Right Bank of the Seine, as well as the part of the Department of the Seine, and the forts situated on the Right Bank.

Conditions for payment of the last 3,000,000,000 (3 milliards) of indemnity

After the payment of 2,000,000,000 (two milliards), the German occupation shall only include the Departments of the Marne, Ardennes, Haute Marne, Meuse, Vosges, Meurthe, as well as the fortress of Belfort, with its territory, which shall serve as a pledge for the remaining 3,000,000,000 (3 milliards) and in which the number of the German troops shall not exceed 50,000 men. His Majesty the Emperor will be willing to substitute for the territorial guarantee, consisting in the partial occupation of the French territory, a financial guarantee, should it be offered by the French government under conditions considered sufficient by His Majesty the Emperor and King for the interests of Germany. The 3,000,000,000 (3 milliards), the payment of which shall have been deferred, shall bear interest at the rate of 5 per cent., beginning from the ratification of the present convention.

Maintenance of German troops of occupation

Art. IV. The German troops shall abstain from levying contributions either in money or in kind in the occupied departments. On the other hand, the maintenance of the German troops remaining in France shall be at the expense of the French government in the manner decided upon by an agreement with the German military administration.

Provisions to be made in favor of inhabitants of ceded territories

Art. V. The interests of the inhabitants of the territories ceded by France, in everything relating to their commerce and their civil rights shall be regulated in as favorable a manner as possible when the conditions of the definitive peace are settled. A certain time will be fixed, during which they will enjoy particular advantages for the disposal of their produce. The German government will put no obstacle in the way of free emigration by the inhabitants from the ceded territories, and shall take no steps against them affecting their persons or their property.

Prisoners of war

Art. VI. The prisoners of war who shall not have been already set at liberty by exchange shall be given up immediately after the ratification of the present preliminaries. In order to accelerate the transport of French prisoners, the French government shall place at the disposal of the German authorities in the interior of the German territory a part of the rollingstock of its railways in such proportion as shall be determined by special arrangements, and at prices paid in France by the French government for military transport.

Negotiations for definitive treaty of peace

Art. VII. The opening of negotiations for the definitive treaty of peace to be concluded on the basis of the present preliminaries shall take place at Brussels, immediately after the ratification of the latter by the National Assembly and by His Majesty the Emperor of Germany.

Administration of occupied departments to be made over to French authorities

Art. VIII. After the conclusion and the ratification of the definitive treaty of peace, the administration of the departments which are still to remain occupied by the German troops shall be made over to the French authorities. But the latter shall be bound to conform to the orders which the commanders of the German troops may think necessary to give in the interests of the safety, maintenance, and distribution of the troops.

Taxes in occupied departments to be levied by and for the use of the French government

After the ratification of the present treaty, the taxes in the occupied departments shall be levied on account of the French government, and by its own officers.

German military authority not to extend to unoccupied territory

Art. IX. It is well understood that these stipulations do not give to the German military authority any right over the parts of territory which it does not actually occupy.

Ratifications

Art. X. The present preliminary treaty shall be immediately submitted to the ratification of His Majesty the Emperor of Germany and to the French National Assembly sitting at Bordeaux.

In testimony whereof the undersigned have signed the present preliminary treaty, and sealed it with the seal of their arms.

Done at Versailles, 26th February, 1871.

(L.S.) BISMARCK (L.S.) A. THIERS
(L.S.) JULES FAVRE

Accession of Baden, Bavaria, and Württemberg

The Kingdoms of Bavaria and Württemberg, and the Grand Duchy of Baden, having taken part in the actual war as allies of Prussia, and now forming part of the Germanic Empire, the undersigned adhere to the present convention in the name of their respective sovereigns.

Versailles, 26th February, 1871.

CTE. DE BRAY-STEINBURG MITTNACHT
BN. DE WACHTER JOLLY

III. DEFINITIVE TREATY OF PEACE (TREATY OF FRANKFORT), MAY 10, 1871
(Hertslet, III, 1954–1963, no. 446)

No. 446—DEFINITIVE TREATY OF PEACE, between France and Germany. Signed at Frankfort, 10th May, 1871.

Table
[Omitted]
(Translation)

Reference to preliminaries of peace of 26th February, 1871

M. Jules Favre, Minister for Foreign Affairs of the French Republic, M. Augustin Thomas Eugène de Pouyer-Quertier, Minister of Finances of the French Republic, and M. Marc Thomas Eugène Goulard, Member of the National Assembly, stipulating in the name of the French Republic, on the one part;

On the other, Prince Otho de Bismarck Schoenhausen, Chancellor of the German Empire, Count Harry d'Arnim, Envoy Extraordinary and Minister Plenipotentiary of His Majesty the Emperor of Germany at the Papal Court, stipulating in the name of His Majesty the Emperor of Germany; having agreed to convert into a definitive treaty the preliminaries of peace of the 26th February of the present year modified as it is about to be by the following dispositions, have agreed:

Line of frontier round the town and fortifications of Belfort to belong to France

Art. I. The distance between the town of Belfort and the line of frontier, such as it had been proposed during the negotiations of Versailles, and such as it is marked on the map annexed to the ratifications of the preliminaries of the 26th February, is considered as describing the radius which, by virtue of the clause relating thereto in Article I of the preliminaries, is to remain to France with the town and fortifications of Belfort.

Rectification of frontier. Cession in favor of France

The German government is disposed to extend that radius so as to include the Cantons of Belfort, Delle, and Giromagny, as well as the western part of the Canton of Fontaine, to the west of a line to be traced from the spot where the canal from the Rhone to the Rhine leaves the Canton of Delle to the south of Montreux-Château, to the northern limits of the Canton between Bourg and Felon where that line would join the eastern limit of the Canton of Giromagny.

Cessions in favor of Germany

The German government will, nevertheless, not cede the above territories unless the French Republic agrees, on its part, to a rectification of frontier along the western limits of the Cantons of Cattenom and Thionville which will give to Germany the territory to the east of a line starting from the frontier of Luxemburg between Hussigny and Redingen, leaving to France the villages of Thil and Villerupt, extending between Erronville and Aumetz between Beuvilliers and Boulange, between Trieux and Lomeringen, and joining the ancient line of frontier between Avril and Moyeuvre.

International boundary commission

The international commission, mentioned in Article I of the preliminaries, shall proceed to the spot immediately after the ratifications of the present treaty to execute the works entrusted to them and to trace the new frontier, in accordance with the preceding dispositions.

Choice of nationality

Art. II. French subjects, natives of the ceded territories, actually domiciled on that territory, who shall preserve their nationality, shall up to the 1st October, 1872, and on their making a previous declaration to that effect to the competent authority, be allowed to change their domicile into France and to remain there, that right in nowise infringing on the laws of military service, in which case the title of French citizen shall be maintained.

Retention of immovable property

They shall be at liberty to preserve their immovables situated in the territory united to Germany.

Amnesty

No inhabitant of the ceded territory shall be prosecuted, annoyed, or sought for, either in his person or his property, on account of his political or military acts previous to the war.

Delivery of archives and documents

Art. III. The French government shall deliver over to the German government the archives, documents, and registers relating to the civil, military, and judicial administration of the ceded territories. Should any of the documents be found missing, they shall be restored by the French government on the demand of the German government.

Reimbursements to be made by French government

Art. IV. The French government shall make over to the government of the Empire of Germany within the term of 6 months dating from the exchange of the ratifications of this treaty : 1. The amount of the sum deposited by the departments, communes, and public establishments of the ceded territories. 2. The amount of the premium of enlistment and discharge belonging to soldiers and sailors natives of the ceded territory who shall have chosen the German nationality. 3. The amount of security of responsible agents of the state. 4. The amount of sums deposited for judicial consignments on account of measures taken by the administrative or judicial authorities in the ceded territories.

Navigation of the Moselle and canals

Art. V. The two nations shall enjoy equal privileges as far as regards the navigation on the Moselle, the canal of the Marne to the Rhine, the canal of the Rhone to the Rhine, the canal of the Sarre and the navigable waters communicating with those channels of navigation. The right of floatage shall be maintained.

Religion. Protestant and Jewish dioceses

Art. VI. The High Contracting Parties being of opinion that the diocesan circumscriptions of the territories ceded to the German Empire must agree with the new frontier determined upon by Article I above, will consider, without delay, after the ratification of the present treaty, upon the measures to be taken in common on the subject.

The communities belonging either to the Reformed Church or to the Augsburg Confession, established on the territories ceded by France, shall cease to be under French ecclesiastical authority.

The communities of the Church of the Augsburg Confession established in the French territories shall cease to be under the Superior Consistories and of the Directors residing at Strasburg.

The Jewish communities of the territories situated to the east of the new frontier shall cease to depend on the Central Jewish Consistory residing at Paris.

Payment of war indemnity

Art. VII. The payment of 500,000,000 (½ milliard) shall be

made within 30 days after the re-establishment of the authority of the French government in the City of Paris. 1,000,000,000 (1 milliard) shall be paid in the course of the year, and 500,000,000 (½ milliard) on the 1st May, 1872. The last 3,000,000,000 (3 milliards) shall remain payable on the 2nd March, 1874, as stipulated in the preliminary treaty. From the 2nd March of the present year the interest on those 3,000,000,000 francs (3 milliards) shall be paid each year on the 3rd March, at the rate of 5 per cent. per annum.

All sums paid in advance on the last 3,000,000,000 shall cease to bear interest from the day on which the payment is made.

The payment can only be made in the principal German commercial towns, and shall be made in metal, gold or silver, in Prussian Bank notes, in Netherlands Bank notes, in notes of the National Bank of Belgium, in first class negotiable bills to order or letters of exchange, payable at sight.

Value of Prussian Thaler

The German government having fixed in France the value of a Prussian Thaler at 3 francs 75 centimes, the French government accepts the conversion of the moneys of both countries at the rate above stated.

The French government will inform the German government, 3 months in advance, of all payments which it intends to make into the treasury of the German Empire.

Conditions of evacuation upon the payment of 2,000,000,000 (2 milliards)

After the payment of the first 500,000,000 (½ milliard) and the ratification of the definitive treaty of peace, the Departments of the Somme, Seine Inférieure, and Eure shall be evacuated in so far as they shall be found to be still occupied by German troops. The evacuation of the Departments of the Oise, Seine-et-Oise, Seine-et-Marne, and Seine, as well as the forts of Paris, shall take place so soon as the German government shall consider the re-establishment of order, both in France and Germany, sufficient to ensure the execution of the engagements contracted by France.

Under all circumstances, the evacuation shall take place after the payment of the third 500,000,000 (½ milliard).

The German troops, for their own security, shall have at their disposal the neutral zone between the German line of demarcation and the Paris enclosure on the Right Bank of the Seine.

The stipulations of the treaty of 26th February relative to the occupation of French territories after the payment of the 2,000,000,000 (2 milliards), shall remain in force. None of the deductions which the French government might have a right to make shall be made on the payment of the first 500,000,000 (½ milliard).

Contributions and taxes

Art. VIII. German troops shall continue to abstain from levying contributions either in kind or money in the occupied territories; that obligation on their part being correlative to the obligations contracted for their maintenance by the French government, in case the French government, notwithstanding the reiterated demands of the German governments, was behindhand in the execution of the said obligations, the German troops will have the right to procure what is necessary to their wants by levying taxes and contributions in the occupied departments, and even outside of them, should their resources not be sufficient.

Maintenance of German troops

With reference to the maintenance of the German troops, the system actually in force shall be continued until the evacuation of the Paris forts.

In virtue of the convention of Ferrières, of 11th March, 1871, the reductions pointed out by that convention shall be put into force after the evacuation of the forts.

As soon as the effective of the German army shall be reduced below the number of 500,000 men, account shall be taken of the reductions made below that number to establish a proportionate diminution in the price of the maintenance of the troops paid by the French government.

Exceptional treatment granted to the produce of industry of the ceded territories

Art. IX. The exceptional treatment at present granted to the produce of the industry of the ceded territories for imports into France, shall be continued for 6 months, from the 1st March, under the conditions made with the Commissioners of Alsace.

Prisoners of war. Number of French troops in and around Paris

Art. X. The German government shall continue to deliver up prisoners of war, making arrangements with the French government. The French government shall send to their homes such of the prisoners as can be discharged. As for those who shall not have completed their term of service, they shall be sent beyond the Loire. It is understood that the Army of Paris and Versailles, after the re-establishment of the authority of the French government at Paris, and until the evacuation of the forts by German troops, shall not exceed 80,000 men. Until that evacuation, the French government shall not concentrate troops on the Right bank of the Loire, but it shall provide garrisons in the towns within that circuit, according to the necessities for the maintenance of public order and peace.

As the evacuation shall proceed, the commanders of regiments shall agree together as to a neutral circuit between the armies of the two nations.

20,000 prisoners shall be sent without delay to Lyons on condition that they are immediately sent to Algiers, after their organisation, to be employed in that colony.

Commerce and navigation. Most favored nation treatment

Art. XI. The treaties of commerce with the different states of Germany having been annulled by the war, the French government and the German government will adopt as the basis of their commercial relations the system of reciprocal treatment on the footing of the most favoured nation.

Are included therein import and export duties, transit dues, customs formalities, the admission and treatment of both nations as well as their agents.

Shall nevertheless be excepted from the above rule the favors which one of the contracting parties has granted or may grant, by treaties of commerce, to other states than the following : Great Britain, Belgium, Netherlands, Switzerland, Austria, Russia.

Renewal of navigation, railway, and copyright treaties, etc.

The treaties of navigation as well as the convention relative to the international service of railways in its relation with the cantons, and the convention for the reciprocal guarantee of literary works, shall be removed.

Reservations of French government

The French government nevertheless reserves to itself the right of levying tonnage and shipping duties (*Droit de Pavillion*) on German vessels and their cargoes, under the reservation that those duties shall not be higher than those imposed on vessels and cargoes of the above-mentioned nations.

Rights of Germans expelled from France

Art. XII. All expelled Germans shall preserve the full and entire enjoyment of all property which they may have acquired in France.

Such Germans who had obtained the authority required by

French laws to establish their domicile in France shall be reinstated in all their rights, and may consequently again establish their domicile in French territory.

Naturalisation

The delay stipulated by French laws to obtain naturalisation shall be considered as not having been interrupted by the state of war for persons who shall take advantage of the above-mentioned facility of returning to France within 6 months after the exchange of the ratifications of this treaty, and the time which has elapsed between their expulsion and their return to the French territory shall be taken into account, as if they had never ceased to reside in France.

The above conditions shall be applicable in perfect reciprocity to the French subjects residing, or wishing to reside, in Germany.

Restoration of maritime prizes

Art. XIII. German vessels condemned by prize courts before the 2nd March, 1871, shall be considered as definitively condemned.

Those not condemned at the above-mentioned date shall be restored with the cargoes in so far as it still exists. If the restoration of the vessels and cargo is no more possible, their value, fixed according to the price of the sale, shall be restored to their owners.

Canalisation of the Moselle

Art. XIV. Each of the two parties shall continue on his territory the works undertaken for the canalisation of the Moselle. The common interests of the separate parts of two departments of the Meurthe and the Moselle shall be liquidated.

National treatment to respective subjects on account of events arising out of the war

Art. XV. The High Contracting Parties mutually engage to extend to their respective subjects the measures which they may consider necessary to adopt in favour of those of their subjects who, in consequence of the events of the war, may have been prevented arriving in time for the safety or the preservation of their rights.

Cemeteries

Art. XVI. The two governments, French and German, reciprocally engage to respect and preserve the tombs of soldiers buried in their respective territories.

Additional stipulations reserved for further negotiations

Art. XVII. The regulation of additional stipulations upon which an understanding is to be come to in consequence of this treaty and the preliminary treaty, will be the object of further negotiations which shall take place at Frankfort.

Ratifications

Art. XVIII. The ratification of the present treaty by the National Assembly and by the Chief of the Executive of the French Republic, on the one part, and on the other by the Emperor of Germany, shall be exchanged at Frankfort, in the delay of 10 days, or sooner if possible.

In faith whereof the respective plenipotentiaries have signed it and affixed thereto the seal of their arms.

Done at Frankfort, 10th May, 1871.

(L.S.) JULES FAVRE — (L.S.) BISMARCK
(L.S.) POUYER-QUERTIER — (L.S.) ARNIM
(L.S.) DE GOULARD

Additional articles. Frankfort, 10th May, 1871

Art.I. Purchase of railways of the east and Guillaume-Luxemburg.

Art. II. Purchase by Prussia of rights and property on Swiss territory of railways of the East.

Rectification of frontier near Belfort

Art. III. The cession of territory near Belfort, offered by the German government in Article I of the present treaty in exchange for the rectification of the frontier required to the west of Thionville, shall be increased by the territories of the following villages: Rougemont, Leval, Petite-Fountaine, Romagny, Felon, La-Chapelle-sous-Rougemont, Angeot, Vauthier-Mont, Rivière, Grasige, Reppe, Fontaine, Frais, Foussemagne, Cunelières, Montreux-Château, Brelagne, Chavannes-les-Grands, Chavanatte and Suarce.

The Giromagny and Remiremont road, thoroughfare to the Balloon of Alsace, shall remain to France throughout its whole extent, and shall serve as a limit in so far as it is situated outside the Canton of Giromagny.

Done at Frankfort, 10th May, 1871.

(L.S.) JULES FAVRE	(L.S.) BISMARCK
(L.S.) POUYER-QUERTIER	(L.S.) ARNIM
(L.S.) DE GOULARD	

Accessions to the above treaty

Baden	15th May, 1871
Bavaria	15th May, 1871
Württemberg	15th May, 1871

IV. PROTOCOLS OF CONFERENCES BETWEEN FRANCE AND GERMANY, FRANKFORT, JULY–DECEMBER, 1871

(Hertslet, III, 1966–1967, no. 448)

Protocol

No. 1. Choice of nationality. Domiciled aliens. Choice of nationality by minors. Competent authority to receive the declaration in ceded territories. Power to natives of Alsace-Lorraine to return to that country after choice of French nationality. Freedom of circulation for those who have not yet made their choice. Question as to their being French or Germans. Pensions. Doctors and chemists. Ministerial offices. Diocesan circumscriptions and religious corporations. Amnesty. Exchange of criminals and lunatics. Execution of contracts, judgments, etc. Wood-cutting in forests of the state. Judicial expenses. Judicial documents. Mortgages. Archives and documents. Patents of invention. Frontier relations. Maintenance and cleansing of waterways; canals; concessions of roads and rivers. Railways of local interest. Transit. Private debts of the treasury. Contributions and requisitions.

Frankfort, 6th July, 1871

No. 2. Execution of judgments. Nationality. Choice by minors. Freedom of circulation to Alsace-Lorraines who have not yet made their choice. Renewal of treaties. Trademarks. Admission of produce from Alsace. Registration and deposit by booksellers. Restitution of funds belonging to communes. Treasury accounts of ceded territories. Local railways. Desaix monument at Strasburg, etc. Railways sequestered during the war.

Frankfort, 13th July, 1871

No. 3. Postal arrangements.

Frankfort, 24th July, 1871

No. 4. Archives and documents of railways of the East (*de*

l'Est). Nationality. Liberation of Alsatian soldiers.

Frankfort, 26th July, 1871

No. 5. Stamps of the mints of Strasburg, Italy, and Colmar. Military pensions. Arrears of pensions advanced by France. Amnesty funds. Renewal of treaties. Definition of the word *Originaires*. Postal negotiations.

Frankfort, 21st September, 1871

No. 6. Canal of salt works of Dieuze. Local railways. Private debts of the treasury. Amnesty funds. Debts of communes and departments. Archives and documents. Bank of France. Amnesty. Machinery for verifying weights and measures. Securities and judicial or administrative deposits. Plans and documents of the railway of the East.

Frankfort, 26th September, 1871

No. 7. Railways sequestered during the war. Definition of the word *Originaires*. Preamble adopted after amendment of official title of President of the Republic. Delay for choice of nationality. Pensions. Amnesty funds. Doctors and chemists. Ministerial offices. Religious corporations. Amnesty.

Frankfort, 19th October, 1871

No. 8. Pensions. Mutual and provident companies. Arrears of pensions advanced by France. Doctors and chemists. Ministerial offices. Amnesty. Mortgages. Diocesan circumscriptions. Patents of invention. Debts and credits of ceded territories. Demands made since the 2nd March. Mixed commission. Transit. Private claims. Bank of France.

Frankfort, 2nd November, 1871

No. 9. Mixed financial commission. Railways from Audun to Longwy, and from Sierck to Mettrich, from Nancy to Château-Salins and Vic, from Avricourt to Cirey. Declarations to be inserted in final protocol. Ministerial offices. Declarations to be inserted in explanatory protocol. Joint stock companies in Alsace-Lorraine and in France. Life and fire insurance companies.

Frankfort, 4th November, 1871

No. 10. Definition of the word *Originaires*. Judicial expenses. Religious corporations. Amnesty. Contributions and demands made since the 2nd March. Bank of France.

Frankfort, 7th November, 1871

No. 10. Definition of the word *Originaires*. Judicial expenses. Religious corporations. Amnesty. Contributions and demands made since the 2nd March. Bank of France.

Frankfort, 7th November, 1871

No. 11. Final arrangements. Definition of the word *Originaires*. Pensions. Ministerial offices. Diocesan circumscriptions. Amnesty. Dieuze canal. Contributions and requisitions. Local railways. Transit. Postal. Alsatian soldiers. Arrears of pensions advanced by France. Pensions funds etc. Patents of invention. Bank of France. Sequestration on funds. Sequestered railways. Explanatory protocol.

Frankfort, 24th November, 1871

No. 12. Definition of the word *Originaires*. Railways, Pensions. Postal arrangements. Bank of France. Patents of invention. Judicial expenses.

Frankfort, 28th November, 1871

No. 13. Ministerial offices. Requisitions and contributions. Railways sequestered during the war. Bank of France. Transit. Postal arrangements. Patents of invention. Railway from Nancy to Château-Salins and Vic. Doctors and chemists. Religious corporations.

Frankfort, 2nd December, 1871

V. CONVENTIONS OF OCTOBER 12, 1871

A. Additional convention to the treaty of peace of 10th May, 1871, between France and Germany. Signed at Berlin, 12th October, 1871.
(Hertslet, III, 1964–1965, no. 447)

[Table omitted]

(Translation)

M. Augustin Thomas Joseph Pouyer-Quertier, member of the National Assembly, Minister of Finances, and specially appointed by letter from the President of the French Republic, dated 6th October, 1871, Plenipotentiary of the French Republic, stipulating in the name of France, on the one side; on the other side, Prince Otho de Bismarck Schoenhausen, Chancellor of the German Empire; and Count Harry d'Arnim, Envoy Extraordinary and Minister Plenipotentiary of His Majesty the Emperor of Germany at the Papal Court, stipulating in the name of the German Empire, have agreed upon the following:

Arts. I to IX. *Customs regulations for Alsace-Lorraine.*

Retrocessions by Germany to France

Art. X. The German government shall retrocede to France;

1. The Communes of Raon-les-Leau and Raon-sur-Plaine, exclusive of all domanial property as well as the communal and private properties enclosed in the reserved domanial territory;

2. The Commune of Igney and the part of the Commune of Avricourt situated between the Commune of Igney, as far as and including the railway from Paris to Avricourt, and the railway from Avricourt to Cirey.

The French government shall undertake the expense of a railway station to be constructed on land chosen by the German government, and which shall be sufficient for military and commercial interests as well as to those of Avricourt.

The estimate for that building shall be made by common consent. The German government will see that it is executed as soon as possible.

Until the termination of the new station, the German government reserves to itself the right of continuing the occupation of the Commune of Igney as well as the above-mentioned part of the Commune of Avricourt.

The boundary commission will be charged with the delimitation of the new frontier.

Art. XI. *Trade marks.*

Art. XII. *Ratifications.*

Done at Berlin, 12th October, 1871

B. Convention of October 12.

Preamble

Article 1

The government of His Majesty the Emperor of Germany engages to evacuate the six departments of Aisne, Aube, Côte d'Or, Haute-Saône, Doubs, and Jura, and to reduce the occupation troops to fifty thousand men, in conformity with the disposition of article 3 of the treaty of 26 February 1871. The execution of these measures will take place in the two weeks which follow the ratification of the present convention.

Article 2

On its part the French government engages to pay in the conditions hereafter determined:

1. Five hundred million francs forming the fourth half-billion of the war indemnity;

2. One hundred and fifty million francs representing a year of interest on the three last billion remaining due by France and falling due the 2 March, 1872, to wit:

[Seven payments of 80,000,000 francs each on January 15, February 1 and 15, March 1 and 15, April 1 and 15, 1872; one payment of 90,000,000 francs on May 1, 1872]

It is well understood that the stipulations of the third paragraph of article 7 of the Treaty of Frankfort of 10 May, 1871, remain in force for the payments indicated above.

Article 3

In case of non-execution of the dispositions in the preceding article, the troops of His Majesty the Emperor of Germany may reoccupy the evacuated territory.

It is, moreover, agreed that the territory of the departments designated in article 1 and evacuated by the German troops will be declared neutral from the military point of view.

Until the payment of the sums mentioned in the preceding article, France will not be able to keep in these departments armed troops other than necessary for the maintenance of order.

The French government reserves to itself, moreover, the right of anticipating the said payments.

Article 4

Ratifications

Done at Berlin, 12th October, 1871.

VI. ADDITIONAL CONVENTION TO TREATY OF FRANKFORT

(Hertslet, III, 1968–1973, no. 449)

No. 449—ADDITIONAL CONVENTION to the Treaty of Peace of 10th May, 1871, between France and Germany. Signed at Frankfort, 11th December, 1871.

Table

Art.

Preamble. Reference to treaty of 10th May, 1871.

1. Choice of nationality by natives (*Originaires*) residing out of the ceded territories.
2. Civil and religious pensions. Military pensions.

3. Execution of judgments. Judicial proceedings.
4. Exchange of criminals. Exchange of lunatics.
5. Expenses of criminal justice.
6. Judicial documents. Reports of sentences.
7. Guarantee of mortagage rights.
8. Reciprocal restitution of all titles, plans, surveys, and documents belonging to communes of new territories.
9. Diocesan circumscriptions crossed by the new frontier.
10. Patents of invention.
11. Appointment of financial commission.
12. Articles free from export and import duties to facilitate the farming of lands and forests on neighbouring frontiers.
13. Recognition by German government of concessions of roads, canals, and mines granted by French government and authorities in ceded territories. Financial mixed commission to take charge of accounts of works on both sides of the frontier.
14. Payment by Germany of expenses of canals of the Sarre, Dieuze, and Colmar. Payment of annuities to old subscribers of the canal of the Rhone to the Rhine. Financial mixed commission to undertake the accounts. Mixed commission relative to canals from the Rhone to the Rhine, and from the Marne to the Rhine.
15. Appointment of mixed commissions for maintenance of frontier waterways.
16. Railways.
17. Customs offices on railways.
18. Renewal of treaties and conventions between France and German states existing before the war. Exceptions. Treaties provisionally applicable to Alsace-Lorraine.
19. Ratifications.

Closing protocol

1. French soldiers and sailors to be liberated on making a declaration of their choice for German nationality.

2. Reimbursement to France of pensions paid by the French treasury since the 2nd March, 1871.
3. Liquidation of pensions, provident and other funds in case one or more of their members make choice of French nationality.
4. Judicial offices.
5. Patents of inventions.
6. Reimbursement of funds belonging to communes of ceded territories deposited in the coffers of Colmar, Strasburg, and Metz.
7. Reimbursement of securities.
8. Recovery of debts by French government.
9. Liquidation by branch establishments of the Bank of France in the ceded territories. Liquidator to complete his operations within 3 months after the ratification of the additional convention. Withdrawal of sequestration of moneys belonging to Bank of France, and restitution in coin. Ratifications.

Protocol of signature

French reservations relative to the right of felling timber in the forests of the states granted during the war on French territory by German civil and military authorities. Declaration of German plenipotentiaries relative to the railway from Nancy to Château-Salins and Vic.

Procès-Verbal of the exchange of the ratifications

Delivery of adhesions of German states to Article XVIII of the additional convention of 11th December, 1871, relative to the renewal of treaties. Declaration of German ambassador relative to copyright conventions and treaties of navigation.

(Translation)

Reference to treaty of 10th May, 1871

The President of the French Republic, on the one part, and His Majesty the Emperor of Germany on the other part, having determined, in conformity with Article XVII of the treaty of peace concluded at Frankfort on the 10th May, 1871, to negotiate an additional convention to that treaty, have to that effect appointed as their plenipotentiaries, namely:

The President of the French Republic, M. Marc Thomas Eugène de Goulard, member of the National Assembly, and M. Alexandre Johann Henri de Clerq, minister plenipotentiary of the First Class; and

His Majesty the Emperor of Germany, M. Weber, Councillor of State of His Majesty the King of Bavaria, and Count Uxkull, Intimate Councillor of Legation of His Majesty the King of Württemberg;

Who, having communicated to each other their full powers, found in good and due form, have agreed upon the following articles:

Arts. I to VIII (see table).

Diocesan circumscriptions crossed by the new frontier

Art. IX. Until the conclusion of the arrangements alluded to in the first paragraph of Article VI of the treaty of peace of 10th May, 1871, it is agreed that the Bishops established in the dioceses crossed by the new frontier shall preserve, in their entirety, the spiritual authority actually vested in them, and shall remain free to provide for the religious necessities of the populations committed to their charge.

Arts. X to XII (see table).

Payment by Germany of expenses of canals of the Sarre, Dieuze and Colmar

Art. XIV. The canal of the Sarre, the canal of the salt works of Dieuze, and the junction of Colmar, which forms the communication between that town and the Rhine, being entirely included within the territories ceded to Germany, the latter takes upon herself the payment of the expenses of those 3 canals remaining due.

The annuities still due on the sum advanced to the French state by the town of Colmar, and by the manufacturers of the east, shall, dating from 1871, be payable by the German government.

Payment of annuities to old subscribers of the canal of the Rhone to the Rhine

The canal of the Rhone to the Rhine being crossed by the new frontier, it has been agreed that the 12 annuities remaining to be paid to the old subscribers on the purchase of their shares shall be divided between the High Contracting Parties in the proportion of the extent reverting to each of the two countries.

Financial mixed commission to undertake the accounts

The commission mentioned in Article XI shall be entrusted with the accounts of the above-mentioned canals, as well as the liquidation of the accounts relative to the canalisation of the Moselle, and of the common interests of the separate parts of the departments of the Meurthe and the Moselle.

The French government undertakes to furnish the commission with all contracts, documents, etc. necessary for the fulfilment of their labors.

Mixed commission relative to canals from the Rhone to the Rhine and from the Marne to the Rhine

The High Contracting Parties shall appoint commissioners, who shall be entrusted with the regulation, in so far as regards the canal from the Rhone to the Rhine, and the canal from the

Marne to the Rhine, of the supply of the dividing mill-courses.

Arts. XV to XVII (see table).

Renewal of treaties and conventions between France and German states existing before the war

Art. XVIII. Besides the international arrangements mentioned in the treaty of peace of 10th May, 1871, the High Contracting Parties have agreed to renew the different treaties between France and the German states existing previous to the war, with the reservation of the declarations of adhesion to be supplied by the respective governments at the time of the exchange of the ratifications of the present convention.

Exceptions

The special conventions between France and Prussia, relative to the canal of the Sarre being excepted.

Neither are the stipulations of the present article applicable to postal relations, which are reserved for a subsequent arrangement between the two governments.

Treaties provisionally applicable to Alsace-Lorraine

It is also agreed that the dispositions of the convention between Baden and France, of the 16th April, 1846, relative to the execution of sentences of the treaty of extradition, concluded between France and Prussia, on the 21st July, 1845, and of the copyright convention between Bavaria and France, of the 24th March, 1865, shall be provisionally extended to Alsace-Lorraine, and that in matters to which they relate, these three arrangements shall serve as a rule for the relations between France and the ceded territories.

Ratifications

Art. XIX. The present convention, drawn up in French and German, shall be ratified, on the one part by the President of the French Republic, after the approval of the National Assembly; and on the other part by His Majesty the Emperor of Germany, and the ratifications thereof shall be exchanged in the delay of one month, or sooner, if possible.

In faith whereof the respective plenipotentiaries have signed it, and have affixed thereto the seal of their arms.

Done at Frankfort, 11th December, 1871.

(L.S.) E. DE GOULARD (L.S.) WEBER
(L.S.) DE CLERQ (L.S.) UXKULL

VII. CONVENTION OF JUNE 29, 1872
(Thiers, *Memoirs*, pp. 367–369, appendix no. 23)

Preamble

Article 1

France engages to pay the said sum of three billion at the times following:

1. One half billion francs two months after the exchange of ratifications of the present convention;
2. One half billion francs on the 1st of February, 1873;
3. One billion francs on the 1st of March, 1874;
4. One billion francs on the 1st of March, 1875;

France may, however, anticipate the payments due on February 1, 1873, March 1, 1874, and March 1, 1875, by partial payments which shall be of not less than one hundred millions but which may comprise the whole of the amounts due at the times above indicated.

In case of anticipatory payment, the French government shall advise the German government one month in advance.

Article 2

The conditions of the third paragraph of Article 7 in the peace treaty of May 10, 1871, as well as those of the separate protocol of October 12, 1871, remain in force for all payments made under the preceding article.

Article 3

His Majesty the Emperor of Germany shall cause his troops to evacuate the departments of Marne and Haute-Marne fifteen days after the payment of one half billion.

The departments of the Ardennes and the Vosges, fifteen days after the payment of the second billion.

The departments of Meuse and Meurthe, as well as the canton of Belfort, fifteen days after the payment of the third billion and of the interest that may remain to be paid.

Article 4

After the payment of two billion, France reserves the right to furnish Germany, for the third billion, financial guarantees which, conformably with Article 3 of the Versailles preliminaries, shall be substituted for the territorial guarantees, if they are accepted and recognized as sufficient by Germany.

Article 5

The interest of 5 per cent. on the sums indicated in Article 1, payable from March 2, 1872, shall cease in proportion as the said sums are discharged, either on the dates fixed by the present convention or before these dates after the previous notice stipulated for in Article 1.

Article 6

In case the number of the German troops in occupation should be decreased when the occupation is successively reduced, the cost of maintaining the said troops shall be reduced in proportion to their number.

Article 7

Until the liberation of the French territory is complete, the departments successively evacuated conformably with Article 3 shall be neutralized from a military point of view, and must not receive any masses of troops other than the garrisons necessary for the preservation of order.

France shall not raise any fortifications in these departments, and shall not extend the existing fortifications.

His Majesty the Emperor of Germany undertakes for his part not to raise any work of fortification in the occupied departments other than those at present existing.

Article 8

His Majesty the Emperor of Germany reserves the right to reoccupy the evacuated departments in case of the non-fulfillment of the engagements entered into in the present convention.

Article 9

The ratifications of the present treaty, by His Majesty the Emperor of Germany, on the one part,

On the other, by the President of the French Republic,

Shall be exchanged at Paris, within ten days, or earlier if possible.

In which faith . . . . . .

VIII. CONVENTION OF MARCH 15, 1873

Preamble

Article 1

The sum of 3 billion having been paid on the 5 billion of the indemnity of war stipulated by the treaty of peace of 10 May, 1871, and that of 1,500 million alone remaining to be paid on the last 2 billion, France engages to pay between now and 10 May,

1873 the 500 million remaining due on the fourth billion falling due on 1 March, 1874 by virtue of article 1 of the convention of 29 June, 1872. The partial payments will not be less than 100 millions; they must be announced to the German government at least one month before payment.

The billion francs falling due, by virtue of the above-mentioned convention, 1 March, 1875, will be paid by France in four installments, each of 250 million francs, on June 5, July 5, August 5, and September 5, 1873. At the same time as the payment of the last installment France will pay to the German government the interest from 2 March, 1873.

Article 2

The dispositions of the third paragraph of article 7 of the treaty of peace of 10 May 1871, as well as those of the separate protocols of 12 October 1871 remain applicable for all the payments which shall take place by virtue of the preceding article.

Article 3

His Majesty the Emperor of Germany, King of Prussia, engages to give to his troops the necessary orders so that the arrondissement of Belfort and the four departments of Ardennes, Vosges, Meurthe-et-Moselle, and Meuse, with the exception of Verdun with a radius of 3 kilometers around that place, should be evacuated completely within a period of four weeks after July 5.

The place of Verdun and the above-mentioned radius will be evacuated within a period of two weeks beginning 5 September 1873.

Until this last evacuation His Majesty the Emperor of Germany, King of Prussia, will have the right to use the road from Metz to Verdun as a military road and to occupy for that purpose as a halting place, the two towns of Conflans and Étain, which will each have a garrison of a half-battalion. The military authorities will maintain at Verdun and along the route of supply the rights that they have exercised until now in the occupied territories.

It is understood that the supply stations will be evacuated at the date fixed for the evacuation of Verdun.

Article 4

France undertakes the expenses of maintenance of the German troops stationed in the arrondissement of Belfort and in the departments of Vosges, Ardennes, Meurthe-et-Moselle, and Meuse, until the day of the complete evacuation of these departments as well as those of the troops stationed at Verdun and in the two way stations until the complete evacuation of these last localities. The number of troops which occupy Verdun will exceed no more than 1,000 men above the number of the garrison which is there at the date of the signing of the present treaty.

Article 5

Until the evacuation of Verdun, the arrondissement of Belfort and the departments designated in article 3, will be, after their evacuation by the German troops, declared neutral militarily and will receive no troops other than the garrisons which will be necessary for the maintenance of order.

France will erect there no new fortifications and will not expand the fortifications already in existence.

In the departments occupied by the German troops as well as in the arrondissement of Belfort, His Majesty the Emperor of Germany, King of Prussia, will have raised no other works of fortification than those which presently exist.

Article 6

In case of nonfulfilment of the engagements taken in the present convention, His Majesty the Emperor of Germany, King of Prussia, reserves to himself the right to reoccupy or not to evacuate the departments and places which are there designated.

In faith of which the respective plenipotentiaries have signed the present act and have affixed the seal of their arms.

Done at Berlin, 15 March, 1873.

(L.S.) VICOMTE DE GONTAUT-BIRON
(L.S.) BISMARCK

Bibliography

ARCHIVAL SOURCES

I. France. *Archives du ministère des affaires étrangères,* Paris, MSS.

A. Correspondance politique :
Allemagne, Vols. 1–11 (1871–1873)
Angleterre, Vols. 753–760 (1870–1872)
Autriche, Vols. 503–507 (1870–1872)
Belgique, Vols. 61–62 (1871)
Italie, Vols. 29–32 (1870–1871)
Russie, Vols. 244–246 (1870–1872)

B. Mémoires et documents :
Allemagne
(1) Vols. 156–158 (Conférence de Bruxelles)
(2) Vols. 160–161 *bis* (Conférence de Francfort)
(3) Vol. 172 (Miscellaneous, 1870–1877)

C. Papiers Favre : Pièces importantes relatives à la guerre, 1871 (unbound).

D. Papiers de M. Thiers au ministère des affaires étrangère : négociations de Francfort, correspondance entre M. Thiers et J. Favre, etc. mai-août 1871 (unbound).

France. *Bibliothèque Nationale,* Paris, MSS, Papiers Thiers (Nouvelles acquisitions francaises) :

A. XXX–XXXII (NAF 20630–32)—Occupation et évacuation du territoire (1871–1873).

B. XXXIII–XXXV (NAF 20633–20635)—Libération du territoire (1871–1872).

C. LI (NAF 20651)—Dépèches relatives à l'occupation du territoire pendant la période transitoire des préliminaires au traité de paix (février et mars, 1871).

France. *Bibliothèque Thiers,* Paris, MSS, Fonds Thiers, 1ère série :

A. XXIV : Lettres de M. Thiers adressés à divers (1824 à 1877), 122 lettres.

B. XXV : Lettres adressés à M. Thiers (1823 à 1877), 43 lettres.

II. Germany. Hauptarchiv d. Auswärt. Amt., Public Record Office, London, microfilm :

A. Frankreich, No. 70. der Krieg mit Frankreich, 1870–1871.

(1) Vols. 100–110 : 1871 Mar. 5–Apr. 26 (Ser. #8309H/1)

(2) Vols. 111–119 : 1871 Apr. 27–June 26 (Ser. #8309H/2)

(3) Vols. 120–130 : 1871 June 27–Dec. 31 (Ser. #8310H/1)

(4) Vols. 131–141 : 1872 Jan. 1–1873 Oct. 10 (Ser. #8310/H/2)

B. Frankreich, No. 72. der Krieg mit Frankreich : Friedens-Verhandlungen.

(1) Vols. 2–10 : 1871 Feb. 14–May 10 (Ser. #8311H/1)

(2) Vols. 11–18 : 1871 May 11–1877 Oct. 16 (Ser. #8311H/2)

C. Schriftwechsel d. Ges. Paris über Zustände USW in Frankreich.

(1) Vols. 2–3 : 1871 July–Dec. (Ser. #8312H)

D. Schriftwechsel mit d. Kaiserl. Botschaft Paris über Zustände USW in Frankreich.
(1) Vols. 1–3 : 1872 (Ser. #8313H)
(2) 1873 (Ser. #8314H)

III. Great Britain. Public Record Office, London, Foreign Office archives, MSS :
A. France : General correspondence
FO 27/1814–FO 27/1863 (1870–1871)
B. Prussia and Germany : General correspondence
FO 64/717–FO 64/720 (1871)
FO 64/744–FO 64/745 (1872)
C. Prussia and Germany : Special mission of Odo Russell to Versailles, Nov. 1870–Feb. 1871
FO 64/737–FO 64/739
D. Prussia and Germany : Embassy and consular archives
FO 244/250–FO 244/253 (1871)

PRINTED SOURCES

Annual Register, second series. London : 1863 ff.

Archives diplomatiques. Recueil mensuel international de diplomatie d'histoire. Paris : 1861 ff.

Bismarck, Otto von. *Bismarck, the Man and the Statesman.* 2 vols. New York and London : 1899.

———. *Die gesammelten Werke,* ed. H. von Petersdorf, F. Thimme, and others. 15 vols. Berlin : 1924–1935.

———. *Letters to His Wife from the Seat of War 1870–1871.* New York : 1903.

Blumenthal, Albrecht von (ed.). *Journals of Field-Marshal Count von Blumenthal.* London : 1903.

Broglie, Duc de. "Mémoires," *Revue des deux mondes,* 7th period, XLIX–LIII (Jan.–Oct., 1929).

Busch, Moritz, *Bismarck in the Franco-German War, 1870–1871.* 2 vols. in 1. New York : N.D.

——— *Bismarck, Some Secret Pages of His History.* 3 vols. London : 1898.

———. *Our Chancellor: Sketches for a Historical Picture.* 2 vols. in 1. New York : 1884.

Castelnau, General de. "Sedan et Wilhelmshöhe," *Revue de Paris,* XXXVI (1929).

Claveau, Anatole. *Souvenirs politiques et parlementaires d'un témoin, 1865–1873.* 2 vols. Paris : 1913–1914.

Doniol, Henri, *M. Thiers, le comte de St. Vallier, le général de Manteuffel. La libération du territoire, 1871–1873. Documents inédits.* Paris : 1897.

DuCamp, Maxime, *Souvenirs d'un demi-siècle.* 2 vols. Paris : 1949.

Ducrot, Auguste Alexandre. *La journée de Sedan.* Paris : 1885.

Evans, Thomas Wiltberger. *Memoirs. The Second French Empire.* New York : 1905.

Favre, Jules. *Le gouvernement de la défense nationale.* 5 vols. Paris : 1871–1875.

Filon, Augustin. *Recollections of the Empress Eugenie.* Paris : 1920.

Fleury, Count (ed.). *Memoirs of the Empress Eugenie.* 2 vols. New York and London : 1920.

France. *Almanach national. Annuaire officielle de la République française.* Paris : 1872 ff.

———. *Annales de l'assemblée nationale. Compte rendu in extenso des séances.* Paris : 1871 ff.

———. Assemblée nationale. *Enquête parlementaire sur les actes du gouvernement de la défense nationale.* 10 vols. Paris : 1872–1875.

———. Ministère des affaires étrangères. *Documents diplomatiques* ("Livres jaunes"). Paris : 1861 ff.

———. Ministère des affaires étrangères. *Documents diplomatiques français.* Commission de publication des documents relatifs aux origines de la guerre de 1914. 31 vols. Paris : 1929–1959.

Freycinet, Charles de. *Souvenirs, 1848–1893.* 2 vols. Paris : 1912–1913.

Gabriac, Marquis de. *Souvenirs diplomatiques de Russie et d'Allemagne, 1870–1872.* Paris : 1896.

Germany. Auswärtiges Amt. *Die grosse Politik der europäischen Kabinette, 1871–1914. Sammlung der diplomatischen Akten des auswärtigen Amtes,* ed. Johannes Lepsius and others. 40 vols. Berlin : 1922–1927.

———. *Politique extérieure de l'Allemagne, publié par le ministère allemand des affaires étrangères,* trans., Henri Audain and J. A. Taillebot. Paris : 1927.

——. *Protokolle über die Verhandlungen des Bundesraths des deutschen Reichs.* Berlin : 1871 ff.

———. *Stenographische berichte über die Verhandlungen des deutschen Reichstages.* Berlin : 1867 ff.

Goldschmidt, Hans. *Bismarck und die Friedensunterhändler 1871. Die deutsch-französischen Friedensverhandlungen zu Brüssel und Frankfurt März-Dez. 1871.* Berlin : 1929.

Gontaut-Biron, Vicomte de. *Ma mission en Allemagne, 1872–1873.* Paris : 1906.

Gouvernement de la défense nationale. Procès verbaux des séances du conseil d'après les manuscrits originaux de M. A. Dréo, ed. Henri des Houx. Paris : 1905.

Great Britain. *Parliamentary Papers, 1870–1871,* C. 244, "Franco-German War, No. 1 (1871) : Further correspondence respecting the war between France and Germany, 1870–1871."

———. *Parliamentary Papers, 1870–1871,* C. 266, "Franco-German War, No. 3 (1871) : Correspondence respecting the pecuniary demands of Prussia on France."

Hérisson, Comte d'. *Journal d'un officier d'ordonnance, juillet 1870–février 1871.* Paris : 1885.

Hertslet, Sir E. *The Map of Europe by Treaty.* 4 vols. London : 1875–1891.

Hoffman, Wickham. *Camp, Court and Siege: A Narrative of Personal Adventure and Observation During Two Wars.* New York : 1877.

Holstein, Friedrich von. The Holstein papers, Vol I : *Memoirs and Political Observations,* ed. Norman Rich and M. H. Fisher. Cambridge, England : 1955.

Italy. Ministero degli Affari Esteri. *I documenti diplomatici italiani.* Rome : 1952–

Knapland, Paul (ed.) *Letters from the Berlin Embassy.* (Vol. II : Annual report of the American Historical Association for the year 1942). Washington : 1944.

Laussedat, Col. Aimé, *La délimitation de la frontière franco-allemande.* Paris : 1901.

Letters of Queen Victoria, Second Series, A Selection From Her Majesty's Correspondence and Journals, 1862–1885, ed. George E. Buckle. 3 vols. London and New York : 1927.

"Lettres à l'Impératrice Eugenie (1870/71)," *Revue des deux mondes,* 7th period, LIX (1930).

Lowe, Charles (ed.) *Bismarck's Table-talk.* London : 1895.

Malet, Edward. *Shifting Scenes, or Memories of Many Men in Many Lands.* London : 1901.

Meaux, Vicomte de. *Souvenirs politiques, 1871–1877.* Paris : 1905.

Memoirs of the Count de Falloux, ed. C. B. Pitman. 2 vols. London : 1888.

Oncken, Hermann. *Grossherzog Friedrich I von Baden und die deutsche Politik von 1854–1871.* 2 vols. Stuttgart : 1927.

The Political Correspondence of Mr. Gladstone and Lord Granville, 1868–1876, ed. Agatha Ramm ("Camden Third Series," Vols. LXXXI–LXXXII). 2 vols. London : 1952.

Radziwill, Princess Catherine. *Germany Under Three Emperors.* London : 1917.

Rémusat, Charles de. "Les débuts de M. de Rémusat au ministère des affaires étrangères (extrait de ses mémoires inédits)", *Revue d'histoire diplomatique,* XLV (1931), 166–192.

Ringhoffer, Karl. *The Bernstorff Papers.* 2 vols : London and New York : 1908.

Rothfels, Hans (ed.). *Bismarck–Briefe.* Göttingen : 1955.

[Salisbury, Marquis of], "The terms of peace," *Quarterly Review,* CXXIX (October 1870), 540–556.

Simon, Jules. *Le gouvernement de la défense nationale.* Paris: 1874.

———. *Le gouvernement de M. Thiers,* Paris: 1878.

Stosch, Albrecht von. *Denkwürdigkeiten des Generals und Admirals Albrecht von Stosch ersten Chefs der Admiralität. Briefe und Tagebuchblatter,* ed. Ulrich von Stosch. Stuttgart and Leipzig: 1904.

Thiers, Louis Adolphe. *Memoirs, 1870–1873* trans., F. M. Atkinson. London: 1915.

———. *Occupation et libération du territoire.* 2 vols. Paris: 1903.

Verdy du Vernois, General Julius von. *With the Royal Headquarters in 1870–71.* London: 1897.

Villefort, A. (ed.). *Recueil des traités, conventions, lois, décrèts et autres actes relatifs à la paix avec l'Allemagne.* 5 vols. Paris: 1872–1879.

Waldersee, Alfred. *Denkwürdigkeiten des General-Feldmarschalls Alfred Grafen von Waldersee,* ed. Heinrich Otto Meisner. 3 vols. Stuttgart and Berlin: 1923–1925.

———. *A Field-Marshal's Memoirs,* trans. and condensed by Frederic Whyte. London: 1924.

The War Diary of Emperor Frederick III, 1870–1871, trans. and ed. A. R. Allison. London: 1924.

Washburne, Elihu B. *Recollections of a Minister to France, 1869–1877.* 2 vols. New York: 1887.

Wemyss, Rosslyn. *Memoirs and Letters of the Rt. Hon. Sir Robert Morier, GCB from 1826 to 1876.* 2 vols. London: 1911.

PUBLISHED HISTORICAL STUDIES

Bismarck's Pen: the Life of Heinrich Abeken. Edited from his letters and journals by his wife, trans. Mrs. Charles Edward Barrett-Lenard and M. W. Hoper. London: 1911.

Bouniols, Gaston. *Thiers au pouvoir, 1871–1873. Texte de ses lettres annoté et commenté.* Paris: 1921.

Brabant, Frank H. *The Beginning of the Third Republic in France. A History of the National Assembly. Feb.–Sept., 1871*. London : 1940.

Brogan, D. W. *France Under the Republic: The Development of Modern France, 1870–1939*. New York : N.D.

Bury, J. P. T. *Gambetta and the National Defence*. New York : 1936.

Carroll, E. Malcolm. *Germany and the Great Powers, 1866–1914: a study in public opinion and foreign policy*. New York : 1938.

Cecil, Lady Gwendolen. *Life of Robert, Marquis of Salisbury*. 3 vols. London : 1921–1931.

Clapham, John H. *Economic Development of France and Germany, 1815–1914*. 3d ed. Cambridge, England : 1928.

Craig, Gordon A. *The Politics of the Prussian Army, 1640–1945*. Oxford : 1955.

Deschanel, Paul. *Gambetta*. New York : 1920.

Eyck, Erich. *Bismarck*. 3 vols. Zurich : 1943.

Fitzmaurice, Lord Edmond. *Life of Granville George Leveson Gower Second Earl Granville*. 2 vols. 3d. ed. London : 1905.

Geuss, Herbert. *Bismarck und Napoleon III: ein Beitrag zur Geschichte der preussich–französischen Beziehungen, 1851–1871*. Cologne : 1959.

Hanotaux, Gabriel. *Contemporary France*. 4 vols. Westminster : 1903–1909.

Hartshorne, Richard. "The Franco-German boundary of 1871," *World Politics,* II (January 1950).

Hazen, Charles Downer. *Alsace-Lorraine Under German Rule*. New York : 1917.

Hazen, W. B. *The School and the Army in Germany and France: With a Diary of Siege Life at Versailles*. New York : 1872.

Herzfeld, Hans. *Deutschland und das geschlagene Frankreich, 1871–1873: Friedensschluss, Kriegsentschädigung, Besatzungszeit*. Berlin : 1924.

Hollyday, Frederic B. M. *Bismarck's Rival: A Political Biography of General and Admiral Albrecht von Stosch*. Durham : 1960.

Howard, Michael. *The Franco-Prussian War: the German Invasion of France, 1870–71*. New York : 1961.

Klein-Wuttig, Anneliese. *Politik und Kriegführung in den deutschen Einigungskriegen 1864, 1866 und 1870/71*. Berlin : 1934.

Lagrange, Abbé Francois. *Life of Monseigneur Dupanloup*. 2 vols. London : 1885.

Matter, Paul. *Bismarck et son temps*. 3 vols. Paris : 1906–1912.

May, Gaston. *Le traité de Francfort*. Paris : 1909.

Morley, John. *The Life of William Ewart Gladstone*. New ed. 3 vols. in 1. New York : 1932.

Mosse, W. E. *The European Powers and the German Question, 1848–1871*. Cambridge, England : 1958.

Newton, Thomas Wodehouse Legh, second Baron. *Lord Lyons: A Record of British Diplomacy*. 2 vols. London : 1913.

Paleologue, Maurice. *The Tragic Empress*. New York and London : 1928.

Pilant, Paul. "Genèse des projéts d'annexion de l'Alsace et de la Lorraine en 1870–71," *Les révolutions de 1884*, XXXI, (1934).

Ramsay, Anna A. W. *Idealism and Foreign Policy. A Study of the Relations of Great Britain with Germany and France, 1860–1878*. London : 1925.

Raymond, Dora N. *British Policy and Opinion During the Franco-Prussian War*. New York : 1921.

Rousset, Lt. Col. *L'armistice de 1871*. Paris : 1927.

Sencourt, Robert. *The Life of the Empress Eugenie*. New York : 1931.

Sorel, Albert. *Histoire diplomatique de la guerre Franco-Allemande*. 2 vols. Paris : 1875.

Vagts, Alfred. *Defense and Diplomacy: The Soldier and the Conduct of Foreign Relations*. New York : 1956.

Valfrey, Jules. *Histoire de la diplomatie du gouvernement de la défense nationale*. 3 parts. Paris : 1871–1872.

———. *Histoire du traité de Francfort et de la libération du territoire français*. 2 vols. Paris : 1874–1875.

Vizetelly, Ernest Alfred ("Le petit homme rouge"). *Republican France, 1870–1912.* London : 1912.

Wallace, Lillian Parker. *The Papacy and European Diplomacy, 1869–1870.* Chapel Hill : 1948.

Winnacker, R. A., "The French election of 1871," *Papers of the Michigan Academy of Science, Arts, and Letters,* XXII, (1936), 477–483.

Index